Library of Peasant Studies No. 1

THE LATIN AMERICAN PEASANT

The Latin American Peasant

ANDREW PEARSE

FRANK CASS : LONDON

First published 1975 in Great Britain by
FRANK CASS AND COMPANY LIMITED
67 Great Russell Street, London WC1B 3BT, England

and in the United States of America by
FRANK CASS AND COMPANY LIMITED
c/o International Scholarly Book Services, Inc.
P.O. Box 4347, Portland, Oregon 97208

ISBN 0 7146 3047 0 (Case)
ISBN 0 7146 4021 2 (Paper)
Library of Congress Catalog Card No. 73–93199

Printed in Great Britain by
Brown Knight & Truscott Ltd
London and Tonbridge

Contents

List of Tables and Figures

LIST OF FIGURES

Preface

The justification of an attempt to treat so broad a topic as the title announces lies in the fact that the region bears the stamp of two related (though distinct) colonial systems, both of which came to an end in the nineteenth century, to be followed by periods in which their economies retained much of the export-oriented colonial character. In fact the importance of the common historical basis can be expressed by saying that it would have been easier to have included the Philippines, also a Spanish colony, in this study, than to have attempted to do justice to Argentina, whose character owes little to the colonial period and much more to post-colonial capitalist development and European immigration.

The book expresses an interpretation of the sense and direction of contemporary transformation, but the method of exposition does not consist of elaborate theoretical development nor of argument with competing interpretative schemes, but rather of the presentation of case material about families, farms, estates, communities, societies, institutions, classes and organisations in the particularity and concreteness of which may be discerned the general trends.

Similarly, the concept *peasant,* taken as equivalent of the words *campesino* or *campones,* though it refers to a variety of cultures and systems of social and economic relations, does have both historical and geographical reality in the Latin American context. And the word, not only in the Latin American context but throughout Asia and Africa as well, evokes a great contemporary problem, namely, how can the rural majorities in the post-colonial countries find a way of coming to terms with the acquisitive expansion of the industrial urban nucleus, which is rapidly undermining their land-bound security, but is niggardly in offering them advantageous places in the new society.

Although this is not a historian's book, it was believed necessary in order to explain the dynamics of the contemporary situation to see it in relation to the structure and institutions of colonial society and of the period of post colonial dependence and penetration by the industrial powers. The presentation is sociological in that it seeks to explain the working out of a process of social transformation and the social forces which are released by the pursuit of common interests by social entities such as classes and territorial groups, and the pursuit of a vision of livelihood by individuals and families.

Some of the case material is from the published and unpublished field work of colleagues, to whom the author expresses his gratitude. And some of the case material presented is a product of research programmes with which the author was directly or indirectly involved during twelve years spent in Colombia, Ecuador, Brazil and Chile, working with FAO and UNESCO. The opportunity for reflection and writing was offered by a Ford Foundation grant and enjoyed as a Fellow of St. Antony's College, Oxford, at the Latin American Centre, from 1968–70.

Geneva
1975 A.P.

I

Land-Labour Institutions in Latin America

The peasant, in the sense of this book, is the agricultural producer and cottage craftsman of pre-industrial and partially industrialised societies, who produces for the provisioning of his own household, and for market exchange, and lives in landgroups (estates, juridical communities, smallholding neighbourhoods or villages and land settlements) with others of his kind with whom he shares certain facilities and services and day-to-day social interaction. Peasantries, therefore, in the sense of landgroups rather than kingroups, or simple neighbourhood groups, were established in certain parts of Highland America before the conquest, and at the present moment, under the pressure of industrial growth and the radiation of urban institutions, are tending to disintegration and transformation.

In our attempt to explain what is happening to peasantries, we shall bring into focus the immediate social and economic context which is the framework within which the individual producer's decisions are made, and the medium through which the press and flow of events and process on a societal and world scale become real forces affecting his life and livelihood. The immediate context is presented as having two aspects. It consists on the one hand of those productive units through which he pursues his livelihood and the institutional conditions of – and conflicts generated by – the several roles which he may be obliged to perform, for instance – landowner, entrepreneur, labourer, trader, manager, tenant, serf, debtor, client, and so on; on the other hand, it consists of the landgroup, deeply moulded by the economic relations required by the productive process, yet sustaining other roles involving values of motivational autonomy. Attention will also be paid to the limitations of his status in the society.

However, *pari passu* with the intensification of the pressure of industrial society on the peasant's landgroups, and the ever-intensifying thrust of the market economy in respect of his product, his consumption and his own labour power, the predominance of the landgroup and the special local conditions of the economic unit tend to diminish, and a process of vertical incorporation takes place in the larger society, so that peasants behave – and therefore have to be explained – in terms of this membership of, and participation in institutions, organisations and movements of an urban based national character, or their resistance to them.

The intensifying penetration of the peasantry and the weakening and disintegration of the landgroup as tutor of peasant decision-making, in spite of its accelerating tempo, is uneven in its operation, and in its effects, on account of the great differences in agrarian structure from one region to the next and the great differences in market pressures. Thus the chronological present often wears the appearance of a stratified outcrop of rock in which various formations from the historical past are present, and especially where in spite of 150 years of republican independence, the social scene wears a colonial character, either by stagnation or regression, or by deliberate conservation.

In order to appreciate contemporary structure and process, and to take these 'outcrops' into account, it is necessary to consider in their proper historical setting a number of social forms to which peasant life has been submitted and which directly or indirectly have contributed to the present scene. The method chosen to do this, of necessity summary and suggestive, consists of presenting and commenting on examples of 'land-labour institutions' which at different stages and in different places in Latin America have performed the central role in the organisation of labour for production and which have, therefore, been central to the social conformation of the landgroup and the conduct of the landgroup's relations with the larger society.

But it will also be noted that these land-labour institutions are products of societies in which the social order is based on different key principles. Thus 'frontier opportunism' may aptly be used to describe the moral climate in which the device of self-ransom described by Las Casas was a possible though temporary recourse. In the same vein, perhaps the class structure of the colonial society is best characterised by the concept of estamental principle, implying the attribution of labour as a status-obligation of a legally discriminated and culturally discrete sector of the population. Although institutions owing their origins to this principle have survived almost to the present day, with custom taking over the generalising mandatory power of the law, it was in general replaced by 'praedial dependence', implying a situation in which access to subsistence lands became conditional upon the delivery of unpaid or ill-paid labour to a particular member of the land-controlling strata. The major tendency of the present day is towards the use of wage-labour as and when required, under conditions of a higher degree of capitalisation and mercantility in agricultural enterprises and of the steady growth of a labour market, as service-tenure systems decay and the pressure of population growth on the smallholdings continues. This does not mean that capitalist forms of production are a novelty, indeed capitalist enterprise has been on the scene in patches since the sixteenth century, though using custodial forms of labour in the absence of conditions producing a labour market.

However, before considering the institutions themselves, it is important to notice certain variations in the initial elements composing the colonial society which result directly from differences in the level of socio-economic organisation encountered in different regions of America by the conquering bands.

Variations in the land-labour situation encountered by the conquering bands[1]

At the very outset, certain different lines of development were established by the conditions of the encounter between the conquering bands and the American populations. These gross differences contributed to the structural foundations which have given a bias to the process of social formation according to certain broadly drawn regions, and which show through even today. And from the same differences in encounter have followed differences in racial stock and in subcultures, which do not, however, correspond to contemporary national boundaries.

What were the elements in these encounters? Much can be said and has been said about the social origins of the individuals making up the conquering bands, and their expectations. Certainly they were people who for some or other antecedent motive were willing to embark on an extremely hazardous enterprise, but who expected with good fortune to reap an uncommon reward in material goods or enhanced prestige and rank; hence the expeditions inevitably lacked members aspiring to such lowly callings as husbandry and artisanship, though such elements did arrive at a later stage in the process of colonisation.

They were colonisers without a labour force. Wherever they arrived, therefore, their first goals were to find subsistence while they collected booty, and secondly to find a labour force and to put it to work on the local resources to guarantee permanent subsistence and to produce wealth, preferably in exportable form, as a long term prospect. When once pillage had run its course, therefore, means had to be found to incorporate the natives in the germinating local society as a labour force, *pari passu* with the distribution of rights amongst themselves to the use of the labour force for wringing from the land whatever it might offer, by collecting, mining and tilling. So colonial society began to take form as the institutional means were found to set a labour force to work for the conquerors.

The conquering bands encountered three characteristic land-labour situations:

i. Land occupied by societies in which locality land-groups are, as regards technology, infra-structure and social organisation, already in conditions to produce and deliver surpluses to maintain artisans and a non-productive élite.

ii. Land occupied by dispersed and uncoordinated locality groups practising some form of rudimentary agricultural production as an integral part of a subsistence system, and

iii. Lands whose transient occupants were not tied to the land by custom of tillage, being hunters and gatherers and who, even if caught alive, were useless as a basic labour force, though individuals might be annexed to domestic families.

The first of these situations was met by the taking over of the apex positions in the society and the substitution of the symbols of authority by those of the conquerors, and the appropriation of the existing means of social control or the elaboration of new means. In order to do this it was necessary to allow the lower levels of existing social organisation to persist, and to collect surpluses both in goods and in labour. This was possible throughout most of Highland America, where intensive sedentary agriculture, with such technical sophistication as terracing and irrigation, had been developed. This belt includes the inhabited plateaux, slopes and valleys of the Highlands of Central and Southern Mexico, Guatemala, Colombia, Peru, Northern Chile and Bolivia. In most of this zone, the contemporary peasant population is markedly autochthonous in stock, retaining many features of social organisation adopted during the colonial period, in addition to some traits that can be traced to pre-Conquest times, and a subject status which the first 130 years of republican rule did little to replace.

The second type of situation mentioned is that encountered in most of the island and coastal areas of the Caribbean, in much of Brazil, in coastal Peru, Southern and Western Bolivia, Central Chile and in Paraguay. Here the conquerors encountered peoples at a lower level of technology who relied on slash and burn agriculture as well as hunting and fishing and were organised in small tribal and kinship groups. Their institutions had little in common with those of their conquerors, and there was little basis for the kind of understandings which made possible a system of indirect rule. Their productive activities were oriented towards a simple subsistence with no allowance in it for creating surpluses and accumulating capital. They could, however, be enslaved or otherwise incorporated in the work routines of the conquerors. It seems that the most important variable here, too, is the degree of intensity of demand for labour, related to the existence of a market. Where for instance, sugar could be cultivated and minerals mined, the inhabitants were impressed by some means or other and organised in work-gangs. But in the absence of a profitable market for commodities in high demand, the European had little alternative to attaching individual natives or families to his own domestic menage, whether by domestic slavery or by some other arrangement. And the more sparsely populated and remote the area of settlement, the less feasible it was to maintain even domestic slavery. Perhaps the logical extreme is to be found in the situation where both European and Indian found themselves facing the problem of uncertain subsistence, and where native skills in the management of creole crops and crafts could be coupled to the exploitation of new tools, seeds and animals brought in by the Europeans. The case of the settlement of Eastern Bolivia in such circumstances is described by Heath (1960), where, although the administrative form of the *encomienda* is used, geographic conditions imposed a simpler way of life. The small number of natives involved, the remoteness of the region from the busy populated areas of coastal and upper Peru, and the absence of Spanish women as companions and wives to the *encomenderos* made these into colonisers obliged to come to terms with the people of the land in the struggle for livelihood. 'It was the custom of the Indians of the land to serve the Christians and to give them their daughters and sisters and to come to their houses in the spirit of kinship and friendship. The Christians were thus served because they had many children and for this reason the Indians came to aid them as to the homes of kinsmen'[2] (Heath, 1960).

The third type of situation was that in which the inhabitants encountered were hunters and gatherers, as in North Mexico, Uruguay and Argentina, whose sparse tribes offered little possibility of conversion into a labour force of any kind. Where there existed the possibility of the production of sugar or of minerals, this was attempted, usually unsuccessfully, but on quite a large scale. But in the absence of either market or infra-structure, they were commonly attached in families or individually to work in agricultural production and domestic crafts for their own and their conquerors' subsistence. Their fate was gradual extermination or absorption, leaving the lands free for any who would work themselves or bring their own labour force with them. In this way, many such regions, colonised more recently, escaped from the rigid colonial mould of land-labour institutions and have experienced a freer capitalist process of development.

A fourth situation occurred where there was the coincidence of a strong demand for an export crop and good natural conditions for producing it, but inadequate labour. This tended to occur in those parts of the second type of area described which were situated on the sea coasts, and thus enjoyed good sea communications for the transport of their product to Europe, i.e. Northern Peru, the Caribbean and North-Eastern Brazil. Where the promise of profits was great and lasting, monocultural production, especially of sugar, was developed on the basis of the slave trade.

To the areas where societies were formed on the foundations laid by the first three kinds of encounter described, Elman Service (1955) gave the names Indo-America, Mestizo-America and Euro-America. To these must be added a fourth, Afro-America, referring to the last situation described, in which the importation of African slaves left a lasting mark on the population.

But visible differences in aggregate phenotype to be met with in the public markets of Buenos Aires, Asuncion, La Paz and Cartagena represent no more than a fortuitous expresion of the much more pregnant structural differences which have followed from variations in the disposition of resources, population and cultural level. Our purpose is not an ethnographic one, and the biological-cultural differences between one region and another are seen to be derived from the structural conditions of the encounter between peoples. But it will be noticed that the two major contrasting agrarian complexes, namely that in which slavery and share-tenure have predominated, supported by a high level of 'mercantility'; and that in which the *encomienda,* the estate, serfdom and service-tenure have predominated, and which are attached to subsistence production, have their cultural and phenotypical correlate in the idea of an Afro-America and an Indo-America.

However, the true significance of ethnic difference is not to be found in inter-regional comparison but rather in the role of ethnicity within any given local structure, especially in connection with the recruitment, maintenance and control of the labour force.

Self-ransom

If in the foregoing we considered some long-term consequences of the structural features of the 'encounter', it is also worthwhile looking at it to discern its immediate effects. For the incursion of the conquering bands and the spontaneous acts to which the situation gave rise tended to harden into procedures of conquest and institutions of governance, and these in their turn could not be lightly made to vanish when the tasks of building a new society were seriously taken in hand. That is to say, while pillage and subjection were in progress, the terms of the new society were being worked out involuntarily, and with little consideration for long-term aims. (We are not referring to cogitations and legal drafting in the royal councils of the peninsula, but the day-to-day process whereby practices become routines and they in turn become institutions, often at variance from their legal charters).

The relation of conqueror to conquered expressed itself clearly in a particular version of the institutions of the ransom *(rescate)* or better 'self-ransom'. The invading bands, unbound by societal strictures in their encounter with the indigenous peoples, set them to hunt out and bring in gold, jewels and precious objects. The way the ransom was carried out is described by Las Casas:

> The conquistadores arrived at the kingdom of Santa Marta (a part of the northern coast of what is today Colombia); they found the Indians working quietly in their huts, villages and lands; and were a long time with them eating and drinking what the Indians set before them, and receiving freely given presents of gold and objects worked by the Indians. And when the time came for the tyrants to leave, this is the way they paid for their lodging: the governor of the tyrants had all the Indians taken with their women and children and put in a large stockade made for the purpose, and had them know that they could only buy their freedom and leave by paying a ransom in gold, so much for the Indian, so much for each of his women and children, and to urge them on, left them without food until such time as the ransom ascribed to each be brought. Many of them sent to fetch gold from their houses and were able to ransom themselves, and were freed to go to their labours and to prepare food in their houses; but again the tyrannous governor sent certain foot-pad Spaniards to catch the miserable Indians, already once ransomed, and put them back in the pen to torture them with hunger and thirst until they should once again ransom themselves.[3]

This kind of institution is obviously only of occasional value to the dominant group, since it cannot operate as a permanent system of relations, nor even of appropriation, and is simply used in initial encounters, until accumulated capital in the form of immediately available treasure has been extracted: indeed the ceaseless hectoring of populations provoked resistance and was in conflict with the aim of permanent settlement based on the exploitation of native labour. (Parry, 1966: 223–4 and *passim*). But the initial grab for tangible wealth played an inevitable part in maintaining the solidarity and morale of the conquerors, who had invested deeply in risk and suffering to reap just such rewards. In any case, it is not unexpected that when one group can exercise complete domination over another, to which the in-group rules of behaviour have not been extended by analogy or by treaty, the dominated group is likely to be used in a purely instrumental manner. This treatment is 'inhuman' in just the same way that the torture and killing of interstitial beings like prisoners of war for the purposes of extracting military information is inhuman. Their marginality consists in their being beyond the rules.

Illustrations of 'frontier' institutions with a similar inhuman quality may be found much nearer, in the case of the Peruvian Amazon Company, a British firm operating during the first decade of the present century for the extraction of rubber from the Putumayo region of Peru. (Valcarcel, 1915). The Company recruited some hundreds of employees who were sent into the *selva* to organise the collection and portage of rubber to river stations by thousands of natives, men, women, and children, of the Borora, Witoto and other nations, under a system of force similar to self-ransom, only perhaps more destructive. The means of coercion used against them included the withholding of food by driving them from their subsistence plots and thus rendering them dependent upon foodstuffs imported by the Company; and whippings, torture and death for failing to deliver sufficient quantitites of rubber or for running away, with the result that many hundreds and possibly thousands lost their lives from hunger and murder. The horrors of the Conquest are liable to be repeated on the thresholds of an acquisitive society as it expands, and for the same reasons, for the two cases share several features in common. In both, the exploiters are attracted by marketable produce of exceptional value which requires only to be gathered. In both, the potential labour force lies outside the bounds of society, and equally outside the accountability of resources: for a brief spell, while the bonanza lasts, labour may be had for the taking. In both, the lines of communication leading from the frontier to the institutionalised watchdogs of morality and legality are overgrown.

Nevertheless, in the course of time the messages from the periphery got through to the centre, in the one case through the mouth of Las Casas himself to the Spanish monarchs, and in the other case by Sir Roger Casement, then at the British Consulate in Lima, to the British Anti-Slavery Society (Valcarcel, 1915). Lest the association of two such notorious agitators for social reform gives the impression that the cases involved are exceptional, it should be insisted that the inhumanity in question is by no means unpredictable behaviour in the type of social setting in which it occurred, and that a cool analysis leads down into some of the core principles of colonialism and colonial ideology, race relations and race prejudice. The myth of civilised man is constantly being exploded by his contacts with outsiders.

Slavery

The system of extortion which we have called 'self-ransom' and the modern system of forced labour referred to, are both executed upon outsiders who remain beyond the pale of society and excluded from the application of its moral norms. Slavery, however, makes it possible to appropriate permanently the person and the labour of the outsider by bringing him physically into it but only as person-property, without rights or patrimony.

The Spaniards established a further system, encomienda, whereby native populations could be incorporated into colonial society as a status group with formal rights and duties. The Portuguese, however, appear to have favoured the slave society outspokenly, considering slavery as the normal condition under which the natives should be incorporated. In 1535, when the Spanish authorities were seeking to put an end to Indian slavery, the King of Portugal gave to Coelho Duarte the right to 'grant lands in *sesmaria* to Christians and to enslave the Indians in order to use them as labour'. (Correia de Andrade, 1964:52).

Slavery, of course, requires certain societal conditions for its maintenance. The slave must be fed and clothed whether or not there is work for him to do. If he is to replace his kind biologically, then women and children, with a much lower productive potential, must also be provided with subsistence. The initial purchase of man and woman requires capital investment, and their surveillance also involves costs, or at least the owner's time. Thus enterprises run with slave labour can only be run profitably in technological and market conditions in which the value of the product is very markedly higher than the value of normal family subsistence production in the local culture and ecosystem.

It is one of the accepted characteristics of slavery that the slave should be an 'outsider' (Levy-Bruhl, 1959:151).[4] An industrial slave system can only with great difficulty be run on the basis of internal recruitment, which would require divesting established members of society of their ascribed rights and duties, exscinding them from their surrounding kinship and transforming them into property. Therefore, a second condition for the maintenance of slavery is the existence of supplies of 'outsiders' and a routine for obtaining them, namely an organised slave-trade. At first, in the course of the conquest, the 'outsiders' could be brought in from the outer unincorporated territories, from the Bahamas, or they might be Caribs, disqualified by their reputation for cannibalism, or the nomadic tribes of Northern Mexico, or those which occupied the hinterland of the north-eastern coast of Brazil. But the momentum of the growing slave-trade itself began to generate free-booting raids and officially sanctioned military operations in which resistance to Spanish arms or refusal to submit to baptism automatically qualified the native as an outsider and hence enslaveable. The conscience-saving device was the famous *requerimiento* or proclamation which was to be read before any military action, calling on the Indians to acknowledge the supremacy of the Church, the Pope and the Spanish kings and to permit the faith to be preached to them. Oviedo the chronicler records the occasion on which it first was used. A conquering band which he accompanied arrives at an already deserted Indian village. Oviedo addresses the leader of the band: '"Sir, it seems to me that these Indians do not care to hear the theology of this proclamation, nor do you have anyone who can make them understand it. Your worship had better put this paper away until we have caught an Indian and put him in a cage, where he can gradually master its meaning, and the bishop can help to make it clear to him."And I gave him the proclamation and he took it, amid the hearty laughter of all who were there.' Oviedo describes the attack, carried out without reading the manifesto, and comments that this procedure was usually neglected. To round off the story, our historian recounts a later meeting with Doctor Palacios Rubios, the learned writer of the proclamation, in which he asks him whether the consciences of Christians were satisfied with the proclamation, 'and he said yes, if it were done as the proclamation required. But I recall that he often laughed when I told him of that campaign and of others that various persons later made' (Oviedo, 1955: Vol. VII, 131–132).

In the Spanish territories, the legal suppression of Indian slavery was attempted and declared on various occasions, especially when its wastefulness of the labour force became apparent and supplies became scarce, so that from the middle of the sixteenth century on, slaves were only taken surreptitiously. In Brazil the *bandeirantes* continued their depth-raids into the interior, until the Pombalian legislation put an end to Indian slave-trading by *'resgate'*, that is to say, by official expeditions into the interior for 'ransoming' Indians held as prisoners by rival tribes.

In comparison with the enslavement of Indians, African slavery came to have much greater importance. According to Mellafe (1964), African labour was especially in demand in the Spanish colonies for gold-panning (in the first half of the sixteenth century) and in general for mining in places remote from Indian labour supplies, for the production of export-crops in the tropical lowlands – sugar, cacao, cotton and tobacco, and in food production for the city markets. In addition, there was a demand for Negro slaves as artisans' labourers, for work in transport by land, sea and river, for employment by public bodies such as royal offices, cabildos, monasteries and hospitals, and as prestige servants of the wealthy and high-ranking.

Thus an important sector of colonial Latin America came to have a very particular set of characteristics as regards economy and the elemental social relationships. The tropical lowlands, close by the continental and island shores, could produce some of the exotic goods which Europe demanded with sporadic voracity. Production could be so lucrative that the colonies could buy their labour from the African slave-trade and produce by means of the highly organised plantation system. But once established, this system of production overshadowed other systems and led to very special consequences in the economy so dominated. In many areas the labour function tended more and more to be assigned exclusively to the slave component of the population, and hence the decline of the idea that the performance of manual labour could be a recognised or respected means to an end for a non-slave. The performance of labour came to be regarded as a last resort, a demonstration of failure, and not a resource which every man has at his disposal to contribute, along with his knowledge, his tools and whatever other resources he may have to hand, to the production of wealth. Slavery meant that one more river had to be crossed to reach commercial entrepreneurship, namely, the obtaining of the capital necessary to invest in labour. As a traveller remarked of the agrarian situation in Brazil at the end of the eighteenth century, 'Although there is abundant land, there are few who own it, since even those who could do so, lacking the 150 reis to buy themselves each a Negro to do the work, would deem it the same to have it or no' (Vilhena 1923 [1802]).

Slave labour was a central and dominating factor in

Brazilian economy for three and a half centuries. It was finally abandoned when important advances were already being made in the cultivation and manufacture of sugar, thus diminishing the labour component of the inputs, and when the production of coffee was being expanded by entrepreneurs who found they could have the labour of European workers for wages and subsistence lands, and without tying up their capital in slaves. Moreover, these labourers, and other free migrants who were given lands in the south of the country added a new element to the population and the culture which helped to break the spell cast by slavery on work-attitudes. Some at least of the migrants brought with them from a cultural background deeply penetrated by the rapid expansion of European capitalism, an image of waxing livelihood for a man and his family, to be achieved by investing his own labour in the enterprise of another, then accumulating a small minimum of capital, and so reaching the position of independent producer. Indeed it was a good historic moment for such aspirations, given the rapid industrial expansion of the Sao Paulo area, and the easy access to land for those who wished to work in the South.

Encomienda

In contrast to slavery, by which outsiders were made a functional part of the productive system but at the same time excluded from formal participation in the society, encomienda stands for a bundle of laws and practices whereby colonial societies were formed by the superimposition of Spaniards and Spanish institutions upon kinships, landgroups and larger tribal and territorial organisations of indigenous peoples. But what makes description difficult is the stormy counterpoint between the use of encomienda as a legal cloak for the crudest and most immediate appropriation of native labour, and encomienda as a society-building instrument.

Let us start by saying that the institution is a blueprint for a form of indirect colonial rule over the greater part of the rural native population by a selected and privileged group of Spaniards, particularly those who had played leading parts in the Conquest or could otherwise win royal favour. The Crown, having pre-empted rights over the conquered lands and peoples, was therefore able to reward the entrepreneurs of the conquest by granting them rights of lordship over native settlements. These rights could be granted for the duration of the grantee's life and that of his heir. He was to receive an annual tribute, stipulated according to the population entrusted and what they were able to produce. He could make use of their 'personal services', which may be thought of as a tribute in labour or as a form of serfdom. He was supposed to take upon himself the christianization and 'civilisation' of his people and also the keeping of order. This did not always imply in effect a deep penetration of the existing systems of social organisation for the first few decades, and many local traditions continued to prevail as well as the rule of native local authorities.

In addition to the granting of encomiendas, Spaniards of all degrees also received land-grants in the form of individual properties – town lots for their houses, *estancias* and *caballerias* for the higher ranking and *peonias* for the lower, etc., within reasonable distance of the towns, and designed to contribute to the subsistence of their population. Moreover, the towns themselves as corporate bodies received commons *(ejidos),* plots of which were allotted annually to those who could use them, and where animals could be pastured and firewood and building materials gathered.

Not all the natives were 'entrusted'. Some landgroups paid tribute directly to the Crown, and were administered by a *corregidor.* Members of these communities produced their own subsistence and the surpluses necessary to pay their tribute and other taxes. They were also liable to labour duties.

In theory, the measures taken fulfilled a number of essential conditions. Productive labour in the society was assigned to the natives and to imported slaves, since Spaniards were culturally unavailable for this function.[5] The Conquistadores both large and small were rewarded. Tribute was paid to the Crown. The Catholic conscience was placated by the administration of liberal doses of the doctrine to the natives, and protective legislation 'guaranteed' fair wages and reasonable treatment.

But the encomienda laws and ordinances could not contain or control the social forces at work, though they came nearer to doing so in certain places as the century proceeded. The two qualifications 'primitive' and 'tamed' encomienda have been used by historians writing about New Granada (Lievano) and New Spain (Simpson, 1966) respectively, to refer to the institution as it worked in the first and second half of the sixteenth century. Under the primitive encomienda, the right to tribute in personal services was used as a cover for the full appropriation of the labour of the 'entrusted' natives of Espanola and Cuba, with little thought even for their survival. The population of Espanola, considered to have attained 100,000 when the Spaniards arrived in the 1490's, fell to 60,000 by 1508, 30,000 in 1554, and by 1570 not more than 500 were left.[6]

The inhabitants of Cuba suffered a similar fate, and in both cases the labour force was replaced by the purchase of African slaves.

The experience of the Antilles lent force to the insistence of the Crown on measures to protect the population and to abolish or at least to restrict personal services. A famous struggle took place towards the middle of the sixteenth century following the publication of the New Laws (1542) between the Crown and the lords-trustees. The Crown had by this time a clearly articulated though Utopian policy aimed at curbing the exploitation of native labour by putting an end to personal services, and royal officials who could attempt to carry out the new policy were sent to the New World. The Crown sought to put an end to forced labour which had become concentrated in the hands of the lords-trustees, and induct an era of free labour, based on the 'just wage'. The Crown was also concerned to regain effective power which had slipped more and more into the hands of the lords-trustees. But by this time the larger part of the economic system had been constructed on the principle of lords and 'entrusted' gangs of natives. Mining, construction, food production for the towns, mines and armies, transport, domestic service in the houses of the townfolk, arts and crafts and, of course, agriculture, all these were founded substantially on the assumed rights of the lords-trustees to dispose of the labour entrusted to them in the manner that seemed most profitable, complemented by the use of slaves. The degree to which encomienda had coalesced into a generalised system of forced labour is seen clearly in the complaint of Viceroy Velasco of New Spain in 1553 about the provision of the New Laws and especially their effect on the labour supply. He writes to the King of Spain:

> The Spaniards are very resentful because the New Laws touch them all. The Council (of the Indies) has declared that it is *personal service* to bring royal and private tributes to this city. Since the greater part of such tributes is in foodstuffs . . . there is much waste in the city, and I find no means of provisioning it, because, if the Indians do not do it, no disposition which I or the Spaniards make will suffice to provide the city even with bread and water, and fodder for the horses, which are

> the strength of the country. Counting the number of people who ordinarily dwell in the city, I find that between Indians and Spaniards, mestizos and Negroes, and outsiders who come to traffic here; there are usually 200,000 mouths [to feed]. Consider, your Majesty, how they are to be fed, for there are not among them a thousand farmers and the city is surrounded by a lagoon, unless [food] be brought in from without. Carts and pack animals are not sufficient; and they have more than they can do [anyway] to provide wood and charcoal, because the Indians have been relieved of bringing it in, which they consider a great bother. The provisioning of this city with wheat and maize – as well as all the other cities in the country – cannot be done unless it be done with Indians . . . As personal services are removed, the necessity becomes as great as that suffered by a city beseiged. (Simpson, 1950:149).

The outcome of the struggle must have been influenced by the realisation on both sides of the continuing demographic decline throughout the empire and the long-term necessity of fostering biological conservation of the labour force. The encomienda was tamed. The use of personal services was severely limited. Royal officials investigated the situation of the entrusted Indians and administered fines and punishments for their continued illegal exploitation, for failure to have the doctrine taught and the churches properly maintained and ornamented, for cruel punishments, enslavement and murder.

The general attack on the encomienda as the main source of labour in the Spanish colonies fostered a number of trends making for the decline of the institution itself, and the growing importance of alternative systems. But the inadequacies of the tame encomienda as an institutional framework for the use of labour are worth considering.

While encomienda in its primitive state created a class of 'lords of labour' whose exhaustive use and abuse of the natives may have contributed to their rapid biological decline, the tame encomienda, with personal services prohibited, was a serious obstacle to capitalist growth and diversification of production. For on the one hand, the native agriculturalist and craftsman, whether working in family or in community, even when he was able to produce surpluses, was obliged to part with them in the form of tribute. And on the other hand, the recipient of the tribute (the lord-trustee), was divorced from the process of production though in a position to accumulate capital, and could not legitimately use the labour entrusted to him in his own productive or entrepreneurial ventures. And though it was possible for them to maintain some sort of style in their city lives from the use and sale of the corn, chickens, firewood, earthenware pots, homespuns, etc., which accrued to them in tribute, with a small proportion in coin, it provided subsistence at a higher cultural level rather than a working capital which could be used in new forms of production. Indeed the possibilities of saving were restricted by the conditions of a quasi-natural economy, the conditions of which were aggravated by the continual draining off of precious metals to the metropolis, and the lack of coin in circulation. Thus, the second half of the sixteenth and seventeenth centuries were characterised by the building up of agricultural productive units bossed by Spaniards (or their descendants) making direct use of native labour, and either circumventing the encomienda arrangements altogether or using the power ascribed to 'lord-trusteeship' to subvert the institution and contravene its regulations. So in the shadow of decomposing encomienda, all the future arrangements of securing labour were experimented with, even the institutionalisation of the free labour market. The nature and operating conditions of these various types of productive relations were of course related to the great variety of conditions prevailing within the colonised area.

In Chile, where continuing warfare against the Araucanian gave an additional feudal touch of a military service obligation to the status of lord-trustee, the rules requiring that native settlements should not be interfered with was systematically contravened by the lords-trustees, who, in addition to their rights in encomienda, obtained land grants *(mercedes de tierra)* and 'set up their *estancias* and croplands *(sementeras)* in the midst of their own Indians' lands from the very first years of the Conquest' (Borde and Gongora, 1956:39). Thus, the lord-trustee, in his alternate role as an agricultural producer and landowner, was able to make use of the labour of the native settlement immediately adjacent to his lands.

The persistence of this tendency even after the abolition of personal services is described (ibid.:32) as 'the drift of the Indians away from their villages and onto the lands of the Spaniards, and the absence of any systematic development of the village economies, which decayed greatly'. And this drift was used to justify the further granting of village lands to the Spaniards.

The encomienda in Chile had served as a framework for the appropriation of native labour especially for mining enterprises, but by 1580 there was little easily available gold left and the native population had greatly declined. This falling off coincided with increased military activity on the southern frontiers, and in addition to the fulfilment of their military duties, the lords-trustees moved into horse-rearing and cattle production under the stimulus of an improving market. Their new line of production required greater extensions of land at varied altitudes and little labour, and fitted the new conditions well (ibid.:49). The taking over of native settlement lands increased and many townsfolk of resources and influence, traders and professionals, obtained landgrants. In this way the great *haciendas* of the Central Valley were formed and became stable and persistent concerns.

The same authors show the patchwork composition of the labour force in mid-seventeenth century. The *encomenderos* still have the use of a reduced number of natives, living in the withered village reserves. A few Negro slaves are to be found in domestic work and crafts such as work in metal or wood, or in animal husbandry, and attached directly to the household, but they were expensive to procure. Two other kinds of natives were found attached to the estate, namely, enslaved warriors (outsiders) from the frontier zone, and *yanaconas.* (In this context the word is used in its earlier sense to refer to natives who had no land-rights or membership of any land-group, as was the case of those who had accompanied the conquering armies as porters, servants and camp-followers. Many of these were in virtual slavery, and a *cédula* was published in 1674 resuppressing slavery.) Others were grouped together in reconstituted encomiendas and given subsistence lands near the cattle pens, serving as shepherds and herdsmen. They were permitted to cultivate their lands with the animals and implements of the estate, but as they were only allowed three days off per year to do so, they cannot be considered as service-tenants but as quasi-slaves, responsible in part for their own subsistence (ibid.:74). Service-tenure in its Chilean form *(inquilinaje)* seems to owe its beginnings to a burst of mercantility in the form of the sudden demand from Lima for wheat which made itself felt after the Lima earthquake of 1687 (Schejtman, 1968: 12, 16–22) and led to the planting of wheat on the *haciendas,* and the need for more labour. Gongora's researches have shown that probably already during the seventeenth century poor families of agriculturalists began to settle as renters on the estate lands, paying for them either in cash or in their own labour, and able to market wheat. These and their descendants were destined to become the main labour force of the estates, and their bargaining power vis-a-vis the proprietor has had its ups and downs, determined mainly by economic factors unaided by estamental subjection or ethnic discrimination, though it comes near to serfdom, especially in the last hundred years. In contrast to the areas of more dense population and higher levels of productive organisation, the Spaniards who were granted trusteeships in what is now Venezuela were unable to exploit a tribute system, and openly continued to use encomienda as a means of submitting and exploiting labour directly. The lords-trustees, as in Chile where population was also more scarce, requested and received of the colonial government either land grants within the areas inhabited by their entrusted Indians, or else applied for trusteeships over the Indians who lived near their land grants. Such, according to Eduardo Arcila-Farias (1957:310–312) was the accepted system of labour organisation until the latter part of the seventeenth century when cacao made possible a link with the European markets, and led to the purchase of slaves for a new form or productive enterprise.

One of the most useful studies of encomienda is a monograph by Juan Friede which traces the short post-Conquest history of the Quimbaya people who inhabited the temperate region around Cartago in the heart of the Colombian Andes. Around the year 1540 the Quimbayas were distributed under their *caciques* and in their settlements, to some thirty lords-trustees, averaging about 500 tribute-paying adults (or 2,000 to 2,500 members in all) per encomienda. Eighty-eight years later 11 encomiendas were still in existence, with an average of eight tributaries in each. During this lapse of time, an extensive human lineage had failed to survive the colonial system, a culture which had been especially outstanding in goldsmithery had been abolished, and a form of colonial administration had worked itself to a standstill.

In the year 1628 a *visita* was practised by a certain Dr. Lesmes, according to the colonial usages of the time. It took him 35 days to make the journey from Bogota to Cartago, where he had his first encounter with a group of lords-trustees who had gathered there to meet him. He finds that in disregard of the royal *cédula* of 1590, they had failed to build their houses and establish their homes in Cartago, and on the contrary either lived in their estates (that is to say, they had received grants of landed property, in addition to their trusteeship) or in more distant cities. 'The visitor exhorts the lords-trustees to build houses [in Cartago] and to establish their presence in the city with their horses and arms, on pain of forfeiting their trusteeships' (Friede, 1963: 178–9). He also notices that the Indians live dispersed through the countryside, which presents obstacles to indoctrination and supervision. He therefore ordered the setting aside of sufficient and fertile lands, with waters and woods, for the construction of a nucleated settlement, if necessary taking lands away from the Spaniards who had occupied them, for this purpose. He adds that these lands should be sown in corn before the people are brought together in the new settlement, to ensure that there is no break in their subsistence, since they had no means of storage at their disposal.

The remaining thirteen lords retain 703 entrusted Indians between them, of whom 119 are listed as *util,* that is to say tribute-paying males between the ages of seventeen and fifty-four) and an additional one hundred and twenty-nine are of the right sex and age but described as 'runaways'. Friede is rightly suspicious of these runaways and the apparent indifference of their lords to their abscondence, concluding that even if some of them had taken refuge from abuses and unjust impositions, most of them had been drawn into new structures of production with the connivance of their lords. Some had settled on estates or ranches as *concertados,* or service-tenants under nominal wage agreements and a greater or lesser degree of subjection; others were working as craftsmen in the towns, others were in the mines, with the lords-trustees in most cases drawing some kind of direct or indirect benefit. Many Indians, especially the *'chusma'* (women and children) had been taken to the lord's residence where they worked as domestic servants. In one case, the Indian village had been as it were turned into an estate farm and rented to a third party; in another the members of the settlement had been transferred as a body to the lord's estate in the hot lands of the Magdalena. A woman is given as a cook to a monastery as a payment in kind for the services of the *doctrinero* of the encomienda, and in another, a man is given out to work to a shoemaker in return for making the shoes of the members of the lord's household!

Thus the demographic decline was accompanied by the drawing off of the entrusted Indian population from their villages and subsistence lands and their absorption either in the domestic households or in the agricultural or other establishments of the lords-trustees and their associates, amongst whom must be reckoned the *corregidores* and other officials whose proper task remained the maintenance of the old structures. In this sense, the lineage of those who had been called Indians merged into what might more appropriately be called 'colonial peasants', whatever may have been their biological or cultural inheritance.

In the dry but irrigated valley of Chancay (Peru), studied by Faron (1967), the early encomiendas were accompanied by the concentration of the numerous but dispersed native population in villages. For a time, under the trusteeship system, uncontrolled use was made of native labour which, as elsewhere, declined rapidly. The situation was altered by the establishment of a Spanish township and the granting of estates to Spaniards (both lords-trustees and townsfolk). A number of the encomiendas were allowed to lapse and the administrative framework was replaced by the *corregimiento* system. As the lands passed steadily into Spanish hands, the natives were forced to become predial dependents of the Spaniards in the classic manner. At the beginning of the seventeenth century the area was linked to the developing markets of Lima across the hills, where there was a demand for beef cattle, loaf-sugar, salt and tobacco, and predial dependence took the form of share-tenure arrangements between the estate owners and the lackland Indians of the villages. And where sugar was produced, the economy could support the purchase and maintenance of slaves. Thus the conditions for mercantile capitalist production came into existence, and the encomienda faded from the scene.

The labour-duty

As the encomienda declined and the role of the lords-trustees as labour lords was subtracted from the institution, one of the formal means of maintaining and developing productive units was the labour-duty, imposed upon male members of native settlements. This took the form of the *repartimiento* or *mita* and functioned to effect a periodic transfer of labour from the native settlements to the mining, agricultural and public works enterprises of the Spaniards. By its regulations, an obligation was imposed upon the settlements to supply a certain proportion of their labour force according to rota for a definite period to the enterprises. The responsibility for the extraction of the labour teams for each stint was placed upon the native chief of the settlement (*cacique, curaga,* etc) while their distribution was the responsibility of local public authorities, who were to allocate rights to use labour to Spanish and *criollo* operators according to criteria determined by the varying interests of the Spanish Crown, modified in practice by local interests and pressures. A good description of the institution as carried out in the early part of the seventeenth century is given by the English priest Thomas Gage (1946: 230–233) who was at that time working in what is now Guatemala:

> The Spaniards that live about that country allege that all their trading and farming is for the good of the commonwealth, and therefore whereas there are not Spaniards enough for so ample and large a country to do all their work, and all are not able to buy slaves and blackamoors, they stand in need of the Indians' help to serve them for their pay and hire; whereupon it hath been considered that a partition of Indian labourers be made every Monday, or Sunday in the afternoon, to the Spaniards, according to the farms they occupy, or according to their several employments, calling and trading with mules, or any other way. So that for such and such a district there is named an officer, who is called *Juez repartidor,* who according to a list made of every farm, house and person is to give so many Indians by the week . . . They name the town and place of their meeting upon Sunday or Monday, to the which themselves and the Spaniards of that district do resort. The Indians of the several towns are to have in a readiness so many labourers as the court of Guatemala hath appointed to be weekly taken out of such a town, who are conducted by an Indian officer to the town of general meeting; and when they come thither with their tools, their spades, shovels, bills, or axes, with their provision of victuals for a week (which are commonly some dry cakes of maize, puddings of *frijoles,* or French beans, and a little chilli or biting long pepper, or a bit of cold meat for the first day or two) and with their beds on their backs (which is only a coarse woollen mantle to wrap about them when they lie on the bare ground) then they are shut up in the town house, some with blows, some with spurnings, some with boxes on the ear, if presently they go not in.
>
> Now all being gathered togethered, and the house filled

> with them, the *juez repartidor,* or officer, calls by the order of the list such and such a Spaniard, and also calls out of the house so many Indians as by the court are commanded to be given him (some are allowed three, some four, some ten, some fifteen, some twenty according to the employments) and delivereth unto the Spaniard his Indians, and so to all the rest, till they be all served; who when they receive their Indians, take from them a tool or their mantles, to secure them that they run not away; and for every Indian delivered unto them, they give unto the juez repartidor, or officer, half a *real,* which is threepence an Indian for his fees, which mounteth yearly to him to a great deal of money . . . If complaint be made by any Spaniard that such and such an Indian did run away from him, and served him not the week part [sic] the Indian must be brought, and surely tied to a post by his hands in the marketplace, and there be whipped upon his bare back. But if the poor Indian complain that the Spaniards cozened and cheated him of his shovel, axe, bill, mantle, or wages, no justice shall be executed against the cheating Spaniard, neither shall the Indian be righted, though it is true the order runs in favor of both Indian and Spaniard.

Writing about New Spain (Mexico) Chevalier (1956) gives the heyday of the *repartimiento* for the purposes of agricultural production as the second half of the sixteenth century and the first third of the seventeenth century. He asserts that powerful pressures were exerted in Spain, especially by the Franciscans, against the imposition of forced labour on the Indians, and that this led to the consideration of other possible strategems for drawing the natives from their subsistence lands. A plan was worked out by the Council of the Indies and Viceroy Velasco II in the 1590's to institutionalise and foster the use of free wage-labour (such labourers were known as *gañanes* or *naborias*) by raising wages well above the level paid for the labour-duty, which was little more than symbolic, in an attempt to attract the natives voluntarily, but they did not respond, thus confirming Velasco's opinion that they would only work if forced to: 'Indeed,' he says, 'the same would be and is true for their own holdings beyond their immediate needs and those of their families.' The Crown policy in the first decade of the seventeenth century coupled an insistence on a generalised duty to labour (meaning, of course, 'beyond subsistence needs') not only for Indians but also for *mestizos* and unemployed Spaniards, with the assertion of the right of the labourer to choose freely his temporary employers and so presumably to encourage the latter to compete in offering the labourer attractive conditions (Chevalier, 1963). It is hard to tell whether this market mechanism ever worked in practice. It is certainly not conspicuous in Thomas Gage's account.

Labour-duty for agricultural production was abolished in 1622–3 but retained as a means of supplying labour to the mines, both in New Spain and in Peru (Rene-Moreno, 1959; Rowe, 1957). Its abolition may be regarded as a victory for a social policy aimed at humanising the lot of the Indian. But it was a Spanish rather than a New World victory. In the 1590's Velasco had said: 'The number of Spaniards grows apace each day: the resultant increase in importance of harvest lands and public works and building projects both secular and ecclesiastical, coupled with the alarming shrinkage of the native population, makes it extremely difficult to support so large a structure with so small a labour force' (Chevalier: 1963). The *repartimiento* proved itself to be an inadequate device for supplying landowners' labour requirements. As the Indian population declined, and the number of entrepreneurially-minded Spaniards and Criollos increased, the struggle to control a permanent labour force for estates and manufactories *(obrajes)* became intense, while the decreasing and disorganised Indian settlements were put under intolerable pressure. So it ceased to be practicable to regulate this struggle for labour by means of continual bureaucratic interventions at the local level. Indeed, the matter was deciding itself by the making and extension of large estates, as autonomous dominated land-groups which acquired their own resident labour force; and the forces harnessed to this new cause were twofold: on the one hand, the engrossment of Indian subsistence lands whereby an increasing number of Indians were obliged to become estate dependents to maintain livelihood; and on the other, the power of the state against the individual who by iniquitous contrivance could be given the permanent status of a debtor and thereby made the thrall of an estate or manufactory.

However, where Indians continued to maintain communal or individual land rights, the labour-duty continued to be used occasionally or permanently, especially by priests and officials of the local administration. Indeed both of these categories of official were expected to make their livelihood by what could be extracted from the peasants of the settlements by one scheme or another, and where they were dissatisfied with the tributes and extortions they could obtain in coin or kind

(Parry, 1966: 209–210), they exacted additional labour duty, either for their own enterprises or on a commission basis for the entrepreneurs in their area. An interesting account of the way in which labour was obtained for a quinine-bark gathering expedition in the lower slopes of the Western Highlands of Peru in the 1860's is given by the French traveller Paul Marcoy. Both priest and governor are able to use their official role to impose the labour-duty, collecting the wages apparently for themselves. One notes also the familiar ill-treatment used to reinforce the *de facto* subjection of the peasants, especially necessary where the imposed duty has no basis in legality.

> All over the vast extent of the Eastern slopes of the Andes, if labour is short, the estate owners who are large scale cultivators of sugar, coffee, cocoa, manioc or coca, have to resort to the most diverse means in order to obtain workers. The most usual consists of arranging an interview with the governor or priest of one of the small towns of the Sierra who for a reward which is not to be divulged, sends through the mountains the number of individuals he needs to till his land or do his harvesting . . . the workers take their wives and children with them. The usual salary is 4 reales for the men and two for the women and food provided. The period of exile in the hot valleys is between three and six months. I used the word exile instead of sojourn because the natives consider it as such, and only undertake the trip for fear of being whipped or thrown in jail. When their exile is finished, these workers return home in worse conditions than those in which they set out. Their fields are unsown, the late snows have broken down their rooftrees; their domestic animals are dead or scattered; they are out of provisions and their clothes are in rags. And as for the money that their labour might have earned them, it was consumed long ago, for the owners are accustomed to open a shop on the estate and to sell (at 75–80% above the town prices) spirits, tobacco and coca to the men, and textiles, ornaments etc., to the women. An account is opened for every worker with a limit judged at the total amount they will earn . . . as a result of this speculation, very little salary is paid at the end, and to some none at all, for instance those who die in the valleys, this averaging about three in every nine: a ditch is dug and covered over, and there is no more to be said.

Marcoy himself went on a quinine-collecting expedition and

asked the governor of a settlement in the Eastern Cordillera to find labour for him. He described what happened:

The priest and the governor summon the people to present themselves for selection after mass . . .

> When mass had been said, the Indians obediently assembled in the square. The inspection began at once. Every well-built broad-shouldered, deep-chested individual was announced to us by name by our agent, who would grasp him by the beard or give him a friendly smack on the cheek, and went over all his bodily and spiritual qualities as an auctioneer would have done with a mule or a horse. The Indian for his part allowed himself to be handled, to be turned round, with a certain complacency.

The priest said that he would reduce the price from four to two reales per day, to be paid to him on return, and asked for each to be given 6 pesos in advance for making a few purchases before they went away, and for a final celebration. It is assumed that none of the final payment would reach the Indians. Marcoy recounts that his porters, recruited in Marcapata, commited acts of destruction against crops and huts on an hacienda on the outskirts of Sausipata. The reason given was that it belonged to the governor of Marcapata, who obtained labour for it by the real or invented misdemeanors of the Indians in that area, who were sent to the estate as to prison for periods of one week to a month. The damage was done in revenge and to lessen the demand for labour.

One of the most recent attempts to meet the economic needs of large farms by means of legalised forced labour as a status duty is to be found in Guatemala. When debt-peonage was finally abolished in that country in 1934, there was a scarcity of labour for the rapidly growing plantation area which had developed in the post-colonial period, and was geographically separated from the old and overcrowded Highland peasant settlements. The shock of this scarcity led to a reversion to something very much like the labour-duty, in the so-called Vagrancy Law (Whetten, 1962:121). It was based on the familiar idea that work must be an obligation for all, and that freedom consists in being able to choose for whom one will work. The law required that all who had neither profession nor trade should be obliged to go to work (mainly on the plantations) for 100 to 150 days each year, exempting only some ten to fifteen per cent of the peasantry – those who were able to prove owner-cultivatorship of a given minimum of land (between 2.8 and 7 acres according to the crop). 'Every worker was required to carry on his person at all times a work-book containing his identification and, if exempt, a note to this effect by the local authorities.' The book contained a record of days worked on plantations. Any person suspecting another of 'vagrancy' could denounce him to the local authorities. Considering that most peasants were illiterate, and that many spoke no Spanish, this legislation delivered them bound to the local officials and the landowners, who could put them to work with the full support of the law. Needless to say, such labour arrangements require a special kind of social order in which to operate, one which we have described as 'estamental'. It is implicit in the law that it is to be applied to the 'Indian' estament, immediately recognisable by the appurtenances of ethnicity, and also already conditioned to accept such impositions, implying exclusion from the enjoyment of the rights of citizens.

Debt-peonage

Unlike the estamental labour-duty, which assigns a whole sector of the population to the obligatory performance of labour, debt peonage refers to the contrived bondage of an individual with no reference to ascribed status or category. It requires a provision in the statute book making it possible to oblige a debtor to discharge his debt by the performance of labour. But if it is to be used systematically as a means of maintaining a bound labour force, it would nevertheless seem to require social arrangements which, like the estamental structure, maintain a handicapped segment in the population, whose members are systematically deprived of the knowledge, skills and alliances necessary to defend their legitimate rights in law.

Once it was legal for a creditor to require a debt to be paid off by means of the performance of labour by the debtor, then a contrived debt and a conniving officialdom could make possible the tying of debtors as labourers to any productive unit.

During the colonial period it was used for recruiting labour for manufactories and estates, and in the nineteenth century, though land monopoly forced increasing numbers of peasants into the estates, debt-peonage was used as an additional means of social control, making labour negotiable as between entrepreneurs without having to take into account the will of the labourer. It was also available for securing labour for outlandish and unhealthy places where even the landless would hesitate to pledge themselves in service-tenure.[8] Debt-peonage, though a colonial institution, is capitalist in character, and near to an arbitrary form of temporary and even permanent individual slavery.

An early example is provided by Vasquez de Espinosa (quoted by Keen, 1955:133–134) in the manufactories of Puebla, Mexico, probably during the second decade of the seventeenth century.

> To keep their mills supplied with labour for the production of cloth and grogram, they maintain individuals who are engaged and hired to ensnare poor innovents; seeing some Indian who is a stranger to the town, with some trickery or pretext, such as hiring him to carry something, like a porter, and paying him cash, they get him into the mill; once inside they drop the deception, and the poor fellow never again gets outside that prison until he dies and they carry him out for burial. In this way they have gathered in and duped many married Indians with families, who have passed into oblivion here for twenty years, or longer, or their whole lives, without their wives or children knowing anything about them; for even if they want to get out, they cannot, thanks to the great watchfulness with which the doormen guard the exits. The Indians are occupied in carding, spinning and weaving, and the other operations of making cloth and grogram; and thus the owners make their profits by these unjust and unlawful means.

After referring to the good intentions of the Crown in sending out mill inspectors to remedy matters, he says that these 'aim rather at their own enrichment, however much it may weigh upon their consciences, than at the relief of the Indians, and since the mill owners pay them well, they leave the wretched Indians in the same slavery; and even if some of them are fired with holy zeal to remedy such abuses when they visit the mills, the mill-owners keep places provided in the mills in which they hide the wretched Indians against their will, so that they do not see or find them, and the poor fellows cannot complain about their wrongs . . . '.

Almost two hundred years later, Humboldt (1822–3: 95–101) was in Queretaro not far from Puebla and visited textile manufactories *(obrajes)* there. Speaking of the labour-force, he enumerates 'free men, Indians and people of colour, are confounded with the criminals distributed by justice, in order to be compelled to work'. (Apparently he is not confounding debtors with criminals, for he describes the system of debt-peonage later).

> All appear half naked, covered in rags, meagre and deformed. Every workshop resembles a dark prison. The doors, which are double, are constantly shut, and the workmen are not permitted to leave the house. Those who are married are only allowed to see their families on Sunday. All are unmercifully flogged, if they commit a small trespass on the order established in the manufactory . . . The manufacturers of Queretaro employ the same trick which is made use of in several of the cloth manufactories of Quito and in the plantations, where for want of slaves, labourers are extremely rare. They choose from among the Indians the most miserable, but such as show an aptitude for the work, and they advance them a small sum of money. The Indian who loves to get intoxicated, spends it in a few days, and having become the debtor of the master, he is shut up in the workshop, under the pretence of paying off the debt by the work of his hands. They allow him only a real and a half, or 20 sous tournois per day of wages; but in place of paying it in ready money, they take care to supply him with meat, brandy, and clothes, on which the manufacturer gains from fifty to sixty per cent; and in this way the most industrious workman is forever in debt, and the same rights are exercised over him which are believed to be acquired over a purchased slave.

As regards the operation of the same system in the haciendas of Ecuador, an interesting description is given by the American, Hassaurek (1868:299) referring to the 1860's:

> In this connection it becomes necessary to explain the system of Indian servitude prevailing on the haciendas of the interior. The Indian farm labourers – and it is only the Indians and negroes who work on the farms, and by the sweat of their brows maintain the white population by whom they are suppressed – are called *gañanes,* or *concertados,* or *peones.* Their wages do not exceed half a real per day, which would amount to about twenty three dollars a year. In addition to this, the landowner is obliged to give each man a suit of coarse common cloth, and a hat, every year. He also gives them a piece of ground which they may cultivate for themselves, and

on which they build their huts, called *huasipongos.* For this miserable allowance they are compelled to work from early dawn until five or six o'clock in the evening. Before beginning their regular work, they are obliged to perform an extra task, such as gathering fuel, repairing the roads, carrying bricks, etc. The extra task is called *faena.* If they absent themselves from their work, the days they lost to their masters are deducted from their scanty wages, and they are in most cases punished for their dereliction.

It cannot be said, however, that the Indians alone are liable to be whipped by order of their masters. Negro and coloured *peons* are generally treated in the same manner, especially on estates remote from cities where they had no opportunity of making a complaint. The estate proprietor is often as arbitrary and despotic as an ancient feudal lord. On an estate on the river Guaillabamba, a sambo peon had run away from his master to try his fortune somewhere else. He was captured before he reached Quito, and his master immediately ordered him to be put in irons, and to receive one hundred lashes.

Besides the labour which they must perform for their masters, they are also compelled to do a thousand little things for their curates, who are generally more despotic and cruel than the landowners. Their wives and children must cultivate the land of the curate, if he has any, and furnish him with servants in addition. Under these circumstances, little time remains to the Indian for the cultivation of his own piece of ground, but his faithful, industrious and untiring wife steps in and does what her husband cannot do. The Indian women, however, are not exempt from labour for the landowners. They must perform their *faenas* like the men although they are not paid for it. It is evident that however cheap living may be in the interior, and however limited an Indian's wants may be, half a real per day is insufficient to maintain him and his family. He needs a hog, or a calf, or a sheep, a *tercio* of barley or corn to grind his raw meal for *mashca;* his wife wants a piece of *bayeta* for a shawl or a petticoat; his children must be baptised, and no credit is given by the curates, who inflexibly adhere to the cash system; a festival takes place in the neighbourhood for which a little money is required; the landowner therefore advances the money or furnishes the necessary articles, and he does so willingly because it is his interest to keep the Indian in debt. An account is kept of all these transactions;

but the poor *gañan,* to whom the art of reading or of writing is a mystery, is at the mercy of the *mayordomo* or *escribiente.* At the end of the year, the Indian not only remains in debt to his master, but the debt for which he was originally purchased has generally increased. It is not usual to settle accounts every year. In many cases it is done only when the Indian, tired of his master, asks for a settlement. He is then taken before a justice, or if it is in a city, to the police station, a balance is struck and the debtor imprisoned, as imprisonment for debt has not yet been abolished in Eduador. His *huasipongo* and the little piece of ground around it, now revert to his master and the Indian remains in jail until somebody else pays his debt, and thereby purchases his services. It is true he might make an assignment of his property, or, as we should call it, take the benefit of the insolvent act; but these are rights which he does not know, and how should he get the money to buy *papel sellado,* and pass through complicated legal proceedings? Moreover the courts would hold that by entering on a new year he made an implied contract to serve during that year, and specific performance would at once be decreed. His new master is generally on hand; labourers are in great demand; the Indian himself has already made an arrangement with his new master before he left the old one (and some Indians are shrewd enough to do this to their advantage) so he passes from one master to the other, a slave in fact though not in name . . .

The Indians of the Ecuadorean Highlands are their working capital the same as negro slaves in other countries. Great sums are invested in their acquisition. A hacienda owner once told me that his Indians owed him S/.13,000 (sucres). Another assured me that his capital invested in Indian labour amounted to S/ 15,000 (sucres). The debts for which they are usually sold vary from fifty to one hundred dollars. (Hassaurek, 1868: 302).

In 1960 the writer visited estates in the province of Imbabura and found that debt-peonage had by no means disappeared. At Sigsicunga estate, the tenant (the proprietor was a relation of his) boasted of his liberal treatment of the *huasipungeros* (service tenants), drawing attention to the fact that his foreman *(mayoral)* was no longer permitted to carry a whip, and that during the few years in which he was running the estate, none of them had tried to escape.

Service-tenure

Debt-peonage was a device based on trickery and class connivance and used for mobilising the repressive apparatus of the state to capture and hold in bondage individual labourers. It has an improvised quality and expresses the spasmodic advance of capitalist enterprise within the institutions of a landed society, of which service tenure is the typical structural feature. The development of service-tenure and the manorial estate represent the main trend following the breakdown of encomienda, and population decline. It represents a powerful social force consisting of a growing number of would-be gentry looking to better their fortunes (in rank and wealth) through the control of land, and its settlement and exploitation by a labour force permanently under their control. This movement may be said to have flowed with irregular insistence for three centuries, that is, from the beginning of the seventeenth century to the beginning of the twentieth century. Moreover, it used more brutally obvious and efficient means than contrived debt, namely the expropriation of native lands and the incorporation of the expropriated peasants on the estates, where they received subsistence lands and rendered service to their lords.

This slow transformation of the social order is not an expression of colonial policy, but rather a result of the growth in power of the strong at the expense of the weak which accompanied the waning of the ability of the Spanish monarchs to control their colonies, and the emergence of an 'aggregate intention' in the colonies diverging sharply from explicit colonial policy. And if it is true that from time to time the colonial government sought to check the process, its local officials were more inclined to go along with the landed proprietors into whose ranks they were able to enter. Indeed it tended to withdraw an ever increasing segment of the society from any direct control by the government, concentrating power in the proprietary class whose members held their landed territories as autarchies. The spontaneous character of these developments, acquiring a variety of appropriate forms in many contrasting local settings, is manifest in the nomenclature of the service-tenure relationship which bears many different names, no single one of which serves anywhere as a generic, though *colono* and *colonato* approaches nearest.

Under customary service-tenure agreements, the peasant receives dwelling and usufruct rights to land for tilling, gathering and pasture, and certain facilities within the boundaries of the estate which allowed him to procure his family's subsistence and limited livelihood, in return for which he (and to a lesser extent the members of his family) must perform agricultural and other services for the landowner, and accept full dependence upon him.

The historical circumstances attendant on the formation of the estate as a landgroup were bound to set an initial pattern for the service-tenure relationship, as can be seen in comparing for instance Chilean service-tenure, *(inquilinaje)*, which grew out of an arrangement of mutual accommodation, (see p.18), with the Highland Bolivian version, forced into existence by expropriations and armed terrorism (see pp. 124–130). Yet in the longer run, the relationship is moulded by factors conditioning the ends for which the relationship exists, of which four seem to be of special importance:

i. The lines of production of the demesne farm and the actual labours which in consequence the service-tenant must perform. This can lead to the harshness of supervised gang labour, but can also lead to a regime in which only rewards can assure that the service is performed with the necessary care e.g. in the management of animals.

ii. The 'level of mercantility' or extent to which the demesne production is oriented to a market, requiring optimum use of resources.

iii. The level of supply of both land and labour, and

iv. The social structure of the larger society, which provides a framework for the relation between the landowner and the service-tenants and a set of sanctions out of which the system of social control is fashioned.

Finally it should be said that the internal dynamic of the structure of the estate landgroup is modified by other factors such as kinship, internal prestige systems and competition, liens based on personalism, accommodation and transactions, giving to each a unique physiognomy.

The service-tenure relationship stands at the centre of the traditional low-mercantility estate which has dominated the agrarian structure throughout most of Hispanic American History. Being pre-industrial in technology, its means of production were almost entirely landbound. Its potential for producing surpluses beyond subsistence needs was limited and its capital requirements minimal. Thus landownership implied exclusive control of resources on which domination was based and was accompanied by control of the nexus linking the estate as a social system with the larger society. Its members were therefore excluded from the independent performance of civic roles, while the state was excluded from intervention in the estate landgroup.

A large part of our analysis of the present condition of the peasantry plays upon the decay of labour systems based on payment in usufruct and their replacement by wage-labour and in some cases share-tenure, contrasted with a few cases in which service-tenants themselves become more effective entrepreneurs than their landowners. The transitional character of the contemporary situation may be seen clearly in two contrasting facts: on the one hand, there are few examples left in which service-tenure as such is the primary basis for an estate labour force: on the other hand, with the exception of some modernised plantation zones, and Uruguay and Argentina, South Chile and North Mexico, whose agrarian structures are post-colonial, there are few estates with a labour force based on pure wage-earning labourers. Most estate labourers still produce some part of their subsistenceon lands made available to them by the estate, or else retain some connection with family members who have access to lands of their own. Though the trend is towards proletarianisation, a rural proletariat in the sense of labourers who have suffered a complete rupture from land as a primary appurtenance of livelihood, is still a small minority.

Share-tenure

The substance of this book is about the contemporary scene, which is characterised by the rapid spread of mercantility and the simultaneous penetration of rural areas by improved transport and capitalist forms of productive organisation. At the same time, during the last decades, most countries have crossed a threshold into a period of surplus in the labour market. For this reason share-tenancy has not been given special treatment in this chapter. There are of course those forms of share-tenure at the subsistence level which are used between neighbours to even out relative inequalities in the matching of family labour to family land, and likewise forms of labour-exchange. But the more important form of share-tenure is associated with high mercantility, an easily marketable crop, and usually a demanding one from the point of view of labour. Share-tenure is therefore very much in the forefront of the discussion of the contemporary scene.

Conclusion

In the foregoing chapter we have outlined some of the main institutional arrangements whereby the peasantry has been set to work, producing its own subsistence, and delivering its surplus products and labour to the non-labouring superior strata and the representatives of state and church. Each institution described is an adjustment made by the power-holders to a limited number of prime factors, among which are the following: the land-labour ratio, the level of mercantility, the availability of capital and the potentialities of the known technologies when applied to the land.

However, it must not be assumed that the peasant was entirely without countervailing power. Though we cannot consider population decline as a positive exercise of power against the viability of the system, yet the desperate hugging of provision lands, the grudging concession of labour, and the transactions, compacts and surreptitious appropriations and encroachments within the structure of the estate, all express peasant resistance.

Changes in the social order are, for example, reflected in the contrast between trusteeship (encomienda) and the labour duty *(mita)* on the one hand, and service-tenure and debt-peonage on the other. The first two of these are clear expressions of the changing policy of the colonial power of the Spanish sovereigns in consultation with their advisors and viceroys. They are the subject of frequent legislation which is concerned with royal revenue and the maintenance of royal power and the role of royal officials, as well as with the protective and religious functions which the Crown took seriously, so long as they did not clash with fiscal interests. The operation of both implies the intervention of government regulation and colonial officialdom in the productive process. In this way, both give support to the existing power structure which continued to rest upon clientism (Miranda, 1969) that complicated concatenation linking the enjoyment of facilities by colonial subjects at all levels to the purchase of the grace and favour of the sovereigns. At the same time, both institutions seem to have failed to foster agricultural production adequately and were characterised by an exaggerated ambivalence as between their norms and their performance. Their decline seems to signify a silent transfer of power from the Crown to local operators, who were able to assemble in their hands various resources, the most important of which was the appropriation of land.

The institutions of debt-peonage and service-tenure (usually disguised behind the legal fiction of officially supervised wage contracts) in contrast, emerge as local initiatives, surprisingly similar in different forms to fit local circumstances and custom, and performed within the quasi-autarchic domains of the growing class of landlords. One of the essential elements in the process of appropriation of lands, involving also the expropriation of native landholders and their subjection within the estate system, was the 'demographic catastrophe' which reduced native population in the more densely inhabited areas, to a fraction of its original size between the initial encounter of the Conquest and the early decades of the seventeenth century. This extraordinary phenomenon disorganised land use and depopulated native settlements. Lands which had once been tilled became open grazing for feral cattle whose increase was uncontrollable, and offered an easy form of subsistence and modest wealth to those who could seize it. But while the native population declined, the number of Spaniards, already conditioned in their livelihood expectations to be usufructuaries of native labour, increased, thus enjoining a much more economical use of this labour. The institution offering this degree of efficiency was that of the service-tenure estate.

So the key to fortune became the individual ownership of land, and the coercive recruitment of labour from diminished reserves, by the expropriation of traditional right-holders. A society was mapped out in which utilised land was divided between native settlements or parts thereof which were successful in maintaining possession of their lands, and the ever expanding estate lands, some of which had entirely enveloped and subjected existing settlements and others of which had created new estate settlements, of dependents, drawn from diverse origins. This process could also be seen on a smaller scale where nucleated settlements had been formed *(pueblos de indios, reducciones)* with appropriate lands for communal and individual use by natives. These, too, suffered the intrusion of poorer Spaniards, *Criollos* and *mestizos* (Mörner, 1965), and others not classified as *indios,* and usually without legitimate land-rights, who nevertheless were able to take over native lands in the course of generations, by fraud, marriage or illegal purchase, or legitimate land grants and *composiciones.*

In the nineteenth century, (especially the second half) the process of engrossment of native lands took on renewed strength, under two distinct impulses – on the one hand, growing demands from Europe for commercial crops increased the pressure for both land and labour, while justification for the freeing of native lands from the protection of communal status was found in liberalism and a laissez-faire view of the solution of the problems of economic growth.

However, it was accompanied by a compensating movement towards the formation of new settlements of smallholders. Some of these resulted from the fragmentation by inheritance of estates in areas where agriculture offered little beyond subsistence. In others, smallholding developed by the sale of marginal land to service- and share-tenants who had been able to profit by commercial agriculture, either in production or services. A third stream was that of internal migration and colonisation in response to a demand for commercial crops, or even for subsistence lands, while the last quarter of the nineteenth century saw great waves of Europeans, (from Italy, Spain, Germany and the Canary Isles) especially in the southern temperate regions, much of which eventually settled on new lands.

In 1888 slavery was effectively abolished in Brazil and debt-peonage disappeared from Mexico in the decades following its revolution, while servile forms of service tenure have survived, until the 1960's in areas of low mercantility. However, in most countries a crucial moment was reached in the third or fourth decade of this century when the supply of free available labour caught up with and overtook the demand, and the labour market replaced coercion and the squeeze on subsistence lands.

In the transformation have concurred population growth boosted by migrations, the overcrowding of subsistence economies, the breakdown of rural marketing complexes involving domestic crafts, steps in the mechanisation of production and transport, and the general tendency to end service-tenures on estates. At the same time, the proprietors of estates have lost their predominance in most governments, and in certain circumstances, peasants and agricultural workers' organisations receive official support. But in order to analyse the conditioning and motivation of the peasant's behaviour, and interpret the social transformation in which he is involved, some further development of conceptual apparatus is necessary.

NOTES

1. The main credit for these ideas must go to the anthropologist Elman Service (1955) viewing the conquest situation through the cultural prism. See also James (1942), Friede (1952), Caio Prado Junior (1965), H. B.

Parkes (1962) and Parry (1966). Also the *Handbook of South American Indians,* edited by Steward, and *Acculturation in the Americas,* edited by Sol Tax.

2. Heath is here quoting an undated communication to the King of Spain from one Diego Tellez which appears in a privately printed *Coleccion de documentos relativos a la historia de America,* Asuncion, 1899–1901, edited by Blas Garay. See also Service (1954).

3. This passage is quoted by Lievano (Vol. I, 13) and the translation is mine. Unfortunately Lievano refrains from citing his sources, and up to the moment I have not been able to find this passage in Las Casas. The *rescate* as an institution of plunder is stressed by the Colombian historian Indalecio Lliévano (1972 p.23), who quotes the foregoing from Las Casas.

4. The Aztecs liked to use their captives for sacrifices and maintained a system of slavery by internal recruitment. But from Katz's (1966:142–148) discussion, it appears to have been a kind of domestic bondage which does not negate his or her free status which 'was conserved in the place where he lived, in his city and his family'. Aztec slavery seems to have maintained an important contractual element, safeguarded by the society, between the 'enslaved' and his master.

5. Aspirations to a status higher than that of labour-giver or handworker were implicit in the system of motivation which brought the early bands of Spaniards to the New World, whatever may have been their position in Spanish society.

6. On the population decline in Mexico see Gibson (1964:403–409), Cook and Simpson (1960), Parry (1966:223–228); for New Granada see Lievano and for Peru see Vollmer (1967).

7. Carmagnani (1963:22) is suspicious of those who attribute the decline of the encomienda towards the end of the seventeenth century in Chile to contagious diseases, seeing its cause in the failure of the encomienda as an effective institution for the allocation of labour, and the consequent destruction of old native settlements and the transference of their populations to the estates *(estancias).*

8. Ben Traven's novel *The Ride to Monteria,* available as a paperback, must be one of the best accounts of the impressment of labour for the extraction of *caoba* wood from the unhealthy tropical lowlands of Mexico. The author has a great deal of sociological insight, and shows that impressment for debt worked out as a covert system of enslavement aided by the authorities, and making use of the ascription of advantages and handicaps by the estamental system.

The contradiction between actual social arrangements, involving thralldom based on ethnic distinction, and the liberalism and equity of the constitutions of the Republics, created a situation of generalised illegitimacy in the operation of institutions governing relations between the powerful and the weak.

II

The Context of Peasant Action

The pursuit of livelihood

In this chapter an attempt is made to present some of the crucial concepts necessary for discussing peasant conduct. A broad and simplifying approach to the problem of motivation is summed up in the notion that man pursues livelihood[1], which is taken to mean the sum of material goods, services and facilities used by a family in the course of its career, or by a man or woman during a lifetime. In addition to connoting such a packet of real goods and interactions, people living in different societies can be expected at any moment to maintain an approximate image of the livelihood for which they are working or which they expect to be their lot and their family's.

For a peasantry, livelihood consists of food, drink, housing and domestic equipment, much of which is made out of the product of family or neighbourhood lands, a certain number of purchased articles, participation in local and regional institutional life, use of the local irrigation, transport and communications system, the enjoyment of some forms of exchange of goods and labour with neighbours, and the rights and duties (however distorted) of citizenship, including the external legitimation and protection of rights of property in land. So the individual, both on his own account and as a member of a family, 'pursues livelihood' continuously and daily, both by means of his economic activity whose outcome he is able to transform into livelihood by domestic appropriation or by exchange, and in his social life by means of his participation in community facilities and the performance of institutional roles.

This approach makes it possible to avoid the pitfalls in the various arguments about whether peasants are 'economic men', whether they are maximisers, etc. The contenders in these arguments are members of societies which are fully monetised, in which expanding production is the norm, and in which nearly all productive effort may be transformed into cash, so that the higher level of cash (or cashable) income, the greater the variety of elements of livelihood accessible; while our peasantries, in so far as they continue to be partially or largely self-provisioning, exert themselves to produce and to obtain a specific set of items composing livelihood rather than seeking quantity indiscriminately. This does not mean that opportunities to increase income or production are lightly foregone; it means that so long as self-provisioning remains the central goal of economic activity, the obtaining of the desired livelihood is a complex operation, especially as regards the allocation of labour-time and land-space to different economic activities, taking into account the unpredictability of weather and the various obligations and liens with kin and neighbours upon which the systematic give-and-take of usufruct, goods and services rests. So the options for improving production will be taken up only after carefully weighing their effect on the other elements of the system.

The 'farm'

The means of livelihood is participation in one or more units of production or 'farms'[2] in such a way as to acquire the right to dispose of all or part of the product, or to acquire some agreed compensation from it. Thus, the form of such participation is the essential relation in a peasant's existence, and defines those interests which he must sustain at all cost. If it were possible to connote 'peasant' by specifying a single relationship to the productive unit and to the other social elements pertaining to the organisation of production, then many of the problems connected with the concept *peasant* would not arise, and it would be possible to move towards generalisations about peasants' conduct by inference from this relation. But the relations linking man to the unit of agricultural production in the pre-industrial situation is complex.

For a farm to establish a routine of production which continues from year to year, even at a rudimentary level, a number of requirements must be met. Land must be available each year, and held uninterruptedly by the producer until the harvest has been gathered. The permanent need for labour implies at least the maintenance of one family's livelihood out of the product. There must also be a known technology of production suitable to the local ecology and the possibility of securing all the production inputs, either from the land and last year's harvest, or by purchase.

It is possible to separate four economic functions which must be performed for agricultural production to take place:

i. landownership: the holding of primary rights to decide the uses of a parcel of land, and the owing of the duties which accompany the rights;

ii. entrepreneurship: the obtaining and committing of labour and resources to particular productive cycles, in anticipation of the right to dispose of the resulting product;

iii. managership: the deployment of productive resources according to a knowledge of productive technique and local conditions, within lines laid down by entrepreneurship, and

iv. the performance of the manual acts necessary in the process of production.

The idea of entrepreneurship used here is wider than when used by the economist since it does not of necessity involve market relations. The action of sowing now to reap next year is the essence of entrepreneurship – perhaps we should call it 'natural entrepreneurship' to distinguish it from the more advanced kind involving the investment of accumulated money and resources in anticipation of the sale on the market of the goods produced.

The concept of economic functions and their apportionment to individuals according to role makes manifest the differences between kinds of production units and also opens the way to an analysis of the relations between social systems and economic behaviour. Thus, in the owner-operated family farm, the unity and coordination of these four roles is related to the structure of the family as a kin group, and to the authority exercised by the father. The contracting of marriage is also an arrangement between two proprietors to join their lands in a single farm and to reproduce labour. Economic roles take their place in a total role-set of the individual, and economic rationality in relation to the unit of production may be contrary to the requirements of other roles. The pre-industrial smallholding is likely to be tightly intertwined with others of its kind and set in an institutional matrix which makes individual autonomous action difficult. Nash (1960) suggests that the problem of peasant development arises largely from the lack of a *firm* or autonomous productive unit. So even if we confine our search for the motivating factors of peasant conduct to his relationship to the means of production, the 'productive role-set' of the individual must be examined closely in order to see the order of importance of the different economic functions which he has to perform.

The organisation of large farms is complex and takes various forms. Landownership is always separated from work, (except when the latter is powered) and may be separated from entrepreneurship as well, while management is diffused through a variety of supervisory personnel. Economic roles are associated with different classes in society, and the relations between the productive roles inside the farm are supported (or hindered) by the relations between the corresponding classes outside it. Proprietorship of pre-industrial estates may be accompanied by lordship, giving to the incumbent extra-economic political power over the members of the landgroup. The relation of trust between patron (entrepreneurship) and steward (managership) may be assured by kinship or pseudo-kinship and the dangers of a manager 'compacting' with the peasant service-tenants in the misappropriation of produce and usufruct may be avoided by the appointment of foreigners or cultural outsiders (Scots, Germans, *mestizos*) as stewards.

Finally, of course, members of the labour force may belong to a subjected estament, or they may be debtors, and thus bound; or they may be organised in peasants' or rural workers' unions or political parties, with their offices in the towns and cities, in which they can obtain added bargaining strength and protection in the enjoyment of their rights. So the four economic roles required by the farm are attached to the larger society, and the interaction between them responds to the changing relations between classes in the society.

Thus the underlying pressures and strains of the agrarian society become apparent when one takes into account the way in which the essential economic functions necessary to agricultural production can be isolated and then seen as components of the various kinds of role-sets guiding the conduct of rural people, according to their 'productive status'. But productive status does not tell the whole story of their motivation, as we shall see.

The rationale of change

Having once established *pursuit of livelihood* as the concept best expressing the guiding intention of most peasant conduct, it is possible to move on to problems of socio-economic change. The process of change is a condition of existence, and infinitely complicated, while its motors and forces are only partially perceived by individual human consciousness. However, the human being is inevitably the main actor and becomes conscious of a part of the larger process at those points when a decision is required of him or her whether to repeat in the accustomed manner a particular act or action sequence, or whether to choose some feasible alternative. Why should the accustomed conduct be set aside and a new and different conduct adopted?

If we conceptually separate *livelihood* as a goal sought, from the technical and institutional means whereby this livelihood-goal may be attained, then changes of conduct are seen: either (i) as a response to a change in the effectiveness or adequacy of the technological and institutional means of attainment of livelihood or (ii) as a subjective change in the actor whereby he comes to modify the composition of his livelihood-goal. This usually means that he becomes dissatisfied with his former achievements and expectations and now desires more or different items in the packet, whether food or clothing, housing or schooling and so on. As we shall see, this subjective change takes place for a variety of reasons.[3] Perhaps the most important and most overlooked is what may be described as the 'deconstraining' of peasantries by the erosion of imposed systems of social control, resulting from loss of power by rural gentry, mobility, the winning of political allies, familiarity with a freer town life, and mass communication and schooling. However, since we have associated livelihood with families, then it must be recognised that changes in the goal-system which orients the pursuit of livelihood take place by the shifting of power from the old to the young, conditioned in a new situation, rather than by a radical change in values by the family head.

Undoubtedly changes in this latter sense take place, and help to explain changes in political behaviour, migration, the pursuit of education, and the adoption of some form of entrepreneurship or commerce related to agricultural production. When once opportunities are perceived, it is not long before horizons are raised.

Decisions to change cropping, technology or the organisation of production are more likely to arise from objective changes in the means – both physico-technical and institutional – of pursuing livelihood, and these are usually changes for the worse. For example, the family's land endowment declines, there is a drought or plant disease, adult sons no longer work willingly for their keep alone, artesanal activities decline because of industrial manufacture of goods, the price of the product falls when production is abundant, etc. Except where land reforms have been successfully effected, there are few places in Latin America where the livelihood of the majority of the peasantry is not in decline. As we shall see, both technological and institutional means of gaining livelihood are proving obsolescent or inadequate, and it is against this background that new techniques, crops, institutional arrangements are experimented with. The peasant, finding himself with diminishing land and increasing livelihood needs, is offered new technologies requiring industrial inputs and capital investment which are beyond his reach. Under these circumstances, innovation when it occurs is frequently a defensive step rather than a confident advance towards more ample entrepreneurship.

So while the peasant takes decisions involving changes in his economic, social and political conduct, the options open to him express the evolution of the local situation, responding to larger economic and social forces in which the individual actor has only a very small hand.

Self-provisioning (or 'autoabastecimiento')

This refers to the faculty of a group to extract the physical requirements for livelihood from the natural resources of the limited area which it inhabits. It implies production for the use and consumption of the producer group. Life based on autonomous self-provisioning is inevitably lived in isolation and at an extremely exiguous cultural level, but as our concern is with peasantries, extreme cases of this kind do not arise since the insertion of the latter in national societies means that they participate in market relations both as producers and consumers. What are the material elements of livelihood which may be extracted by cultivation or collection from the land, fashioned or processed by received techniques, and consumed or used? Soil, rock, waters, flora and fauna can provide for house-building, containers, utensils, many tools, rope, textiles, dietary, medicines, ceremonial objects and secular ornaments. Peasant material culture, including daily consumption, is made out of a combination of local materials worked by received methods, and articles imported from other areas with different ecosystems or from industrial sources, whose inventory begins with iron tools, salt and matches and goes on to include goods of all kinds which are substitutes for or complementary to locally made goods, according to cultural expectations and economic necessity. The most important elements of subsistence, and those which concern us most here, are sources of water and supplies of energy-giving foodstuffs of vegetable or animal origin, with an adequate storage and preservation system where supplies are not available all the year around. A number of creole plants whose cultivation and use has been elaborated by autochthonous cultures, and some imported ones, have provided and still provide the main substance of this dietary.

Throughout the Amazon and Orinoco basins, and elsewhere in fertile moist tropical soils, *manioc* or cassava serves as the main subsistence crop, though it is low in proteins and fats and therefore provides poor nutrition. But is is easy to plant and rich in bearing and can be left in the ground without danger of rotting for a reasonable time, and so can be taken out and used as required. It can also be milled into coarse flour, though the manual process is laborious. Different varieties of dry beans are used for subsistence in Brazil, Chile, Colombia, Venezuela and Central America, doing especially well in climate without extremes. Some kinds require only four months from seed to crop. Maize is the most common of the subsistence crops and grows in many well adapted varieties in most parts of the continent. In the Highlands of South America as in the temperate latitudes of the South, the potatoes and similar tubers form an important part of subsistence, and ingenious methods of preservation by natural freezing and drying are still used in the Andean Highlands.

Wheat, introduced by the Spaniards, serves the subsistence needs of the Chilean peasantry, while the banana, of more recent diffusion, is used in some of the wet tropical areas. Some of its varieties are productive where very little else will grow, like the *topocho,* a small plantain which thrives in the Upper Orinoco Plains and is the mainstay of the cattle ranchers of this inhospitable area.[4]

On the basis of an assured supply of carbohydrates and whatever else the land may offer, the peasant household economy is constructed, and necessities which the land does not afford must be obtained by exchange. So over and above the package of goods destined for family consumption, plus next year's seed, surpluses must be produced to provide the cash or the kind for the purchase or barter of these additional consumer goods, for capital replacements and whatever rent or tax payments may be required. These surpluses may be in the subsistence products themselves or in some cash crop or product not consumed by the family but in market demand.This is what Manning Nash (1960) has called the adjunct export economy and the majority of our smallholders uncomfortably straddle subsistence and commercial production in this way. But in places where pressure on land has become intense, livelihood cannot be maintained even by a combination of subsistence and market production, and the peasant must further supplement his income by sale of his labour on the market, in neighbouring estates or in seasonal migrations, or else by craftwork, using materials obtained from outside, or by himself turning to trade. Indeed some of the toughest entrepreneurial striving comes from peasantries whose land base has been reduced far below the minimum necessary for export-adjunct economies like the pig-dealer butchers of Quinchuqui, Ecuador and the Quiche traders of Santa Maria Chiquimula, Guatemala (see Chapter VI).

The most serious incompatibility between the self-provisioning principle and industrial conditions is the threat of a rising population, made possible by public health measures, producing a relative decline in land available, or a *declining resource-ratio.* If this condition is accompanied by a rapid expansion of the economy, then the excess population of subsistence areas may be absorbed in the urban labour force. But the two trends do not necessarily coincide. In Java, for instance, the tenfold increase in population during the last 150 years has extended and intensified self-provisioning production in conditions which have diminished per capita production and made it necessary to substitute first maize then cassava for the preferred rice in certain areas, on account of the higher carbohydrate yields of the latter (Penny, 1969:73). Haiti appears to have been in the grip of a similar process of decline, aggravated by deterioriation of the soil by erosion from ill-use and over-use for the past 50 years (Moral, 196l:114–123). Other areas of declining self-provisioning agriculture can be found in parts of all the Highland Countries, especially where smallholding communities are of long standing, and have suffered encroachment by the estates.

In order to see the role of self-provisioning in the social formation of rural society, one must stress the axiomatic nature of the coupling of the individual family to a specific piece of land from which a central core of subsistence may be drawn. This umbilical relationship is the core of the security which the peasant family looks for in pursuit of livelihood. Nearly all rural families (and most families *were* rural) had access to some specific provision ground – *roça, conuco, milpa, chacra, huasipongo, topo, ración de tierra, pegujal, sayana, jardin,* etc. – from which the major part of the family's food requirements was drawn. Moreover, the terms under which the peasant family held rights of access to its land largely defined the extent to which the family disposed of its own labour force and the structure of the group to which it belonged. The guarantee of such rights by the state involved duties to the state – duties of service, of tribute or taxation. The sharing of such rights within a juridical community implied a set of formally institutionalised arrangements and mutual obligations with the rest of the members. The concentration of individual smallholdings in a geographical unit of land involving inter-dependence leads to the development of exchange and cooperative arrangements, and institutions of control and decision-making about common locality problems, until such time as institutional penetration by the larger society fosters the individualisation of each nuclear family and economy. And in the absence of either communal or individual right of possession, the concession of usufructuary rights in alien lands may carry with it a heavy load of obligations not only to pay rent in services, in cash or in kind. Possession of subsistence lands has constituted the peasant's life-line, and alien control of it can spell subjection.

Thus, the 'paleotechnical' low-mercantility estate of the landed society also rests on self-provisioning, having a labour force made up of the members of families whose labour is considered a service-rent for their provision grounds and other facilities (pasturage, water, wood-gathering, etc) which the estate grants them, whether or not they are subjected as serfs or debtors. This is what is often referred to as the 'traditional hacienda'. Though internal arrangements are based on the self-provisioning principle, and can have a pre-capitalist and feudal character, the proprietor is likely to maintain limited capitalist relations with the market.

Up to this point, self-provisioning farming has been considered as an element of security for the peasant, and as a universal concomitant of rural family life in paleotechnical conditions. However, the oscillation between bursts of export production of exotic crops for the metropolitan or world market and reversion to local complexes of self-provisioning family economies linked together through small towns by marginal exchanges, is perhaps the dominant theme in the economic history of Latin America, providing the prime motor of change until the development of a national market system began to make itself felt. And it has been emphasized recently that the characteristic weakness and dependence of Latin American economies are due to the fact that the great productive initiatives have answered the growth needs of various external mercantile, industrial-capitalist and monopoly-capitalist systems, with complete disregard for the growth needs and impulses emanating from the peoples of these territories. This has accentuated the drastic, indeed catastrophic, nature of the oscillations (Frank, 1969).

This is not the place to review the growing literature on the subject, but we may remind ourselves of some of the products whose profitability in Europe and North America generated bursts of extractive entrepreneurship in different climatic zones for shorter or longer periods, and while they lasted, dragged the fragile local economies in their wake, submitting their thousands of peasants from the four corners of the earth to regimes of forced labour. The classic image of the character of the export economies appears in the work of the Bolivian historian of the nineteenth century, Gabriel Rene-Moreno, writing about the *mita* or forced labour system used for the silver mines of Potosi from 1575 till 1812. 'In its two and a half centuries' career, that enormous slave-machine passed creaking over the things of its times, splitting cobble-stones, splintering pavements, unsettling bridges and spattering with mud the faces of its drivers . . .'.

The greatest of them was sugar, whose cultivation in the New World changed the course of African history as well. Cacao, indigo, and tobacco in the colonial period, and coffee, cotton and rubber in the nineteenth and twentieth centuries all galvanised the economy of certain areas for limited periods, only to leave them in disarray as the impulse subsided.

The most extreme form taken by the colonial export economy, in which *mercantility* reaches its greatest intensity, is the plantation, with the advance of which subsistence systems go into abeyance or are pushed out to the fringes, and high mercantility separates the economic enterprise from the social life of those who participate in production, leaving its workers, coerced or tricked or bought at the lowest price and brought together in settlements on the estates, no more than interstitial space for social life set between rigid measures taken to ensure that cheap, manageable labour be available whenever required. On the slave plantation, tendencies to form permanent unions and domestic families had no opportunity to thrive, and so offered no permanent basis for a system of family subsistence. Moreover, slave owners were loath to allow commercially profitable labour to be spent in individual subsistence lots, except of course when markets decline and the cost of the maintenance of slaves is a burden on income.

Gabriel Debien (1956:124) quotes an eighteenth century planter in Santo Domingo as saying in his correspondence that he obliges every slave to make a garden for his own nourishment, and that he allows him free time at midday for this purpose, as well as Sundays and holidays. But the reason given is not an economic one but connected with the system of social control; *('je ne veux point qu'ils sortent de l'habitation')* he does not wish them to leave the grounds of the estate.

One of the systems used in Brazilian slave plantations was that of inter-planting subsistence crops between the rows of commercial crops, i.e. cassava between the cane and corn between the cotton rows, a practice which continues in modern share-tenure agreements. Thus, the organised estate labour force produced subsistence crops more economically for its own labour force.[5] Subsistence crops were also produced by praedial dependents occupying peripheral lands of the estates, and selling provisions to it, or delivering them under share-tenure arrangements. Indeed the *engenho,* or pre-industrial slave plantation in Brazil, combined the sugar producing enterprise oriented to the market with various subsistence and local exchange types of dependent productive unit, while the capitalist producer-entrepreneur was liable to find greater satisfaction in lordship than in entrepreneurship, and his title 'Lord of the Mill' commemorated this penchant (Lins do Rego, 1966).

But while commercial export production provides examples of escape from family self-provisioning, the latter nevertheless remains the rule under conditions of rudimentary productive technique and transport, and low mercantility. However, with the growth of the national markets and improvements in technology during the last decades, service tenure arrangements in which the labour force lives from its own provision grounds, have become increasingly cumbersome and resistant to rationalisation for market production, and have largely been dispensed with in favour of wage labour, thus taking the self-provisioning element out of estate agriculture and increasing the trends toward rural proletarianisation. But, of the smallholder sector, only a very small proportion has controlled sufficient resources and credit to participate fully in the market economy.

The peasant's problem with the market is that successful production requires the use of industrial inputs, which in their turn require the risks of credit – remembering, of course, that credit has for 400 years been the noose of enslavement. Certainly the chances of the market are not sufficiently favourable to lead to the abandonment of self-provisioning production, which therefore continues to take up both land and labour, so that the market directed effort is half-hearted.

On the other hand, the subsistence system no longer provides a reasonable way of life because of the breakdown of the exchange systems of the natural economy, and the rural market complex, making money necessary for nearly all kinds of exchange.

Thus the reliance of the peasant on the land for his own immediate provisioning, or his desperate aspiration to obtain that reliance, must never be forgotten in attempting to analyse the motivational systems involved in changing agrarian structures. Relationship to the market through production of a commercial crop can not necessarily be interpreted as a striving for commercial entrepreneurship (c.f. Ortiz, 1963 and Manning Nash, 1966:81 on the adjunct-export economy) and in many cases continues to be a means of complementing a self-provisioning family economy.

One of the situations in which commercial entrepreneurship makes its appearance in our data is the result of excessive impoverishment and fragmentation of subsistence lands which so diminishes the possibilities of livelihood by agriculture or by crafts that marginal ambulant trading is a last recourse compatible with retention of community membership and hence of cultural identity (Herbert, 1969). In most smallholding peasant communities of our days, under conditions of rising population, increased monetisation and rising land values, agriculture is frequently in pathological decline. The resource base is usually insufficient for effective commercial agriculture, land is too dear to permit the consolidation of holdings into more viable units, and the desperately retained self-provisioning sector of the farm is insufficient to provide food for the whole year round. Nevertheless, insecurity prevents its abandonment. It is both life-belt and mill-stone.

The landgroup

An indispensable social unit of this study is what we have called the landgroup. It consists of *a group of families forming part of a larger society and living in permanent interdependence, interaction and propinquity by virtue of a system of arrangements between them for the occupation and productive use of a single land area and the physical resources it contains, from which they gain their livelihood.*

The core of the system consists of a set of norms, compatible with arrangements prevailing in the larger society, about the distribution and transmission of rights of access to the land and its resources, about thoroughfare, about the application of labour to the land and about participation in the product of labour, land and the natural increase of stock. This core forms a basis for the usual and varied gamut of institutions and customs by which a large part of the daily material, social and spiritual needs of any small permanent human group are met.

In terms of the historical career of societies, the landgroup sets in as kinship ceases to be the primary organisational factor of social cohesion and as settled agriculture becomes the main support of livelihood. McBride (1923) draws attention to the fact that the Spanish encomienda in Santo Domingo consisted of grants of rights to use the labour of kinship groups and clans, identified by use of the names of their *caciques* or chiefs, while in Mexico the rights distributed in encomienda were to the use of named indigenous settlements. This difference expresses the fact that in parts of Mexico a more complex stage had been reached, in which the landgroup was already a main basis for social organisation. The *calpulli* (meaning kinship group) was already established on lands which were recognised as belonging to it, and practising sedentary agriculture, very often as part of a larger settlement, when the Conquest of Mexico took place. He comments, 'What originally had been kinship groups later on became place units, the land that was occupied tending to supersede blood relationship as the bond of union.' It is also true that in the Maya, Inca and Chibcha regions, comparable developments had been going on (Urquidi, 1966:113; Posada, 1967). Certainly under the impact of the rough reorganisation carried out by the Spaniards, kinship as a main principle of social organisation at a level more extensive than the domestic family rapidly gave way and in spite of the forced movements of population induced by the system of mita, the landgroup, with a tendency to endogamy, steadily became the prevalent form.

On the other hand, the landgroup does not survive industrialisation and urbanisation. Occupants of villages in contemporary developed societies are not essentially or exclusively interdependent and their relations have little to do with dependence on a common land area for livelihood, and the variety of needs which in the pre-industrial stage the landgroup met are now satisfied segmentally by large urban-based networks of services and local branches of national institutions and associations. Thus, the landgroup takes the place of the kinship group and disintegrates as its members are incorporated into the industrial society. But between these two thresholds it is the immediate but not exclusive social environment of the non-urban majority. It is the main receptacle through which culture is received and participated in. It contains the reference groups by which limits on behaviour are set and models given. The behaviour of the individual peasant and the way he reacts to changes in the wider physical and social environment must be explained largely in terms of the accommodation of his landgroup to the situation. And if it is reasonable to discuss the rationality of decisions, then this can only be done if full allowance is made for the peculiar set of controls and expectations which the landgroup imposes.

Its members who go out from it take with them a set of predispositions and expectations which they learnt within it, and the impulses that penetrate it from without – from the larger society – are interpreted, evaluated and utilised according to established customs and dynamic patterns. The landgroup is therefore the tutor and conditioner of the behaviour of its members. For these reasons it is central to the study of the peasant; indeed the concept makes possible a definition of 'peasant' as 'those who belong to landgroups, performing labour and gaining their livelihood in agricultural production for use and exchange'. The actual performance of agricultural labour, given certain generalised cultural characteristics in Latin America, sets upward limits on his social status. The fact that he produces for use and exchange implies that he has a commitment to work the land and is not simply a worker looking for a wage. His actual tenure status is not specified, and he may be proprietor, proprietor's kin, occupant, service-tenant, communal usufructuary, share-tenant or even cash-tenant so long as he belongs to the landgroup. He is not, however, a non-labouring proprietor, nor a supervisor or manager, though persons occupying these positions have come out of peasant families, and might be described as peasant in a cultural sense. It defines him, or her, as an individual who lives within a certain kind of community, is quasi-exclusively formed by it, and has a certain land-tenure status within it.

If the word 'peasant' can be used for making generalisations about common cultural traits or political attitudes or ways of responding to situations, this is only possible because of the existence of a permanent group of *semblables* through whom these characteristics are transmitted to the individual. To discuss 'peasant behaviour' implies 'landgroup'.

We must also bear in mind that the emergence of generic terms for peasant accompanies the appearance on the stage of people who think in terms of 'societies' as wholes and 'social classes' as parts of them, and who wish to communicate their views about the state of the nation (rather than a particular region with localised social terminology) for the purposes of analysis, mobilisation, political action, etc. Let us consider the concept 'peasant' in Brazilian society.[6] The currently used equivalent in Portuguese is *'campones'*, but this seems to be of recent diffusion. Candido uses the word *caipira* for country folk, 'people of rustic culture' (1958:7–8) and explains that *caboclo* used in the phrase *cultura cabocla* by Emilio Willems, is encumbered with a racial meaning (the mixture of Portuguese and Indian, or acculturated Indian) and is therefore inconvenient. Morais recounts that the name 'peasant leagues' was applied to the movement associated with Juliao by hostile newspapers, attempting to put the fear of God into the public by using the name of the banned communist organisation of the 1940's. The name stuck, and a well-disposed lady deputy asked Juliao to talk about the peasants as *ruricolas* in place of *camponeses,* in order to avoid shocking people's political susceptibilities. This suggests that the word was used by the communists as a direct translation of *paysan, bauer,* etc. from the vocabulary of the European political left, and therefore first reached the public ear with this connotation. Kalerv Oberg in 1957 was writing about *'O campônio marginal'* and uses the word *campesino* only adjectivally in the sense of rustic/rural (1957:118–132).

Landgroups are differentiated most significantly by the degree of internal monopolisation of land, a variable which splits them into two types – the estate landgroup, in which a single family or proprietor owns all the land, and landgroup in which most of the families have rights to communally owned lands or are individually possessors or proprietors of varying extensions of land. The two categories are so distinct from one another that for the most part they are treated separately.

The estate, then, may be described as a dominated land-group, in which proprietorship or control of land is separated from labour. And since proprietorship appropriates surpluses above subsistence, it requires a system of social control supported by the society in which it is set. It is inevitably a vertically differentiated class structure. It implies and requires the proprietor's control of the nexus functions linking it to the society in respect of exchange and administration, thus adding to proprietorship a type of lordship. The system of social control becomes the backbone of the internal structure (see Chapter III).

In contrast with the estate are landgroups in which the possession of land is dispersed. These might be categorised 'communal' and 'common' landgroups to distinguish those in which land is held legally in the name of the group as a whole from those in which each family has its own tenure arrangements. But a judicial distinction of this kind is not an actual and operative one as regards social solidarity and defence of proprietary right today. Even where traditional lands are held communally, individual families have effective and heritable possession, and cases are rare where communal authority is strong enough to reallocate lands which are effectively held by individuals since such communal authority is exercised by those possessing the largest extensions, and least interested in redistribution. Existing communal tenure in practice is usually confined to grazing and gathering rights on non-agricultural land, or the distribution of shifting plots. In Ecuador, where communal rights were permuted into allodial rights in the last century, many communities of smallholders maintain a high degree of group solidarity and have maintained their corporate nature to the point of being able to prevent the individual sale of lands to outsiders. In contrast, many of the Mapuche 'communities' in Chile are superimposed legal fictions, in which the names on the communal roll do not correspond to the actual possessing families, so that the so-called communal land tenure of the *reducción* simply has the effect of permanent insecurity of tenure amongst those enjoying *de facto* possession. So since formal communal ownership is normally accompanied by effective family possession and use of agricultural lands, we shall adopt a single category of 'smallholders' landgroups' to contrast with estates.

Nevertheless, within the smallholders' landgroup there is a very important variation in the degree of interdependence and solidarity which has to do with continuing degrees of control of resource allocation and political organisation, and the exigencies of common defence against the exterior. Its internal solidarity is strengthened by the fact that its toponimic unity and shared transport system is recognised and used by its neighbours and by the local secular and ecclesiastical authorities for practical purposes, though it is seldom an administrative unit. Among the generic names it enjoys are: *anejo, asentamiento, ayllu, barrio, capilla, caserío, colonia, comuna, comunidad, ejido, estancia, ex-hacienda, parcialidad, poblado, reducción, resguardo, vecindario,* (Spanish) and *bairro, linha, vizinhancà* (Portuguese) and *habitation* (French). Contrary to general belief, the landgroup is most commonly a dispersed settlement[7] with each smallholder living on his lands. The exceptions to this include those whose water supplies are concentrated in a limited area, and some of those with pastoral economies which may have a central dwelling nucleus. The liaison or *nexus* function with the exterior in administrative matters is performed either by some internally appointed leader or representative, such as the *jilacata* or the *general secretary* of the peasant union in the Bolivian *communidad* or *exhacienda* respectively, or simply by a member of the landgroup nominated by the external organ which requires the liaison, such as the *comisario* of the Colombian *vereda,* nominated by the mayor *(alcalde)* of the municipality, or by an officer elected by the members of the landgroup by due process established by the authority of the state, like the President of the *Comuna,* which is the juridical form which the Ecuadorean *parcialidad* may adopt to represent its interests. Although marked differences in the amount of land held by each family soon come to characterise any smallholders' landgroup making for differences in levels of consumption and power, there are a series of factors tending to counter-balance greater inequalities or land monopolies, assuming that the level of production is low. One of these is the fact of kinship. The chances of heredity are likely to interrupt a process of accumulation of land by a single family during several generations, since the custom of inheritance by all the heirs is general, and sooner or later fragmentation is likely to take place.[8] Kinship solidarity may soften the asperities of economic logic.[9] Though land is the key to the realisation of values, these do not reside exclusively in domination, and the enjoyment of respect and consideration can also be achieved by succouring one's poor relations and by the fulfilment of other expected public obligations. In any case, a leap out of the peasantry into an unlabouring proprietorship is unthinkable where technology is rudimentary and productivity low, since it would involve the appropriation of the surpluses of too many landless peasants to be practicable. And the larger peasant proprietor lacks the social ascendancy to utilise the forms of legitimate or connived-at coercion by which the gentry has been able to secure its labour force.

The paths most likely to be followed by the fortunate peasant are either the accumulation of cattle, which requires little additional labour in proportion to the amount of land held, or to let out parcels of land in excess of his use-capacity to the landpoor or landless in return for a part of the product or labour at harvest time or even for a small cash rent, but these arrangements are not sufficient to raise him out of the peasantry to a non-labouring proprietorship; his upward path leads towards the practice of commerce or investment in some capitalised service (such as milling or transport) in which case the peasant type of economy is retained rather than the estate-type and individual economic advance takes place through 'service entrepreneurship'. In areas where the estamental system continues to dominate the scene, the peasant may be effectively excluded from these entrepreneurial opportunities, and in these situations it is common to find the prevalence of *fiestas,* fostered by priests and traders in alcohol, music and the paraphernalia of tawdry pageantry, effectively absorbing surpluses, and ensconced as part of a historically created set of cultural expectations and mechanisms for distributing status.

The rural town and the nexus function

Peasant interaction with society is mediated by the rural town. It owes its existence to the fact of convenience of access and is therefore a transport and communications junction, serving also a nucleated centre in which can be assembled a set of functions connected with economic exchange, administration, taxation, the sale of services and some specialised manufactures and crafts. There is also (in Hispanic America) a historic cultural disposition to build rural civilisation from the town outwards. It will have some sort of administrative status, such as capital of *municipio* or canton, or seat of a sub-prefect or sub-delegate of police. Its relative size in relation to the area it serves is an indicator of the degree of development in the area. An extreme case of economic stagnation in the interior of Sao Paulo, Brazil, at the end of the eighteenth century is described by Antonio Candido (1964) in which the rural town lodges no more than 25 families of the thousand living scattered throughout the area of its governance.

Vis-à-vis the rest of society, the landgroup members have many common interests. These are economic, in regard to the selling price of their surpluses and the purchasing price of their consumer goods and services, as well as in regard to taxation and other impositions of the state. They are interested in the common amenities of their land and communities, as regards control of water, transport facilities such as roads and bridges, and health and education services. They require common political representation. They also look to the town for entertainment, sociability, the legitimation of their property rights and the symbols and paraphernalia necessary for acts of worship.

The population of the towns live from these nexus functions – those to do with the administration, performed by local government officials, tax-collectors, constables and registrars; commercial functions such as the purchase of the peasants' products for resale, retail distribution of consumer goods, tools and other agricultural inputs, money lending, ecclesiastical office, teaching, the purveyance of services. Most of these are extractive from the peasant's point of view. As regards crafts, some of these are widely diffused skills or else performed by one or other member of the landgroup, such as maker of adobes, guitar player, midwife or baker, but family self-provisioning does not encourage a high degree of specialisation, and the more demanding crafts are likely to have their exponents in the town – the mason, the harness-maker, the lock and gunsmith, the joiner, the shoemaker and the players of brass instruments.

Some of what the peasant requires of the town implies an open market situation in which supply and demand fix prices. In some cases, there is direct exchange, using money, between producer and consumer, as for instance, where landgroups tend to specialise in craft production of goods needed by the peasants, such as ceramics or textiles. But in seeking the satisfaction of many of his requirements, the peasant is at a serious disadvantage. Many of the services are petty monopolies. And where they are offered by several persons, the townsfolk are in a better situation to come to price-fixing agreements, while the peripheral situation of the peasant leaves him in the weaker position in these encounters. And even where there appear to be the elements of free competition between traders for peasants' custom, it is more common to find a kind of clientship, involving the permanent tying of the peasant, as producer and consumer, to an individual trader, who acts as his agent and adviser in some of the more difficult transactions with the larger society, in the intricacies of which the peasant is no adept. This relationship may be starched out with ceremonial sanctions such as co-godparenthood or formal drinking. But more than anything else, it is likely to involve credit. So the peasant may become permanently dependent, and at a disadvantage in bargaining.

It is not only in trade that the peasant is handicapped, but also in his dealings with the administration. During the colonial period it became a firmly established procedure that local ecclesiastical and secular authorities should live by what they could extract from those who were committed to their charge, and a whole system of gift-giving, fining, forfeits, labour days, were added to the official tributes, tithes, taxes and fees. Where estamental division of the peasantry from the townsfolk still persists, so do these practices.[10] The teacher or nurse who receives a regular salary from the government every month is still something of a novelty.

In areas where smallholding predominates the townsfolk, therefore, constitute a class whose economic interests consist of what they can take from the flow of goods and services between the peasants of the discrete landgroups and the rest of the collective. They are able to take advantage of their insertion in the circuits of communication, their knowledge of the ways and language of the institutions and bureaucracies through which goods, power, little privileges, political influence and jobs are correlated, circuits to which the peasant may not be connected. They occupy the vital crossroads. And although competitive amongst themselves, they maintain certain solidarity norms in regard to their dealings with the peasants who constitute their livelihood.

Does the separation of dispersed landgroups from nucleated nexus towns coincide with class differences? This raises a complicated set of questions which we hope will become clarified by the analysis of case material, and by giving attention to the threefold penetration of landgroups by the hitherto sporadic and scattered bursts — and the present unrelenting pressure — of com mercial relations, accompanied by intensified communication-interaction and the impulse to institutional incorporation. The interest in economic class, just as in membership of land-groups and towns, and in identification with ethnic sectors, is of course directed to their competing roles as conduct-guiding matrices making it possible to explain peasant conduct and decision-making.

Ethnos

Peasant status in society is also complicated by 'ethnicity'. In four of the countries, the majority of the rural population is still overtly or covertly referred to as *'indio'* or *'indigena'*, almost four and a half centuries after the Conquest and their incorporation in the colonial system, and in most of the others these terms are used to refer to some sector of the peasantry or even to some characteristics of the peasantry. They imply cultural and biological American (as opposed to European) antecedents and there are two major stereotypes or commonly accepted explanations of the situation. One of these is frankly racist, and still claims the adherence of most non-peasants in these societies. *Indios* are members of an inferior, or at least degenerated race, and with the exception of rare cases of specially gifted people, they have not got the necessary inherited equipment to compete with those who are wholly or partly of European race in civilised pursuits.

This view of things is likely to be accompanied by a paternalistic attitude in situations where the people referred to are incorporated in the productive system as purveyors of labour, and by a liquidationist attitude where they occupy lands coveted by entrepreneurs with access to capital.

This racist explanation is probably unacceptable to the readers of this book, and there is no need to use space showing it to be untenable. It must be recognised, however, as functionally maintaining the privileges and standing of the class immediately superior to it in life chances.

The second stereotype – and in this case it pretends to the title of 'model' – is more sophisticated, yet in many ways misleading. Indians are envisaged as the biological and cultural descendents of the pre-Conquest peoples who have managed to maintain an essential core of their ancient culture or cultures and though by a process of acculturation they have adopted in a modified form many of the traits and institutions of the white or mestizo ('Western') hispanic culture of the societies forming their social-political setting, yet they remain essentially different as a result of this cultural persistence. They are still *Indians,* and their tenacious clinging to tradition creates very serious social problems, preventing their full integration in the society and therefore retarding 'development'. Thus, for instance, James Payne (1965:224) writing about the agricultural labour force in Peru says 'At the center of the difficulty is the Indian (in the Sierra), who, whatever his condition may have been during the Inca empire, has not succeeded in making himself a successful or productive part of modern society' — thus assuming the existence of a cultural biological entity in modern society, in direct descent from some part of pre-Conquest society. This view falls short of a just historical appraisal of the degree of disorganisation and re-organisation and incorporation to which the conquered peoples and their immediate descendents were submitted.

The misleading character of the continued use of phrases like 'indio' and 'indigena' lies in the suggestion that the characteristic features of the colonised are to be attributed to their racial and cultural origins, rather than to their situation in the colonial order around which the re-working of their culture took place. Indeed there never was a single Indian culture any more than an African culture. It is true, however, that most of the Highland populations formed parts of agrarian societies which could be administered and exploited in certain ways. The Spaniards broke up existing realms which had articulated and integrated the cultural diversity of kingroups and landgroups, replacing them by their colonial structures and adminisative institutions. In the process of making a colonial society, they destroyed all the accessible cultures, considered as whole systems of behaviour, though individual landgroups were able to retain many sub-cultural traits, largely deprived of their significance. The process of submission and incorporation in the colonial society altered the essential setting in which people performed and made decisions by radically changing the social context of kinship and the structure and authority-system of landgroups, by making new demands on existing agricultural systems, by the destruction of religious symbols and the liquidation of religious leadership. And in so far as certain values (or preferences) persisted, these came to have a different generative significance when the set of alternatives to which the preferences were applied, were themselves altered. At the same time the colonial system soon began adding new dominant elements to the culture of the colonised, partly by indoctrination and implantation of new institutional and technical means, and partly by the reactions of a defensive character to the violence done to their customary way of life by forced settlement, custodial labour systems and indiscriminate exactions. It is difficult to exemplify this aspect of cultural formation, but one expects examples to be found in attitudes and practices to do with group solidarity and the integrity of the group's land rights, and also in the form of acceptation of many of the implanted cultural traits. Thus the behaviour of the peoples submitted to these forms of colonisation must be explained primarily by the way the colonial system rearranged the relation of families and land-groups to their social and natural environment.

If *indianness* can be used to denote any significant cultural common ground (as opposed to particularities) this owes its origin to the Spanish colonial system as it operated in the Highlands and not to the manifold pre-Hispanic antecedents. The importance of this cultural re-formation is recognised by the anthropologist Alfred Metraux (CLAPCS, 1960:73) who writes:

> The cultures of the Quechua and Aymara peoples as they appear to us today are constituted out of traits fundamental to the sixteenth and seventeenth centuries. Their social, economic and religious life, turned upside down by every kind of novelty introduced by the Spaniards, at a certain stage reached an equilibrium which has lasted till our days, once again to be threatened by economic transformations

though he does not draw the reasonable conclusion that the situation of the 'indian' could better be understood by changing the name to 'colonial peasants'.

The process of structural transformation in Peru was recognised by Valdez de la Torre (1921) who says:

> The Incaic village communities or ayllus suffered considerable mutilation because of the wars between the conquerors, misery, epidemics, the assignment of *repartimientos* to the support of industries and public services, race mixtures, and the arbitrary gathering of several *ayllus* into a single newly created village. The result of all these factors was the loss of the bond of fictitious kinship maintained until then by tradition. It came about that the Indian communes were deprived of their ancestor worship and of their feigned kinship, their

common agrarian interests being now their sole bond save that forced upon them by the political and administrative machinery of the colonial government.

Means (1932:162), who quotes the Peruvian author, supports this view, and sheds light on the change of content in the ayllu, so often referred to reverently, almost mystically by 'indigenists':

> The minor government's chief object was that of getting the most possible work out of the natives. As a result of this the character of the ayllus – originally kinship groups of either real or feigned consanguinity – changed into a labour association in which the Indian officials came to be hardly more than bosses of workmen, or, in the higher ranks, collaborators with the *corregidores* in the extraction of tribute.[11]

As to the generality of this process of uprooting and forced re-settlement, with its implications of control, taxation and indoctrination, we may cite Magnus Mörner (1967:93) who asserts that:

> From the latter part of the sixteenth century onward, the authorities both civil and ecclesiastic, had devoted much energy to gathering the Indians into landholding villages or towns all over Spanish America. These reducciones soon housed most of the Indian population. Though they had lost their status as missions, these settlements were supposed to remain *pueblos de indios,* or Indian communities, as differentiated from villages or towns of the 'Spaniards' (non-Indians).

One of the earliest observers to identify the sources of homogeneity in native culture of the colonial period was Vitoriano de Villalba, inspector of the Audiencia of Charcas, who was especially concerned with the social effects of forced labour service in the mines of Potosi. In 1792 he writes:

> Visitors to the Equatorial regions, the tropics and the temperate south will not find Indians who will answer their questions with a definite Yes or No, but rather with ambiguous expressions like 'who knows?' or 'just so', etc., as if they distrusted the question and feared giving weapons to the questioner which might be used against them. Their submission to public humiliation, their distrust and the concealment of what they have and know, is the same in all parts, and this uniformity

> defies latitude and climatic differences and must be attributed to some moral cause itself superior to physical differences . . .

Language is frequently pointed to as a cultural element which has shown great persistence, but it is important to remember that the widespread use of Quechua is not proof of cultural continuity. Theodor Wolf (1892) asserts that the dense Highland population of what is now Ecuador was in the second half of the sixteenth century comprised of tribal groups and *'mitimaes'* (settlements of families from other areas) brought in from Peru – and that the Inca regime had been unable to liquidate the ancient differences between these peoples, while the superimposed Peruvian influence had been wearing off since the conquest.

> The first diocesan synod, held in Quito in 1583, disposed that catechisms be composed in the indians' mother tongues, since they did not understand the language of the Inca (Quechua), and suitable persons were nominated to write these catechisms in the vernacular of Canar, of Puruhay, of Quillacinga and of the Pastos and others. Bit by bit Quechua came to be spoken generally, especially by estate owners and missionaries, who obliged their peons and parishioners to learn the *lingua franca* since it was easier for them to learn one than three or four different American tongues . . . and the same thing happened in the regions of Napo and Canelos and even as far as the Mainas missions.

The point of view sustained in this section seems to be supported by George Kubler (1946: Vol.II, pp.331–410) when he comments on the rebellions connected with the name of Tupac Amara, saying:

> . . . the most significant aspect of the Indian rebellion is its striking lack of formal indigenous cultural content . . . at all points the late Colonial Indian philosophy of rebellion found its limits within the horizons of Spanish institutional culture. In essence, the Indians wished to capture Spanish institutions, not destroy or displace them by others.

In spite of his very useful work, Kubler leaves the issues cloudy by keeping cultural duality at the centre of the picture rather than finding his explanations in the dynamics and conflicts of a unitary social system.

The estamental society

To speak in the broadest possible terms, the colonial system was based on the division of society into statutory ascriptive estaments (or 'estates'), each of which performed distinct economic functions, having different parts to play in the production of wealth, different duties to pay tributes and taxes, and different rights in the consumption of the social product. Estamental division was also a basis for recruitment to different administrative and ritual offices in the society, and a principle underlying appropriate behaviour between individuals and groups. Such a system required the maintenance of visible cultural differences, especially in dress, to ensure that members of each rank behaved in the manner appropriate to their station. It also inevitably implied segregation. Birth was the normal means of entry to the estament, but it was also possible for the individual to pass from one estament to another, provided he could adopt the cultural requirements of the new estament and had sufficient influence to legalise the change.

The first main line of division was that between the conquering Spaniard and the American native, and the conquest situation itself gave to the system its dimension of dominion and subjection. It was not long before this initial dichotomy between conquerors and conquered was complicated by distinctions brought in by creolisation, miscegenation, the importation of Negro slaves, the separation of natives from their traditional lands, recruitment of forced labour for the mines, the growth of town life and the purchase of 'whiteness', but birth-rank continued to be the mechanism canalising the attribution of roles and status in the society.

The efficiency of the system required the upkeep of certain boundaries between the differentiated sectors. The Spaniards had soon found that the controlled social order of the native settlements they established could be upset by the intrusion of freer elements looking for fortune, and pursued a policy of segregation between two theoretical 'republics', one of Spaniards and the other of indios, which took the form of separate town settlements (Mörner, 1969: 169).

Even though the strata multiplied, the most numerous remained the indios. In Peru, one may distinguish three main categories of indios, differentiated by the liens attaching them to the colonial society. Two of these categories were defined by their headship and membership respectively of landgroups recognised by the colonial government as pertaining to the native peoples and their descendants and given judical status as such on the grounds of the sovereignty exercised by the Spanish Crown over the whole territory and its inhabitants. Ordinary members had rights to usufruct of land and to the protection which encomenderos and Crown officers were supposed to afford whilst owing tribute, labour service and other duties to the Crown, the colonial officials and the local priests. The hereditary headmen *(curagas* and *caciques)* were differentiated by privileges in regard to the amount of land allowed to them and a degree of exemption from services, taxes and duties, and they were expected to act on behalf of the colonial power in the government of the landgroup. The predominance of this stratum lasted well into the nineteenth century.

In addition to headmen and members of legally recognised landgroups, there was a third category known as *yanaconas* consisting in part of descendents of domestic slaves from the Incaic period, and in part of natives who, through the misfortunes, uprootings and mobilisations of the Conquest and the early years, had no usufructuary landrights in recognised landgroups. These yanaconas were related to society by their attachment and subjection to individual Spaniards or to corporate bodies. Official attempts were made to tax them, and to impose on their 'owners' payments in manumission of the labour duty or mita. But these measures were not effective, (Penaloza, 1953–4:137) and the yanaconas became the nuclear labour force of the Spaniards' agricultural enterprises. They were granted subsistence lands so that they could provide for themselves, since the absence of intense market relations made their maintenance as slaves impracticable, and thus the estate became a dominated landgroup, based on servile service-tenure.

But as individual agricultural enterprises were extended the number of yanaconas was increased, not so much from the original stock as by the number of indios from reductions and communities who sought refuge in the estates to escape the vexations of their protectors, the civil and ecclesiastical authorities and above all from the cruel mita. Apparently estate serfdom was preferable to the hazardous freedom of the community, offering as it did the uninterrupted pursuit of agriculture, and the security of family provision grounds and flocks of cattle. In this way the indios were differentiated into free and bound, a distinction which has survived until today, or rather yesterday, and is verbalised as *llactaruna* and *haciendaruna,* or 'landed folk' and 'estate folk'.

By the end of the colonial period, the multiplication of legally sanctioned ranks had become impossibly complicated. In the struggle for fortune, the Spaniards retained the advantage over others by their links with the court and its power brokers near the source of royal patronage. They used rank endowed by place of birth against possible competitors amongst the creoles, who in their turn used legalised purity of race against contenders of mixed descent. Those less favoured by birth had recourse to power derived from landholding, trade and minor office to make advantageous alliances and to buy themselves up the ladder of rank. By the Wars of Independence, as is well known, the excessive advantage enjoyed by the Spaniards was put an end to by the combined efforts of the wealthy creoles and the middle strata, and under the Republican constitutions, universal citizenship was introduced, limited only by the continued existence of slavery. But though the minor estamental restrictions and distinctions about which the middle sectors exercised their lifesmanship were abolished, the deeper division of society between those to whom was allotted the function of rural labour and services and the rest of the society was not abolished and that division of the society which the Spaniards had deliberately fostered persisted.

In the case of Bolivia, for instance, the Trujillo Decrees of 1824–5, expressing the liberal views of Bolivar and some of the other leaders of the new republics, set out a policy as regards landed property and taxation which made no distinction between groups, thus turning away from the estamental principle in legislation, and looking forward to a single common citizenship with universal rights. However, the significance of the proposed land and taxation arrangements was not apprehended by the communards as an advantage to be grasped, and they were opposed by the 'rich Indians' and *caciques* (traditional community headmen) whose privileges they implicitly attacked (Penaloza, 1953–4:264–265). And in practice the various elements of the dominant sector were loath to do away with those features of the social organisation which provided for public and private labour requirements gratuitously or at low cost, or in return for the use of subsistence lands, and also provided a large part of public revenue.

New decrees were promulgated in 1829 in which once again the ethnic status indigena is named; in which limited servile labour obligations were assigned to the sector of the population described as *indigena* towards the persons of the parish priests and certain local administrative officials. The post duty and the duty to provision rest-houses *(tambos)* are also imposed as rotating services lasting one year (Reyeros, 1963:113–117). Indeed the duties legally imposed were not overwhelming. It was important, however, that ethnic character was used as a criterion for the automatic allocation of handicaps and advantages, and so could be extrapolated to all aspects of social life and used to put the backing of the state behind the exploitation of the labouring population. But the history of republican legislation concerning the rights and duties of *indigenas* about land, obligatory services and taxation is complicated though not very relevant.

In reality a body of practice took form out of the persisting features of the colonial order which apparently varied greatly according to local custom and conditions, and in areas of low mercantility and continuing ethnic separation, tended to a particular set of structural relations involving the domination of the primary producer by landowners and townsfolk (traders, clergy and officials) and faciliatating the appropriation of surpluses, arbitrary extortions and the engrossment of lands. It is this systematic aspect of social relations which we are referring to as 'estamental', the two estaments (estates) of the Republican era being:

i. indios, indigenas, etc., who are 'the peasants' in the estamental areas, and divisible into smallholders (llactaruna) and service estate tenantry (haciendaruna), and

ii. the rest, the citizens, those who with varying degrees of advantage and disadvantage according to class, but under no absolute handicap, participate in the civic institutions.

Further observations follow in which the estamental system is treated as an ideal construct or referential model usable for analysing situations of ethnic separation in those parts of Latin America to which we referred in the first chapter, using Service's term as Indo-America.

The immanent social purpose of the estamental system as operated in the countries considered, is the exclusion of that sector of the population which performs the more lowly tasks of production and service from right-bestowing citizenship, and its submission to a general handicap as regards the value and voluntary disposal of their labour, the sale of their product and their possibilities in any competition for scarce resources or facilities, whether physical, cultural or moral, for the apparent benefit of the *citizens,* and especially of the categories enumerated above in whose hands the management of the agrarian sector rests.

The exclusion and handicapping depend on the identification of the sector as an *ethnia,* that is to say, as people of different culture and different nature, and therefore calling for different treatment. In primary group relations each individual has an identity which evokes an appropriate (status-wise) response from those with whom he interacts, but for a status system carrying such sharp differentiation of rights and duties to function at the impersonal societal level, universal status marks are essential. But since difference in phenotype based on racial origin provides no operative guide to rank in the system (in contrast with South African apartheid), peasant vesture, in spite of its mainly Spanish origins, plays this critical role in the ordering of relations. Thus, any random encounter between peasant and citizen is guided by the prescribed estamental norms, and mutual recognition of the appropriate estamental dress sets off a total set of appropriate behaviours. In Bolivia, after the Gran Chaco War, as peasants began to adopt citizens' dress, an estate owner is reported to have accepted this change of custom, but to have insisted on the use of *indio* vesture when the peasant went to town in an attempt to ensure that he should continue to be treated in the city according to the status which the proprietor wished to continue imposing upon him (Clark: 1968).

Could the subjected status then be put off simply by a change of clothes? Formally, yes, if 'a change of clothes' is taken to mean the grosser externals of culture. The fragility of the system becomes immediately apparent when estamental areas find themselves faced with a growing urban or industrial demand for labour, or when presented with other conditions favouring the (by no means easy) cultural 'change of clothes'. Indeed, the indio estament has continually 'leaked' – to mines, to the towns, to the frontiers and to the coastal plantations – as Kubler (1952) has ably demonstrated. Also in many areas estamental distinctions have been allowed to dissolve, since Independence as before it, though in most cases the effect for the peasant was not one of escape, but rather of proletarianization, by the loss of his lands. But its long survival in areas in which the conditions of the landed society have persisted without critical intrusions of capitalist-industrial enterprise required the operation of other mechanisms of control.

The system requires the apportionment of roles in the society, and restricts the entry to or adoption of many occupational, political and ceremonial roles. Citizens are held to the appropriate roles, and excluded from indio roles by the 'laws of social gravity'; they do not choose voluntarily to lower their status. On the other hand the indio is driven by the search for livelihood, and the arriviste ethos which pervades the citizens, to aspire to citizens' roles. The individual may emigrate and enter the citizen world, but this means radical excision from his kingroup and a marginal isolated position in the citizen sector, unless the canal of mobility is already well institutionalised.

He is taught early in life (by a socialisation process well adapted to the realities of the structure) which occupational roles will be permitted to him. If, in spite of socialisation, he aspires to a 'citizen' trade or profession, no institutional paths or stairways are available. (The owner of Pocoata estate, Bolivia, always hired artisans for building work from the capital, preferring to pay wages rather than risk his service-tenants learning a trade, and so gaining access to urban roles.) The perimeters of the lower estamental territory are carefully guarded, and a periodic *beating of the bounds* awaits the pioneers, e.g. the beatings administered to indios who went to school in Coroico to learn Spanish (Barnes, 1965), or who walked across the central plaza in Otavalo (Parsons, 1945) or who accepted an oppositionist political role in countless cases, or who wore inappropriate garb or shoes in Moya, Peru, before 1930. Fuenzalida (1969:29) refers to 'a tacit sumptuary law'.

The policing of the perimeter, and the difficulty of access to most of society's roles, tends to the acceptance of confinement in the estament. Moreover, the landgroup itself, strongly endogamous and offering some minimum usufruct of land as well as cultural identity, provides a basis for living which is not easily abandoned (Herbert, 1969). This inward-facing character is also discussed in Chapter IV on Bolivia.

Estamental division is kept up by making relations of reciprocity involving mutual trust between individuals on each side impossible. Such relations would imply a principle of equity quite contrary to the exclusive presumption of civic rights by the dominant sector, which is justified by difference in 'nature'. However, mutual recognition of humanity in the encounters of daily life, and the patent fact that individuals do change estament, weakens these prohibitions. In-group pressure is therefore exerted on the individual to prevent the formation of peer-relationships and loyalties with the other side, since they threaten the internal solidarity of the estaments, required on the one hand to maintain the 'universal conspiracy' of the citizens, and on the other, to defend collective interests of the dominated. It is in this functional sense that racial prejudice is fostered and comes to play an important part in maintaining in-group solidarities and continued separation. It is necessary as a weapon against the member of one's own group who endangers solidarity by establishing alliances with members of the other sector. It is also necessary as a way of pronouncing and justifying the suspension of the ground rules of interpersonal relations of one's own collective in dealing with members of the other collective. So contact relations become conventionalised under pressure from a public opinion within each group always on the watch for the individual who is seeking his own advantage in some special relationship or alliance with the other group, and thereby endangering the position of his own. Thus, cross-estamental personal relations are prestructured in conventional moulds expressive of domination and subordination, and precluding the development of personal confidence.

The system also inevitably implies a societal condition which can best be described as 'institutional ambivalence', so that all institutional acts have two faces, two forms, according to which estament is involved. The estamental system excludes the *indio* from any direct influence in the power structure and the political and administrative roles upon which it rests. The institutions of the dominated are 'second class compartments' which do not connect with the centres of decision-making, but only refer inwards, to intra-group regulations. An approach must be made to a citizen intermediary within the prescribed mould of dominance and subordination, and in this way the connection is inevitably one of dependence. The mechanisms which preserve the gap in personal relations ensure that there is no place for an intercessor who belongs to the citizen estament, yet will keep faith with the *indio* client. If the estamental system is 'functioning perfectly' the intermediary must in the long run show that his actuation on behalf of the *indio* is really for the benefit of the citizens. The absence of effective intermediaries can be seen in Condarco's account (1965) of the struggle of the 'communidades' in Bolivia for their land, and the role of Pando. Similarly in the Tocroyoc incident, the *indios* found no citizen intermediary, and the last word in the dialogue was the exhibition of the murdered leader's body on the church tower (ibid:314). (This was the true and ultimate language of estamental domination.) And the existence of citizens who take the part of the indio in Convencion (ibid:317–321) and Cochabamba (ibid:281–283) reveals the decay of the system, as the grounds for conflict *within* the citizen sector are more urgent and meaningful than an artificially maintained estamental *apartheid*.

NOTES

1. *Livelihood:* The word is derived from *liflad* (Old English) meaning *life-way* or course, and also *subsistence.* I am using it for the sum of what is consumed in a lifetime by a human unit and it is not to be confused with 'means of livelihood'. It is confined to goods, services and use of facilities and eludes quantification, though quantitative indicators can be found in a given social situation for many elements of livelihood. It refers to kind and quality as well as amount. Livelihood is linked to social status since in a given social situation, a certain range of livelihoods is regarded as appropriate to a certain status.

The second syllable *hood* seems to be an orthographic accident and has not the meaning of the suffix *hood,* as in neighbourhood, nationhood, etc.

2. Analysis of the structure and internal dynamics of the 'unit of agricultural production' and the 'estate' has aroused interest. See Stinchcombe (1968), 'Agricultural Enterprise and Rural Class Relations', Baraona's discussion of the subject in *ICAD Ecuador* (1965: 50–77), and also S. Udy, *The Organisation of Work.*

3. This is discussed in Chapter VI, while the 'deconstraining' of a peasantry is one of the themes of the chapter on Bolivia.

4. Perhaps the least complex subsistence system is that of the cattle herders (gauchos) of the temperate plains of what is now Argentina, as they were in the early nineteenth century, before the open range Pampas were squared up by barbed-wire fences. Most of their food, furniture and implements came from the cattle and horses themselves, both of which were to be had in almost unlimited supply – hides, fat, bones, horns, skulls, meat, mane, etc., supplied most of their wants, leaving only a few elements of material life to be obtained outside the immediate environment – saddle and spurs, poncho, knife, spit and cooking pot, and *mate,* to digest the unrelenting meat diet. Captain Head, an English mining manager, who travelled to and fro across the Pampa on horseback in the 1820's, is a keen observer of their self-provisioning system:

> The huts were built of mud and covered with long yellow grass . . . the immediate produce of the soil (and so blended in colour with the face of the country that it is often difficult to distinguish) . . . The hut consists of one room, in which all the family live, boys, girls, men, women, and children all huddled together . The door was a gap in the wall, covered by an extended hide. When supper is ready, the great iron spit on which the beef has been roasted is brought into the hut, and the point is struck into the ground. The guacho then offers his guest the skeleton of a horse's head, and he and several of the family, on similar seats, sit round the spit, from which with their long knives they cut very large mouthfuls . . . The hut is lighted by a feeble lamp, made of bullocks tallow, . . . on the walls are hung on bones, two or three bridles and spurs, and several lassoes and balls . . . (Head, 1826)

5. Correia de Andrade (1964) mentions various systems of inter-cropping subsistence with cash crops, (e.g. 1964, p.149), and interesting combinations are found in contract planting, e.g. for cacao, coconut and coffee, where the tenant must plant and care for the tree until it comes to bearing, meanwhile using the lands for family self-provision. The existence of these forms of production is frequently lost sight of in the census returns, and the persistence of subsistence agriculture for the labourer in commercial agriculture is thus overlooked.

6. The Brazilian illustration is weakened by the fact that groupings of family-sized properties and areas occupied by a relatively independent peasantry are rare in Brazil (except for the recent European settlements in Sao Paulo and the south), a country dominated by slavery until the late nineteenth century. In the present century, though most rural workers have been excluded from property owning, they have had access to provision lands and consequently have had characteristics of a peasantry, though a dependent one.

Not unexpectedly, ideological debate forms around the meaning of the word. Caio Prado Jr. (1963) insists on the need for careful discrimination as regards the classification of Brazilian agricultural population, especially if deductions are to be made in Marxist terms about political conduct derived from class position (RB.47:1–13). He is particularly concerned about omissions and confusions in the 1963 Rural Labour Statute, and the underlying assumptions of the 'land reformists'. Labour relations in agriculture, he says, are very complicated because payment may be made in money, land usufruct or a part of the product and varies as between different lines of production and different regions, and changes with time. Later he insists on the danger of confusing 'the man employed on the large estate with the *real peasant* who is both worker and executor of tasks, and director of both, as the European peasant was, whether or not he owned the land'.

Our use of the word peasant is less categoric, and therefore can apply to all who labour with the exception of those who have no access to land on their own account, and who live from wages in towns and cities. But these are still exceptional conditions. Most labour is precariously resident, retains provision grounds, fighting for the little security that these afford in a way which clearly demonstrates their *peasant* bias, or better said, they fight for a more perfect peasanthood. But Caio Prado, Jr. gives insufficient importance to the self-provisioning element, not only in the cash and service tenancies, but also in the share tenancies. That is to say, the share tenant is a commercial producer, but he obsessively retains a part of the land for his own provisions, his life line, or plants his provisions between his commercial crops. And so long as neither commercial production nor wage-earning, nor a stable combination of these two, offer him some year to year security he remains a peasant in his political outlook. He wants land though this is often expressed as a desire to have *um bom patrão* through whom access to both land and some cash income may be obtained. Peasanthood is manifest in outlook, behaviour and social organisation, which are regulated by the fact that at least a part of livelihood and security are looked for from the lands to which they have access and in which they work.

This means that the agricultural proletarian non-peasant is only found where a high level of mercantility and technology exist and where the labour force is almost entirely wage-earning. This is the case in many parts of the sugar producing zone where increasingly the workers live in *ruas* (like the Uruguayan *rancheríos*), interstitial line villages or straggling suburbs. While this full degree of proletarianisation is quite advanced in the Caribbean island territories, and to a lesser extent, in the Caribbean littoral, it is rare in most of South America, save in Argentine, Uruguay and the extreme south of Chile (Tierra del Fuego).

In Cuba, the pressure put upon service-tenants by the sugar corporation during the 1940's was tantamount to expulsion, and led to the growth of such villages, like the one – *Manga-larga* – described by John du Moulin (1965:27): 'One group (of plantation workers) settled on the outskirts of Ranchuelo, on public lands by the roadside . . . and so established a settlement which, being a single line of huts stretching out for more than 1 km., is known as 'the long sleeve'". This is one of the ways the landgroup disintegrates.

7. In the course of his excellent book, Barrington Moore writes (1966: 468 – 9) 'though the system of scattered individual settlements also occurs quite widely, it was not the predominant form anywhere except perhaps in parts of the United States in colonial and frontier times. In itself this is one of the grounds for refusing the designation peasant to American farmers.' This surprising lapse does at least draw attention to the peculiarity of the Latin American situation, in which the village, rather than the dispersed settlement, is the exception. Its most important implication is the social separation of aggregates of families of cultivators from all other classes. It also gives the *nexus* idea an operational value which is confused and overgrown in villages: and it makes necessary the idea of a *landgroup.*

8. A historical exception is to be found in the colonial period where the *curaga,* or hereditary headman, was allowed to practice *entail (mayoragzo)* so that accumulated landholdings could be passed on from generation to generation. According to oral tradition, in some of the landgroups *(parcialidades)* of Otavalo, Ecuador, *curagas* became land monopolists and oppressors, probably with the connivance of the colonial officials. But in this case, they already enjoyed a status set above that of rest of the peasantry in such a way that their control of communal lands put the landgroups in question into the 'dominated' category. I also heard similar complaints made about the contemporary situation of a headman in one of the *resguardos* of the Tierradentro zone of Colombia, but was unable to make any further investigation.

A further exception is to be found amongst the North European colonists who recognised, and were culturally pre-disposed to accept, the necessity of maintaining the integrity of the landholding, bringing up one child only to take over the farm and training the others to seek some other livelihood. This observation was made at Huillinco, Chiloe, Chile, amongst third and fourth generation Dutch, Germans and British.

9. Thus, for instance, community development has had its success where its organisers have offered the means of realising obvious community ends – (school, water, transport, renown), but programmes wittingly or unwittingly bringing about a redistribution of resources to farms and firms, have either served to reinforce or strengthen the existing order of domination, or have been rejected, with or without, before or after conflict.

10. The mechanisms of separation seem to dissolve with the extension of market relations and the growth of capitalist enterprises, requiring greater mobility of labour. Lievano (Vol. II: 208–209) refers to the policy of the Spanish Crown in the latter eighteenth century as one of demolishing the protected indio settlements *(resguardos)* to free labour for mining and commercial agriculture, and so to counteract the rising wages of existing free labour. In this case, the escape from the estamental condition was a change for the worse for the peasant, since it usually

meant the loss of his lands as well as his cultural separation. But its long survival in areas in which the conditions of the landed society have persisted without critical intrusions of capitalist-industrial enterprise required the operation of other mechanisms of control.

11. This system seems to have reached its height in the forced distribution of consumer goods, *repartimiento de generos,* in the late eighteenth century. Official posts such as that of corregidor were purchased, and charged their incumbents with a heavy burden of debt which they had to liquidate before beginning to make a profit. The peasants were legally bound to buy merchandise at inflated prices which they did not require or choose, and coerced into payment by the public, power. In his famous letter to Areche, the Spanish Visitador, in 1781, Jose Gabriel Tupac Amaru complained of having to accept not only fabrics at three or four times their usual price, but useless inappropriate surplus including pairs of spectacles, blue powder, playing cards, estampitas (?) (Lewin, 1957:475; Lynch, 1957:57–58, 196–198).

In Ecuador, local government officials continue to live off the peasantry. The teniente-politico of the parish of Quichinche told me (1960) that he earned a salary of exactly two and a half times the price of the daily paper, and charged any service performed in agricultural produce: when in special need he would arrest drunks and fine them on the spot, taking their ponchos if they had no money, thus bringing the administration of the law very close to highway robbery.

III

The Transformations of the Estate

An estate may be defined as 'a single landed property on which live various families, drawing their livelihood from agriculture performed in one or more units of production (farms)'. They are likely to be submitted to a framework of control of some description by disposition of the *persona* in whom control of the land is vested.

The importance of the estate in the landed society was brought out in Chapter I. However, under contemporary conditions of market and productive technique, the estate, as a source of livelihood for its proprietor by various and complicated traditional forms of disposition of land, and the power which accompanies its possession, is in decline, and land is being re-allocated by one means or another to entrepreneurs as one amongst various factors of production. In this chapter, some of these transformations are looked at from the point of view of the way in which societal change produces changes in the estate and the system of socio-economic relations which rests upon it, and the effects of these on the peasantry.

It is convenient to distinguish estates according to the way economic production is organised, that is to say, according to the relationship – estate : farm. The two obvious categories are multifarm estates and manorial estates.[1] The multifarm estate, though not thought of as typically Latin American, is found significantly and widely under special conditions. The lands of such an estate are entirely given over to small tenants who produce for subsistence and market, or in advanced technical conditions and high mercantility, for the market alone. They arise frequently where conditions for economic large scale production for the market present difficulties to the owner of the estate, because of marginal natural conditions or indifferent market prices, and especially where a high labour input is required. The tenant may pay a cash rent derived from the sale of his commercial crop or of the surplus from his subsistence production, or more usually he will deliver a portion of the commercial product to the owner, e.g. tobacco production in Colombia and in Cuba before the Revolution, cotton production in Brazil, vegetable products in Chile, etc. In some cases the tenant farmers exercise free entrepreneurship and can meet their obligations to the proprietor by the simple payment of a rent. In such cases they may develop positions of strength which can threaten proprietorship, as in the two rather special cases described further on. But share-tenants may not be able to develop entrepreneurship for lack of credit. In such a situation, they become dependents of the proprietor who secures their family labour with a prior investment of a credit for initial subsistence needs and whatever inputs may be required, and the due share of the crop, which he commercialises. Thus he avoids managerial responsibilities and wage costs, and has his labour share the risks of a bad crop as well as the stunted advantages of a good one. In this kind of estate, therefore, the landowner may be a simple *rentier,* or he may combine proprietorship with a role of commercial entrepreneur, making use of proprietorship to achieve dominating advantage in his business operations with his labour-tenants.

The second type we shall call the manorial estate and it is associated with situations of low mercantility. It consists of the owner's farm enterprise ('demesne farm', '*empresa patronal*') producing for the market but also for various local needs, including provisions for his household and for compensating his workers; the subsistence farms of the service-tenants who form the greater part of his labour force; and probably some additional market-directed enterprises on a share-tenure basis, using resources not exploited by the owner, such as woodlands for timber, firewood and charcoal, reeds for basketry and matting, quarries, sandpits, etc.

The concentration of resources in the estate, the political power in its proprietor, and his disposal of cash and credit may attract or coerce families and individuals into positions of dependence, each paying their labour stint whether they live on or off the estate. Thus, a manorial estate may consist of an agglomeration of productive enterprises of various sizes, degrees of efficiency, of various orientations to the market, etc., all tied together by the use of resources controlled by the proprietor, whose own productive organisation probably overshadows the rest.

The relations established in the exploitation of these resources provide the guidelines for and motivation of the system of interpersonal and intergroup relations which forms about the estate. However, its processes do not take place in isolation, and four factors immediately strike the attention as directly affecting the internal structure of estate-relations: supply of labour available outside the estate, and conditions governing it; supply of land and access to it; the market for goods produced on the estate; and the societal order in which the estate is set. While the operation of the first three of these factors is not obscure, the fourth deserves further consideration. In addition to market relations, the estate is socially linked to society by the fact that all who perform productive roles within it, whether of ownership, managership, entrepreneurship or work, also have a status in the society outside which adds to or subtracts from the power with which they can pursue their goals within the estate. This is true of the peasant whose lowly rank in the society gives him very little bargaining power in the estate, and of the peasant ranked as 'indio', who suffers a set of universal handicaps, weakening his position still further. And it is also true of the peasant who is also a member of a union, with its headquarters in the capital city.

Much more significant and generative is the position of the proprietor. He may be assumed to have social ascendancy since acquisition of the property, whether by grant or inheritance or the legalisation of *de facto* possession or by purchase, implies high rank or effective power or wealth. Moreover, his role as estate proprietor in the landed society has carried with it important political roles, and has implied equally important commercial ones, and the advance of industrial conditions has made him at least partially a man of the city, of whose various interests landed proprietorship is not necessarily the chief. Nevertheless, to the proprietor, the estate and the demesne farm are instrumental and must serve for the realisation of his goals. They may be an adjunct to his commercial or industrial enterprise, a form of capital or a holding against inflation or tax-saving, they may provide him primarily with the status of a landed gentleman, or with a political base. So at the centre of the estate with its various categories of persons and families seeking livelihood and pursuing their life's goals, there is a central relation between patron and peasant.

Though there is inherent conflict of interest between the two about access to resources and the division of the product and in connection with the peasant's freedom and the patron's intention to control, the predominant power of the patron, where it is legitimised and supported by the state and rendered effective through a working system of social control, maintains a situation of stasis and is a context for compacts and accommodation between apparently conflicting interests. But factors both internal and external to the estate may undermine the balance achieved, or interfere with the mechanisms of control, leading to open conflict, a resetting of positions, and to minor or major change in structure or to disintegration. The elements which play leading parts both as props of a continuing accommodation and, in themselves changing, as factors of change in the estate, will be discussed at greater length in the cases which follow.

The most important single factor affecting the internal structure and organisation of the estate is the level of mercantility, that is to say, the intensity of the market demand for the products which it can produce. When prices are high, then the owner or entrepreneur is likely to devote all available resources to producing, processing and transporting the product in question to the market. He is likely to find credit without difficulty, and will have increased incentives to use whatever technical means as may be available to maximise production.

If on the other hand there is no more than a sluggish local demand for certain estate products, then the productive activities of the estate will be largely absorbed in subsistence both at the level of the self-provisioning labour force and the more lavish use of rustic resources by the owner and his entourage. Dominion over his estates and the enjoyment of the political power that his realm brings are the rewards of this kind of lordship.

The pre-industrial estate and its demise

The manorial character which many estates acquired and maintained so long as mercantility remained at a low level is shown in an account by McBride (1923) of a traditional estate in Mexico in the early 1920's before the Land Reform really began to take effect. He asserts that 'the actual return in money is often very small . . . the economic value to the owner lies in the supplies which it furnishes, the cheap service which it provides for his household and the amount of money which he can obtain on a mortgage . . . The typical estate aspires to be self sustaining . . . '.

a. An example from Mexico

The estate occupies vast and varied lands making possible the production of most of the material goods required for rustic life – valley lands for grain, mountainsides and higher alpine meadows for grazing lands of flocks of cattle, horses, sheep and goats, and higher still, the property must include the sources of the mountain streams and ensure the irrigation system of the estate against interference. The resources include forest for timber, stone and lime for building, clay for *adobe,* coarse grass for roofing, salt, wild fruits and herbs for household use, and so on.

The landlord belongs to the country's aristocracy, and ownership helps to guarantee him his status, though landlordship is only one of a number of roles which he plays in Mexican society. His visits to the estate are occasional, and he cannot be said to have an entrepreneurial function, nor does he look to the estate for a money income, but rather to the enjoyment of an ancestral patrimony as an end in itself.

His labour force consists of families each of which is given a provision ground (*milpa,* used especially for raising corn) and a hut, and allowed to keep a pig or two and fowls. This does not provide for livelihood, and the peasant is more a labourer than a service-tenant, receiving wages for his work. However, these wages do not open up the possibilities of commercial relations in the larger society since they are paid in scrip which has value only in the estate 'truck' stores. Thus, the landgroup is a complex one, with some division of labour and internal exchange, with crafts and workshops in addition to agriculture. Commercial relations with the larger society are controlled by the landowner through the store *(pulpería)* and the direct sale of the estate produce. Moreover, many of the elements of nexus with the larger society were contained within the estate (church, school, post office) and belonged to the power-realm of the landlord.

What held the peasantry to the landgroup which offered them so little? Debt-peonage, which was contrary to the constitution of 1857, had been abolished in 1917. But this had not generated a movement away from the estates. Although an agricultural labour market was fitfully making its appearance at this time in Mexico, it did not offer feasible alternatives to the isolated illiterate peasant at a distance from the source of demand. His provision ground was some small reassuring link with Nature the giver, and probably more attractive than the distant promise of wages.

The low level of mercantility may also obviate sharp conflict between patron and peasant in regard to land and labour. The provision grounds in no way compete with alternative land-use plans of the patron. Nor is he under an economic imperative to extort the maximum labour from the peasant on his demesne farm. The effective control of the 'societal' nexus by the patron and his stewards limits the group as a field of action, depriving the members of external reference points, and creating accommodation to the system, and 'routinism'.[2]

Given the quasi-institutionalised routines which accrete to subsistence production, undisturbed by a competitive market, can the pre-industrialised service-tenure estate adapt itself to a general advance in technology and style of living by means of internal reorganisation and the improvement of productive methods? This question is discussed by Bourricaud (1962) in connection with the Highland Peruvian estate he visited. It is described as having an extension of 35,000 acres and operates on a pure service-tenure system amounting to an easy-going serfdom under the reigning 'estamental' conditions.

b. An example from Peru

Its work force is self-supporting, producing quinoa, potatoes, meat and textiles for its own consumption, with a sale of surpluses to make up deficiencies, while its landlord sells his produce to the market for cash. This labour force is made up of 150 service-tenants and their families, who work as shepherds, each one minding a part of the flock for the patron, and fulfulling other work obligations in the cultivation of a subsistence reserve of quinoa and potatoes (available for sale to the peasants in case of need) and in some forms of domestic service. In return the peasant may keep a certain number of sheep of his own with the landlord's flock, and has a usufructuary right to a private plot of land for subsistence crops and access to such firewood and building materials, and so on, as the estate affords.

On what does the viability of the landgroup rest? Primarily on praedial dependence established by the landowning class by quasi-monopoly of land. Was the estate superimposed upon a communal landgroup established by the Spanish colonial authorities for entrusted Indians, or were the service tenants drawn to the estate by having been deprived of their rightful lands or by the harrassments of *corregidores,* priests and the *Mita* for the mines of Upper Peru? Unfortunately this is not revealed but the solidly institutionalised relations within the dependent peasant community suggests to us the first explanation, i.e. that it is a 'captured' community (see Chapter IV, pp.120–122).

What it offers to the peasants is subsistence land which could not be obtained elsewhere, some possibilities of micro-entrepreneurship, and the solace, strength and partial protection of belonging to a community with a minimum of day-to-day interference. Bourricaud points out that the solidarity and legitimacy of this community gives it a considerable bargaining power vis-a-vis the landowner, for instance, the possibility of initiating a lawsuit in case of breaches of custom by the landowner, of hanky-panky with the flocks or of connivance with outside cattle thieves. Indeed, labour for stock-raising always requires qualities more easily elicited by consent than coercion.

And what are the goals which possession of the estate fulfills for the landowner? As in the previous case, possession of an estate endows him with social rank, and provides rent to facilitate the enjoyment of its status. Says Bourricaud:

> The *hacendado* does not worry overmuch so long as the income he can get out of his estate seems to him sufficient. Instead of thinking in terms of profits, that is to say of the maximisation of the excess of receipts over costs, he thinks in terms of rents, that is to say, of an income capable of sustaining a certain style of life. The estate has assured the upkeep of his family in Arequipa or Lima, and allowed him to keep up his social position . . . until recently the stimuli were neither numerous nor pressing to encourage the patron to take much interest in the administration of his patrimony, much less to introduce new methods.

The characteristic trend of the Mexican estate, making towards an alteration of the nature of the entreprise, was the persistent impoverishment of the soils, by overuse and lack of conservative management, and consequently the steady fall in yields. In the case of the Peruvian estate, what Bourricaud remarks on is the changing society which causes the *de facto* obsolescence of the traditional style of landlordship as a means to the social rank desired by the owner. Times change, and keeping up socially requires more income for the modernisation of style, not only of town-life, but also of the conduct of the estate. Our landlord is forced into defensive innovation by the fall in the price of common *(chusca)* wool resulting from the introduction (by go-ahead entrepreneurs) of improved stock yielding a finer wool, and also from the deterioration of rural-urban terms of trade through slow inflation. Moreover, his prestige is endangered if he does not maintain such fine animals, or if he does not practice artificial insemination like Senor X. The peasant is less interested in a finer wool since his market exchange is a sideline, and his manner of spinning and weaving is adapted to the use of *chusca:* he has little interest in giving to the finer sheep and their offspring the additional care which their sensitivity demands; and he has little sympathy for the patron's claim to the best pastures, relegating the peasants' animals to the second best; nor for his attempts to enclose these pastures, thus changing the whole system in such a way as to dispense with the need for so many shepherds. Our Peruvian *patron* was not able to undertake such drastic reforms, and must contemplate the decline of his economic and social position in so far as it rests upon this estate. Not so his neighbour, a Scot, who expelled most of his peasants, forbade the remainder to maintain their own flocks, and multiplied the estate's revenue by the scientific production of fine sheep. The shepherds who remained also enjoyed increased prosperity in higher wages. The stranger, untied by customary obligations and local limitations of resource-perception, is the likely entrepreneur.

c. *An example from Chile*

Our third example of a declining manorial estate comes from Chile, and is described by Ramirez.[3] In this case, it is the sheer rigidity of a complicated system of particularistic service-tenure arrangements which resists the economic reorganisation necessary for survival in conditions of rising mercantility and monetisation, especially in the absence of a patron capable of taking radical measures.

Santa Clemencia consists of a great fan of land spreading upwards from the irrigated flats of the central valley into the Andean Cordillera, with only one tenth of its 5,434 hectares in irrigation. Variegated in its geophysical characteristics, it is also varied in production and in entrepreneurship. The upper stretches are exploited by six share-tenants extracting lumber *(quillay)* and manufacturing charcoal, while the rough mountain pastures are used by the service-tenants' sheep, goats and pigs. Tuna (a cactus bearing a marketable fruit), oranges and lemons are grown in the irrigated lands, on a rather small scale.

Most of the irrigated lands are devoted to natural pastures for fattening beef cattle and dairy farming on the one hand, and for annual crops such as wheat, maize, sunflower and beans on the other. Chickpeas are also grown on the non-irrigated lands.

This great variety of lines of production is accompanied by a rather rigid specialisation of labour according to different activities, including a high proportion of personnel occupied in purely supervisory roles. This is made ncessary by the separation of the labourer from the benefits of production, and the lack of incentives to produce in greater quantity or better quality. The labour force is deployed as shown in Table 1.

The service tenants *(inquilinos)* were under an obligation to work on the estate lands, or to pay a labourer to replace them, all the year round, and indeed at some season of the year to provide a second worker. The 41 'volunteers' form a labour reserve, and consist of members of the service tenant's family, or possibly 'lodgers' *('alojados'* or drifting landless men) quite commonly found on the estates. It is usual for the service tenant to be paid in consumer goods, in rights of usufruct of estate lands and in wages. He receives a house and small garden of about 1000 square metres, a plot of land of perhaps one hectare, a daily meal and a ration of flour and rights to pasture one or more head of cattle, and to collect firewood. The volunteer receives a money wage only, and in the slack season he is usually liable to be unemployed.

The multiplication of supervisors, partly due to a kind of Parkinson's law boosting escape from disdained manual labour, the number of servants, and the 'specialists' whose activity can only be spasmodic, resulted in a greatly inflated labour-

TABLE 1

USE OF LABOUR FORCE – LA CLEMENCIA

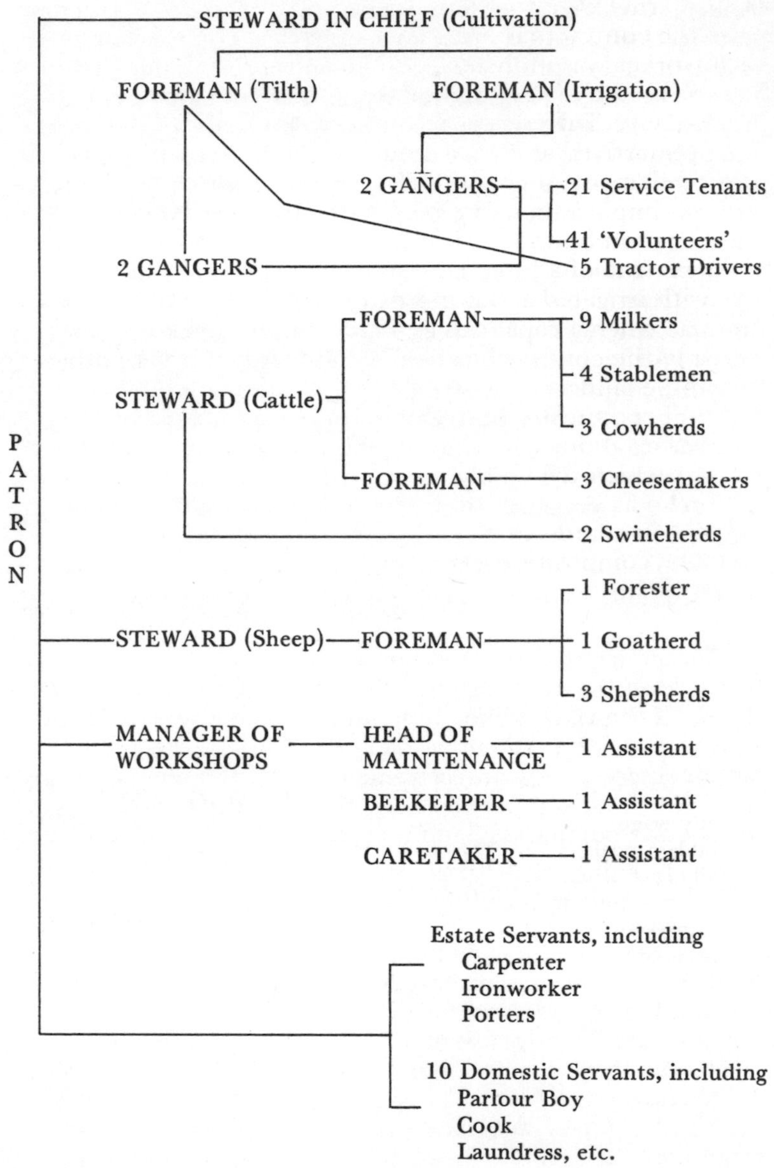

force, and the researcher reckoned that there was a surplus of 5000 labour/days per year. And of the 125 persons employed, only the 21 service-tenants were permanent general purpose workers.

The structure also is a very good example of particularism since the contractual relation between the entrepreneur and each worker was individual and idiosyncratic rather than standardised by categories of skill, or degrees of individual productivity. Differences in forms and amount of payment had been arrived at by individual negotiation expressing a complex of elements such as loyalty, favour, caprice, length of service, simple bargaining skill by the worker and pragmatic manipulation by the landowner to forestall united action. This was true of a long standing dispute between service tenants with irrigated and non-irrigated land respectively since the time when a canal was constructed on the estate; and certainly the continual in-fighting and elbowing for position within the landgroup absorbed the energies and interests of its members, turning their attention always inwards, so that murmuring about land reform and unionisation of rural workers which fell upon their ears from outside had aroused little echo as yet, even though their incomes were well below regional standards.

The composition of the payment of one of the gangers is given below:

TABLE 2

BREAKDOWN OF UNDER-FOREMAN'S PAY

	Escudos per day
His daily wage	2.450
His midday meal	–
His daily loaf of hard-tack	0.140
His garden – (one acre)	0.125
His pasture rights – (for one cow and four pigs)	0.120
His allotment – (two acres)	0.500
Monthly allowance of flour – (6 kgs.)	0.078
Monthly allowance of beans – (8 kgs.)	0.258
Yearly allowance of wheat (or approximately	0.383
one kg. per day)	0.383
TOTAL (not including midday meal and house rent)	4.054
	(or approximately 27p)

While the amount in each case is determined by *particular* arrangement, each of the employees receives his salary in these forms.

For service-tenants, the daily wage varies from 1.730 to 6,000 escudos or 11p to 45p. Everybody who wishes, including the volunteers, receives an allotment, and these run from half an acre to two acres, the majority being of one acre. The total land in allotments is 55 acres, mainly irrigated land, following the scheme of rotation of the estate.

La Clemencia is an anachronism and faces imminent crisis. It consists of a complex of 59 small farms run by service tenants and employees, six share-tenants' farms, and the estate farm. The productivity of the latter is so low that wages in cash (excluding usufruct of land) had reached 55% of the operating costs, so that after paying his taxes and the interest on loans, and taking out domestic expenses, the patron had little left for reinvestment: indeed the report asserts that the estate is already consuming its own capital and has entered upon a carer of disintegration. The patron, an aged man with little remaining interest in the estate, has up to now successfully warded off unionisation, but pressure from the service tenants for increased use of resources and higher wages is inevitable.

In the case of La Clemencia, it should be made clear that the social situation of the patron had a lot to do with its decay. As he was more than 80 years of age at the time of the study, he was going towards 70 when the minimum cash wage was introduced. Up to that time he had been able to pay his labour force almost entirely in usufruct of the ample lands of the estate, and in estate-grown wheat made by unpaid labour into the farmers' daily bread *(el biscocho)*. Using mainly pre-industrial methods his operating costs were low and he could enjoy a rustic lordship in ample style, with few worries and a reasonable income. The security and permanance of the pre-industrial estate was radically upset as urban industrial interests came to predominate in national legislatures.

Entrepreneurship grasped by estate peasants

The two cases which follow are examples of peasant entrepreneurship emerging from an estate as the patron's entrepreneurship falters.

a. A case from Chile

Rafael Baraona's study of this estate is valuable for the light it sheds on several aspects of our problem:

i. the tricks played by inheritance in the ascription of lordship;

ii. some problems of patronship and of fitting together or separating the three component roles of owners, entrepreneur and manager; and

iii. a possible mode of transformation of the structure of an estate when it links up with a strong market.

Santa Catalina fell into the hands of an Italian who in the last quarter of the nineteenth century was about to retire from a successful career as an industrialist in the city of Santiago. He thereupon moved to the country with his wife and twelve children, and devoted himself to running the estate. Its twelve thousand odd acres, climbing up the Andean Cordilla from a small wedge of irrigated land in the Central Valley below, was obviously suitable for the traditional cattle-raising system of the region. This involved the use of the natural pasture composed of the mountain grass and shrubs at different altitudes at different periods of the year, and recourse to conservable fodders from the irrigated lands when the natural pasture was exhausted or dried up.

On the death of the Italian patron, his sons showed little interest in farming, and patronship fell collectively on his eight daughters, who performed in this role throughout the first fifty years of this century, until the last survivor, a widow, retired to live in Santiago in 1950, leaving the estate to a religious order.

No doubt the story of this epoch of petticoat rule is enchanting, but unfortunately it has not been written. However Baraona is able to report that the sisters managed operations by direct contact with their service-tenants (*inquilinos),* some of whom were promoted to the usual specialised and supervisory positions (such as foreman, warehouseman, caretaker, cowherd, irrigation minder, etc.) that they managed the estate according to the traditions established by the praxis of their father, unresponsive to the currents of new technology and improved husbandry which were flowing through the Central Valley. The system operated by the sisters is typical of areas of low mercantility where there is a class monopoly of accessible land. Wealth is created by the national reproduction and growth of cattle, feeding mainly upon natural vegetation.

Labour is required for the conservation of the feeding grounds and for the care of the cattle, and it is drawn from the landless peasantry who may be paid in grants of usufruct of subsistence plots without much expenditure in money. The product moves itself on its own hooves to the market, over long distances if necessary, where it is sold for cash. The working capital required, once the herd is established, is minimal. Though epidemics may cause hunger and privation, bankruptcy is not likely to be a threat. In these circumstances it is frequently the quantity of cattle owned which brings prestige to the owner, rather than other prestigeful goods bought with the proceeds of the sale of cattle.

The study which we are using as source was carried out in 1966, when the estate had already been managed by stewards serving the new owners (the religious order) for fifteen years. During this period the estate was rather belatedly stirred by the new and intensified currents of the national market, in the form of a demand from the capital for vegetables and garden produce which can be grown in irrigated lands. The appointment of a steward marked the re-sorting of the component roles of patronship. Entrepreneurship had been of a very low order during the rule of the sisters, who had, nevertheless, been owners and effective (though inefficient) managers. In the new circumstances, ownership was assumed by a corporate body, seated in Santiago, while managership was delegated to a paid steward. Neither the corporation nor the steward had strong reasons for assuming the risks and responsibilities of running a highly competitive enterprise, in spite of the large monetary profits which this could be expected to bring.

Nevertheless, in spite of the unenterprising posture of the new patronship, the estate as a collectivity of producers was drawn into a dynamic market relation, and entrepreneurship arose from the ranks of the peasant service tenants. One of these, who made tomato-sticks for sale to a neighbouring estate which had already developed commercial market gardening, acquired enough knowledge, confidence and motivation, to begin growing tomatoes and other vegetables for the market on a small patch of land conceded by the steward under share-tenure. Only after two years of demonstrated success did others copy his example, and this with the encouragement of the steward, who immediately saw the advantages for the estate. To accommodate this new development, service tenants were permitted to become share-tenants, receiving plots of irrigated land, in addition to their provision grounds, and in accordance with their entrepreneurial capacity as judged by the steward. As this process ran its course, the estate acquired a new structure which showed up clearly in the study. The estate farm proceeds on its unspectacular career, stock-raising and milk accounting for two-thirds of its product and green corn and wheat for the remainder. But the larger part of the irrigated lands have been handed over to 20 of the service-tenants on a share-tenure basis, with the result that their total product is nearly double that of the estate farm, and comparing net profits we find that the peasants make E.347,000 as compared with the patron's E.58,000. However the payment by the peasants of half the crop in rent changes the picture, so that in the final accounting the peasant sector receives E.207,000 and the patron's sector E.198,000. Of the 30 service-tenants, including eight who had supervisory functions, 20 had been able (with the steward's encouragement) to take up share tenancies, and of these eight had been able to make savings and buy parcels of land of their own, and ten of them hired labourers to 'pay their obligation' while they worked on their share tenancies and properties. And at crop times they used to hire between them an additional 30 day-labourers.

TABLE 3

PATRON AND PEASANT SHARES IN THE ESTATE ENTERPRISE

	Patron	Peasants
Division of arable land	38.5%	61.5%
Division of pasture (mainly natural)	88.0%	12.0%
Division of total labour input	43.0%	57.0%
Division of value – total production	29.0%	71.0%
Production per man/day by sectors	E.18.80	E.32.90
Value of production per hectare of cultivated land	E.924.80	E.3,963.00
Final shares in net income	44.5%	55.5%

One of the conditions accompanying the growth of dynamic commercial relations is the process of sharp economic differentiation between individual economies. Taking the whole group of service-tenants and monthly paid men, a few of these have remained in poverty, lacking even the implements necessary to cultivate all of their provision grounds, while others have been able to get together the necessary capital to become successful agricultural entrepreneurs. (This phenomenon is given more attention in the section on smallholding peasants.) The most successful of the service tenants set out with cultural expectations of a higher order than his fellows, being the son of a small proprietor. His superior social position also endowed him with attributes which contributed to his getting a job in the monthly-paid category as storekeeper *(llavero)* on an estate. His persistent search for land to exploit himself finally led him to Santa Catalina, where in addition to his service-tenancy, he was given the plot of land in share-tenure on which he successfully planted tomatoes and sweet corn. At the time of the study, he was cultivating 14 acres of estate lands on his share- and service-tenancy, owned parcels in two other places, had his own hired men and was owner of a lorry. His income was at least ten times that of the poorest tenant.

The failure of the corporate ecclesiastic owners to exercise an adequate entrepreneurship delivered the intiative to the peasants, and in the short term offered an easy and lucrative solution to the owners. However, it is not likely that the new entrepreneurs will tolerate the excessive share rents they are obliged to pay, and will before long, and with the help of the Land Reform, obtain ownership.

b. A case from Ecuador

A further interesting case of the emergence of entrepreneurship from the tenants of a multifarm estate occurs in the ICAD (1965) report on Ecuador in which a cocoa producing enterprise is faced with the prospect of the destruction of its trees by disease (*monilla* and witch's broom) if unable to raise the technological level of production, particularly in respect of prophylaxis.

The labour system used is that of contract-planting, common enough throughout Latin America and the Caribbean for the purpose of clearing the land, planting and cultivating a permanent crop until it reaches bearing age (and therefore income producing) with the minimum of capital investment. This is the method which has been generally used by proprietors who wished to have as their main crop coffee, cocoa or coconuts which take several years to bear. It is also used for clearing land and planting pasture and is a form of short-term service-tenure. However, the present case is significantly different from that described for Brazil,(p.109)where the tenant in return for his clearing and planting was compensated by rights to make charcoal and to plant provisions only. In the Ecuadorean case, the tenant was allowed to plant market crops in addition to provision, and received payment for the bearing trees on delivery.

An effective response to the attack on the cacao trees by the diseases mentioned would have meant integrating the whole planted area under a single management in place of the patchy and unequal multi-management exercised by the contract planters, and the undertaking of cultivation with the necessary sanitary measures on a large scale. This would have meant a complete and costly re-organisation of productive relations, and might have been attempted by the proprietor if the critical moment of decision had not coincided with a rapid decline in the market price of cacao. So the proprietor (a bank) took the alternative step of relinquishing the entrepreneurial function of cacao producer and turning the contract planters into cash renters and entrepreneurs of the failing crop. This policy led to a movement by the tenants (as they had now become) in favour of their proprietorship of the lots they worked, and in effect the bank decided to parcel out and sell the whole estate to the 286 tenants, each of whom held an average of 13 hectares.

The division of the land proceeded, but before it was completed a new position crystallized and took body amongst the tenant-purchasers. Why should they pay a commercial price for land whose value was mainly due to their own labour during the preceding 30 years? Why pay a proprietor who hardly even visited the estate, simply enjoying the proceeds of the sale of cacao, in whose production he had not even invested? The struggle that ensued became a *cause célèbre* in which the peasants were reasonably successful in the bargain they finally made with the bank.

Perhaps three factors should be taken into consideration comparing this relative peasant victory over a great proprietor with the situation of the complete dominion exercised over the peasants, say, of Camaçari. The peasant tenants who became proprietors were scarce labour in a frontier situation where unused land was available. They received cash payments on delivery of cacao, and thus at certain times disposed of capital. And they were able to organise themselves. The aggressive attitudes of these tenants (*finqueros* and *arrendatarios*) to the landlords were generated by the process of colonisation, in which ownership goes to the person who takes possession and organises the elements of production – the 'frontier mentality'. To them the passive rent-collecting stance of the landlord deprived him of his moral rights. In these new lands there existed no class monopoly sanctioned by tradition.[4] Finally, the tenant was owner of the plantations, works (canals and fences), tools, houses and installations, while the landlord owned only the land. The tenants were already entrepreneurs and capitalists.

Commercial estates in a situation of surplus labour

a. A study of a group of estates in Guatemala

The next case consists of a group of twelve commercially-oriented estates of fairly recent origin in Guatemala. They represent a unique constellation of the familiar factors of landowner role-set, market, labour supply, etc., and are especially interesting in relation to their interaction with existing smallholding areas and the development of a class of agricultural labourers. This research was carried out in the ICAD programme during 1962–63 by Manger Kats, and was complemented by studies of 25 families of smallholding peasants living in the Highlands from which the labour force for the estates was drawn. Six of the estates, on the Pacific coastal plateau, produced tropical crops such as sugarcane, cotton, kenaf, lemon-grass, rice, as well as cattle, while the other six situated on the intermediate mountain slopes were in coffee. The coffee estate of St. Lucia is described briefly below.

The estate contains 450 hectares of which 150 are in coffee, 50 in pasture and ten in sugarcane, the remainder being in forest. The landowner has a business as a coffee exporter in Guatemala City, and is also partner in a much larger coffee and cattle estate elsewhere. In consequence he spends only a few days per year in St. Lucia. His steward, however, goes to the capital every four weeks to settle problems of the estate, and enjoys responsibility and independence. He is to be found in the estate office mornings and evenings, and for the rest of the day he rides all over the farm on horseback.

The estate employs forty labourers all the year round, who at first sight appear to be service-tenants since they have provision grounds. But considering their size (approx. 450 square metres) and the fact that they are granted only after two years of work with the estate, their importance is more in providing an additional reward encouraging stability than in substituting cash wages. The labourers live with their families in huts belonging to the estate. The daily wage paid is Quetzal 0.65, but some jobs go by piece rates. The labourer receives only about three-quarters of his wage in cash, the remainder being deducted in respect of rations and other perquisites received.

During the coffee harvest, the labour force is doubled by the employment of a few of the casual labourers who have settled in the vicinity and a larger number of migrant labourers from the mountains, driven to supplement the incomes they obtain from their minute smallholdings. These are accommodated in crowded sheds.

The immediate supervisors of the labourers are known as *caporales* while the different lines of productive labour fall under foremen, responsible directly to the steward.

The tropical lowland estates are described by the ICAD report as 'speculative', and their owner-entrepreneurs look for profits by being able to react nimbly to fluctuations in international prices. They are able to play this game because they can rely upon flexible supplies of both land and labour. Of the total croplands they hold, only 44% is in commercial crops, and reserve lands are put down to sown pasture on the contract system, and used for raising and fattening cattle at a fairly low technological level. Labour for sowing pasture is obtained by offering the growing land-hungry population small parcels of land (1 — 2 hectares) on verbal contract of share-and-service tenure for one or two harvests, which are paid in a proportion of the corn crop, and the terminal sowing of pastures, so that at the end of the period of renting they are at the disposal of the estate for cattle. Labour for the commercial crops is mainly seasonal, and the same migrants who harvest coffee on the mountain slopes above pass on to the tropical estates which need them immediately after the coffee harvest is finished.

These arrangements result in a symbiotic relation between the Highland peasant areas on the one hand, and the mountain slope and coastal plateau areas of commercial farming on the other, which is characterised by the most spectacular inequality and injustice to be found anywhere in the world, and where the family living on estate labour frequently earns a wage which is one hundredth part of the income which the proprietor family draws from the estate – a situation which can be explained by the conjunction of four factors operating at this historic moment in the national economy-society:

i. the continued survival of the familiar estamental system in its own peculiar Guatemalan form, which has made it impossible for the impoverished peasantry to break out of their subsistence ghettoes and the ascription to the labour function.

ii. a national rural labour surplus due to the increasing peasant population in the Highlands which seems to have increased by 40% between 1950 and 1964 (Hill and Gollas, 1968:9) and the declining fertility of their lands.

iii. the accessibility of rich tropical lands requiring capital for their exploitation, and

iv. the development of capitalist farming which, though not notably efficient, has escaped the dead weight of traditional particularist service-tenure systems of the Andean Highlands by spreading out in areas hitherto unpopulated yet easily linked to the market.

The subjection of the peasants by a variety of refinements on the debt-peonage system was underlined by the institutional changes following Independence, and it was only in 1877 that a new legitimation of this subjection was sought. In that year the Reglamento de Jornaleros provided a new legal framework for debt-peonage and compulsory labour on private estates. The most artful device was the 'work-book' or *livreto* which the worker was obliged to carry with him, in which were inscribed (in letters which he could not understand) a record of his debits and credits, thus enabling the public authorities to apprehend him at any moment and return him to his late 'employer', on pretext of his being in debt. Thus, any peasant seeking wage work with a proprietor was liable to be pressed into obligatory labour with the full authority of the law (Whetten, 1962).

As the demand for labour grew, and the unwillingness of the peasants to seek wage work understandably continued, a means was sought to pry them from their holdings, and it was created in the Vagrancy Law, passed in 1934, when debt-peonage was abolished. This simply imposed labour as a status-duty of those known as 'Indians', due to proprietors who were not so known. The actual definition of the status distinction was not explicit in the law, but implicit and readily understood by those whom it concerned, because the society was officially an 'open' one, though covertly its estamental character was retained. All persons who had no trade or profession, and who were not already employed or owners of less than a certain extension of land, were obliged to seek work on an estate up to a certain minimum number of days per year: and once again, a work-book was required, in which the land-labour and ethnic status of the bearer was given, along with the number of days of obligatory work required. And once again, the public authorities were enabled to take summary action against anyone (of the implicitly and explicitly intended status) whose book did not give evidence of fulfillment of his obligations. Up to 1945 the estates continued to rely on forced labour. The constitution promulgated in that year managed to be vague on labour duties but the history of custodial labour in Guatemala was at an end. From then on, labour had to be secured for the plantations by the mechanisms of a labour market, which was rapidly growing as population overtook fertility in the subsistence lands.

Passing over Arbenz Agrarian Reform Law, so soon undone with the aid of the U.S. intervention, it is interesting to look at the situation as regulated by the labour market, as it was at the time of the ICAD study in 1962 – 63. Indeed, no other suasion than deprivation is needed to make peasant labour available to the estates. This is immediately obvious from the figures on land distribution.

Of the first two categories shown in Table 4, comprising 88.4% of all units, most are inadequate to provide family subsistence, and most of them belong to the Highlands. In the study area, it was found that while the family usually disposed of 600 man/days, all the necessary labour needed on the holding was approximately 110 man/days (and 128 in the Lowlands). Peasants interviewed claimed on the average 233 man/days worked off the holding by members of their families, in crafts and commerce but more especially when they migrated at harvest time to the estates. The study revealed the curious fact that even these 110 man/days on the family holding were often worked by wage labour. But one third of the inhabitants of these peasant neighbourhoods are landless families, in addition to the microholders, and these could be paid at

TABLE 4

NUMBER, AREA AND PERCENTAGE DISTRIBUTION OF AGRICULTURAL UNITS IN GUATEMALA
(by size)

Type of unit	No. of units	%	Total area (hèctares)	Area as %	Average size per unit (hectares)
Micro-holding	74,270	21.3	28,600	0.8	0.4
Sub-family holding	233,800	67.1	504,600	13.5	2.2
Family holding	33,040	9.5	500,800	13.5	15.2
Estate (medium)	7,060	2.0	1,167,500	31.4	165.4
Estate (large)	520	0.1	1,519,300	40.8	2,921.9

Source: ICAD (1965) from 1950 census

Q 0.40 or Q 0.20 with food, while the peasant owner could sell his labour to the estate at Q.50.

What were the Highland peasants able to produce? The average income was composed as follows:

Imputed value of corn, beans, etc. consumed by family	188
Cash value of produce such as wheat, chickens, eggs, etc.	136
Total family income	324
or Q.54 per capita	

It is estimated that 160,000 peasants, mainly younger men, go down every year, first to work in the coffee harvest, and when that is finished, to the coastal estates, and perhaps 3000 of each yearly wave remain, some hoping to live throughout the year on harvest earnings and other sporadic jobs for the remaining months, others looking for lands which they can rent and cultivate. Thus, for the Highland peasant averaging

Q 324 in a year's operations on his holding, the additional Q 260 earned in craftwork, petty trade and wages, mainly on the estates, is a very important addition to his annual income, which now reaches Q 584, putting his family per capita income at Q 97.35.

The direction of the tendency towards loss of land by the peasantry is noted by Feder (1971:55 – 60) who points to the increase in landless labourers between the 1950 and 1964 census from 69 to 140 thousand. One such peasant gave some account of his life and work (ICAD Guatemala) and it follows at the chapter's end.

A similar condition of exclusion from the land in east and north-east Brazil makes profitable the inefficient cacao plantation described below:

b. A case from Ilheus, Brazil

Before the great cacao market began its clamorous demand at the end of the nineteenth century, the Ilheus area of the Atlantic coast of Brazil, to the south of Bahia, enjoyed no important external market relations. Its sparse peasant population lived by subsistence agriculture and a coastal trade in cassava flour and wood. So the first planters of cacao were small people, 'anonymous men, men without history', pioneers who penetrated by the numerous rivers, clearing out the undergrowth and planting their cacao in the shade of the remaining trees, or using bananas for this purpose. They continued to plant subsistence crops even after their cacao had come into bearing. But the prices for cacao and the reputation of the zone soon attracted other tougher characters, armed with rifles and the 'caxixe' (or fraudulent title to land), who dispossessed the family planters and drove many into the remoter hillsides.

As fast fortunes were made, and as the new barons fought one another for the land, labour soon arrived from the arid backlands (or *sertões*) driven by frequent droughts and the need for cash, and both land and labour were exploited to the maximum. In 1930 prices slumped, but picked up again with the Second World War. The characteristics of this agricultural episode have been a lucrative but fluctuating export market, a highly suitable land area with an extending frontier, the initial absence of a powerfully ensconced landowning class used to a traditionally rigid heritage of land-labour institutions, and a plentiful supply of labour. Cacao production has been extractive and uninhibited, and the organisation of production has responded to these conditions.

During 1962, seven cacao estates were studied in the ICAD programme, and an account of some aspects of one of these, call Boa Vista, is given below.[5]

Land ownership and entrepreneurship was exercised by an old man living in a city of the north east, his active son, who visited the estate for half a day every two months, supervising its operations, exercising entrepreneurial functions in association with his father, and transmitting decisions to a steward. This latter lives on the estate and organises the day-to-day operations, having authority to draw and dispose of a limited amount of money per month, to hire and fire labourers, to appoint them to their tasks, and generally to look after the cultivation and processing. The actual relations between father and son as regards participation in all aspects of patronship were not revealed. The steward who had served the family for 52 years, received a salary of about twice that of a labourer, the best house on the estate to live in, a small lot of land for his own cultivation, an annual bonus and three litres of milk per day. He was also owner of a primitive sugarcane mill, worked by draught-animals, and a shed equipped for the milling of manioc flour, both of his own entrepreneurship but built on the property of the estate. He had also been able to purchase a piece of land of 18 hectares of his own in a neighbouring municipality, on which he kept a permanent wage-worker and a contract worker busy in the cultivation of cacao.

The landlord owned three other estates, on one of which he was known to have 500 head of cattle. Like him, six of the seven landlords in the group studied had two or more estates. His son was partner in a firm of distributors of agricultural equipment and building materials.

The particular nature of the key relationship of the steward to the owner should not be overlooked. The steward, now 64 years old, has been working for the family for 52 years, and considers that he 'is as it were one of the family' *(sou como se fosse membro da familia)*. This is a possible sentiment in Brazil, where it was usual for a land-owing family to embrace within the bonds of kinship various ranks, including for instance the patron's illegitimate children (by slaves or servants) and foster children *(filhos de criação)* from poorer families, with restricted rights and augmented duties.

In spite of his acquired sense of kinship with the landlord, the administrator is a long way from him in terms of social class, being of humble rural origin, a man who learnt reading and writing only after he was grown up, and who has allowed most of his children to grow up illiterate. His house contains no radio, book nor newspaper. He always has followed a traditional routine in the cultivation of cacao, but in recent years he has become aware of more scientific ways, through his contact with visiting agronomists.

Of the 260 hectares of the estate, 136 are cultivated, about 100 being planted in cacao. But more than half of the trees are more than fifty years old, and consequently yields are relatively low. In the harvest of 1958–59 the average yield was 27 arrobas, in the 1961–62 harvest 15.8, and in the 1962–63 harvest it fell again, to 8.1. The average for 1962–63 (the year of this study) was 20.3. Declining production owed a good deal to successive years of drought, but also the bad condition of the ageing trees. The estate also has the usual sheds and appurtenances for storing, fermenting and drying the cocoa beans.

The number of permanent workers employed is 19, including the steward, who is distinguished by receiving a monthly salary rather than weekly wages. Four are single, and live in bachelors' quarters, and all the rest are married, living in houses provided by the landlord. They receive their wages, work 8–10 hours five days a week, and most of them have the use of small garden plots of about half a hectare, in which they grow beans, manioc and a little sugarcane or vegetables. They are also allowed to collect firewood on the estate. With few exceptions, cultivation of the garden plots, usually done on Saturdays, or else attended to by some other member of the family, is for family consumption. In all the seven estates studied, there was a single case only of a worker who had developed market-gardening and was receiving a reasonable income from sales in the town. It was a rarity for entrepreneurship to emerge from this form of service-tenure.

There was no sort of formal agreement between the workers and the landlord about the terms of their employment, and their working hours were determined by the administrator. The key to control was the threat of immediate dismissal if workers did not do the work expected of them, or behaved in any way unacceptable to the steward. Other labour was always waiting at the gates. Wages paid for the day's work were Cr$ 221 on this estate, as against an average of Cr$ 251 on the seven studied, but both these figures fall short of the legal minimum daily wage, even allowing for the owner's right to deduct 30% for the provision of housing. The value of the garden plot (which not all workers enjoyed) and the right to pick up firewood might be claimed to offset the deficit. But this can hardly be taken seriously since the wages paid to workers with and without garden plots were the same. And if such allowances are made against the house and the garden, then they are so high that the worker pays off the capital value of both in about four years.

The technical level of production was very low and 60% of the operating costs were in labour. In the year of the study, despite declining yields, a net income was obtained by the owner-entrepreneur amounting to 30 times the wages of a permanent worker, though entrepreneurship only required attention at the estate a few days in the year, and management could be entrusted to a familiar of no more than peasant status.

What did a labourer receive for his part in production? Joao Bautista is depicted as representative. He is a sickly man with bad teeth, married with five children under 16. His work clothes are ragged but he has a shabby suit to go to town in. He has a midday meal of dried meat with plantain and eddoes, and he sups off coffee, and what is left over from lunch. The single men get the same salary as those with families and are consequently better off.

The most remarkable feature of the situation, and that which contributes most to the excessive inequality, is the overwhelming power delivered to a landowner with some access to capital, by the surplus labour situation, and consequently the practice of immediate dismissal as settlement of a disagreement.

The ridiculing of minimum salary laws, the virtual absence of any rights on the part of the worker, the exclusion of the vast majority of peasants from access to the land and the consequent desperate search for wage work to buy daily bread has delivered to the patron a complete and arbitrary domination, and engendered a fatalistic submissiveness in the peasant, whose only alternative is migration to the south.

Old estates and new agriculture in juxtaposition – Bahia, Brazil

In order to penetrate more deeply into the Brazilian agrarian situation we shall use data from a monographic study done by Maria Azevedo Brandão on a municipality on the north-east side of the Recôncavo, or bay-coast which forms the immediate hinterland of the city of Salvador, which was done in connection with the ICAD study (1966). The *municipio* lies on the margin of the massape soils so excellently suited to the cultivation of sugarcane, and its history up to 1940 was dominated by the 'tidal' effects of the export market for sugar, whose 'flow' meant that the cultivation of cane reached out to patches of marginally suitable soils within the *municipio* itself, and whose 'ebb' caused a withdrawal, and a return to the production of goods necessary for servicing the nuclear lands devoted to sugar-monoculture and a sinking into primitive shifting subsistence by a large part of the labour force. Since 1940 a series of changes has taken place resulting from the growth of a national industry in Brazil, and the expansion of the town of Salvador as a market as well as the penetration of the country areas by more highly organised, technically advanced forms of capitalist production.

The production of sugar by slave labour grew rapidly in the sixteenth century, and by the seventeenth century the plantation had become well established as a system of productive organisation, a micro-society and a form of settlement. After a spasmodic career in the seventeenth century, due to bad crops, difficult transport, a smallpox epidemic and a famine due to failure of subsistence crops, the eighteenth century opened in conditions of considerable prosperity, but Caribbean competition caused a general decline in prices, while the goldrush in Minas Gerais caused a run on slave labour as well as on other commodities, and consequently the prices of these rose. There was also a migration by *lavradores, moradores* and technicians who preferred to seek their fortunes in the mines (Hutchinson, 1957:39).

This time large scale sugar production disappeared from Camaçari for good, though within the Recôncavo the state government was financing the construction of sugar-factories *(usinas)*. Capitalised operations fell off and productive activities re-formed themselves around family subsistence and extraction. Where lands were of better quality and still contained some forest cover, estates were maintained as single properties, their owners letting them out on a cash or share-tenure basis for the making of charcoal and shifting subsistence agriculture. Poorer estate lands were allowed to fragment, or fell into the hands of renters, or were simply abandoned. The natural economy prevailed again with the sale of charcoal meeting cash needs.

During this century the export market for sugar has recovered twice (during the two World Wars) but it has also lost its overriding importance with the growth of a national market not only for sugar but for other agricultural commodities. The present situation therefore must be seen in terms of master trends and events of the national scene.

The Napoleonic wars renewed the demand in Europe for sugar from Brazil and this was strong enough in Recôncavo to lead to the planting of canes in Camaçari – not continuously, but in patches of marginally suitable soils. This was accompanied by a reconsolidation of large estates (of as much as 2000 hectares) as plantations, and the development of subsidiary economies to sugar monoculture – in the provision of firewood, draught animals and their pasture, and subsistence crops for the labour force. A report about Vila de Abrantes at the beginning of the nineteenth century speaks of the inhabitants being *moradores* who produced cassava and other provisions, and also were occasional fishermen and hunters.

After the Wars of Independence, from 1825 onwards, decline set in, leading to the abandonment of cane planting in the municipality, though the estates were not at this stage broken up. Unsuccessful attempts were made to grow tobacco and coffee, but the situation was one of stagnation, probably aggravated by the cholera epidemic of 1855, while wage labour tended to move towards the coffee areas of Sao Paulo.

However the American Civil War once again created favourable market conditions, and a new expansion of cane planting in Camaçari took place. The mills began to grind again until the Abolition (of slavery) put an end to the plantation system on which sugar production rested.

Following Maria Azevedo's account of Camaçari,[6] the factors which have impinged most on the agrarian socio-economic structure of the areas have been three:

i. The growth and expansion of the national industrial complex. This has not had the magnitude of the industrialisation of the Rio–São Paulo area, but important growth has taken place, including the expansion of the petrol industry in the Reconcavo, and the further rationalisation of productive methods in the cultivation and industrial processing of sugar. It has also introduced other technologically modern forms of agricultural production into the country, so that they are available to entrepreneurs who may be in a position to use them. This has already resulted in the intrusion of new kinds of farms into the area in the form of intensive coconut monoculture and a few scientifically managed dairy herds, both with considerable capitalisation. They are using new techniques of production and showing little inclination to adapt themselves to the subsistence system.

ii. Secondly, the growth of the city of Salvador, and the *prospects* of urban (and suburban), industrial and agricultural advance, have led to the raising of land values and consequently to land speculation.

iii. The government has intervened in the designless pattern of change impelled by these factors, organising a land settlement scheme on purchased properties, and setting up three colonies of middling producers to supply the growing city market with food. The first of these colonies contained a high percentage of Italians, whose cultural conditioning led them to expect to produce commercially for the market and to live on their entrepreneurial rewards, rejecting from the start the use of their own land and labour for their own subsistence. It had also endowed them with knowledge of the means of producing garden crops. Other colonists were either Brazilians from other areas, about whom no data is given, or itinerant local tenants of the subsistence tradition.

In the first place, when the government proceeded to the expropriation of the large estates and let it be known that lots could be applied for, the peasants of the neighbourhood did not respond because they were not told that credit facilities were available. Secondly, it did not occur to them that the expropriated estates would no longer be available for their shifting subsistence activities once distributed to the new smallholding colonists. Thus, the new situation was not perceived as threatening their existing means of livelihood, nor as a feasible alternative form of livelihood, offering better prospects of security than the uncertainties of the old system.

Meantime some of the colonists began operations. It was demonstrated that no immediate payment had to be made for the land, and that the new ventures of both Italians and Brazilians could prosper in selling to the city market. At the same time, land for subsistence became scarce, so local tenants were persuaded to apply for lots, and often obtained them. However, the possession of their new parcels was welcomed rather as an opportunity to pursue their customary routines with greater amplitude and security, and not as an opportunity for experimenting with novel techniques and crops, certainly not for abandoning subsistence cropping, the core of their material security.

The tenants, therefore, on taking up possession, began the familiar work of burning and charcoal making and proceeded to the planting of their provision grounds, but with no improvement in techniques on account of the absence of credit, and no increase in the scale of production on account of the limits set by the available family labour. Moreover, by tradition older sons did not cooperate with their fathers in the 'family farm', but were expected to find their own provision grounds which were made to measure for one man, and dependents. This still left most of the land idle, and the colonists were then under pressure from friends and relatives to fulfil their traditional obligations of renting out some of these lands. Thus the new regime became a perpetuation of the old. A further element of cultural persistence was the form in which the land was perceived, i.e. as a 'reservoir' of resources from which one could take out the means of livelihood each year and which nature would renew. Customary alienation from proprietorship, and the apparently unlimited character of the resource, led to a fundamentally extractive attitude rather than to husbandry.

The tenants who sub-rented lands were obliged to leave the colony, since regulations did not permit renting until the land had been fully paid for. Several of those who received compensation for crops sown and work done invested the money in small shops, which were soon in liquidation since credit for hungry friends could not lightly be denied. The tenants were soon on the lookout for lands to rent again. The 'survivors' were those families in which a number of adolescent children made up an effective labour force, and one or two families which entered with some capital acquired in petty commerce.

The patches of commercial agriculture beginning to appear in the colonies and in the technically managed coconut plantations and dairy herds also created a demand for wage-labourers, some of whom were recruited from the local peasant tenants, and others from migrants from the *sertão*.

The success of commercial agriculture was linked closely to ability to get credit for the high operational costs and the increasing labour required. The result was a much sharper economic differentiation between the new farmers and their labourers, than between the traditional proprietors and tenants whose production remained low. High productivity made no difference to labourers' wages, since the labour surplus continued.

The study of Camaçari shows the superimposition of a modern agriculture, using industrial techniques and capitalist organisation, upon pre-industrial commercial and self-provisioning production, and the decline of these. With the opportunities offered by the government-financed colonisation scheme, a small number of traditional peasant families seem to have been able to become capitalist farmers, but without this kind of assistance, there is very little prospect of the evolution of the peasantry towards technically improved commercial farming. The continuous population increase, and the disappearance of spare lands for subsistence, leaves the two main alternatives as wage-labour and migration.

Estate peasants and livelihood - some notes

The case studies do not make it possible to assert trends in the peasant situation in any sort of statistical order, and much of the census data is difficult to interpret in this sense. The value of the case material is that it brings one imaginatively closer to the human experience, shows the interaction of factors producing changes in estate economies and consequently in social relations, and certainly demonstrates the predominance of the estate as a crucible in which larger socio-economic forces meet, interact, and define new situations and destinies for the peasants who find their livelihood upon them.

In four of the eight cases, some portion of the service-tenants on the estate obtain access to sufficient land and credit to develop entrepreneurially. The circumstances favouring this transformation are: in one of the Chilean cases, market penetration creates a demand for vegetables, and the estate owners decide to deliver the new entrepreneurial possibilities to enterprising service-tenants. This decision is in line with the present trend in Chile, where it is reported that between 1955 and 1965 the number of service-tenants halved. The number of share-tenants did not increase much but the land per share-tenant rose from 8.9 to 14.3 hectares. This expansion came out of the idle estate lands.

Why should the proprietor deny himself the rewards of entrepreneurship? His action is part of a remodelling of his economic organisation, especially to avoid the fate which overtook the proprietor in case No.3 (La Clemencia). Labour rapidly became expensive as a result of minimum-wage legislation, compulsory social insurance and unionisation. Many patrons sought to mechanise the estate-farm and to shed the entrepreneurial responsibilities for horticulture, receiving an immediately saleable rent-in-kind, and thus easing the credit problem of their main operations. It was found that the share-tenant (frequently a service-tenant in an additional role) obtained his labour supply more cheaply than the patron could, first by drafting his own family and, when additional paid labour was needed, using pensioners, men without papers and social marginals.

The Ecuadorean cacao growers have also become smallholding commercial farmers. They owe the opportunity to accumulate capital by contract-planting to the frontier situation and the consequent labour scarcity; their advance to independent entrepreneurship to the poor state of the industry; and, finally, their proprietorship of the land to their own intense political campaign.

But there is little sign of the growth of peasant entrepreneurship within the export-oriented estates with an abundant labour supply at their gates. On the Guatemalan estates, the permanent workers cannot be described as service-tenants, being allowed only 400 square metres of land. And in the cacao estates, the level of technology is so low that labour accounts for 60% of cost of production, so that profitability becomes a matter of the tightest possible squeeze on wages, and the concession of 400 square metres for provision grounds is a real contribution to the minimum food-basket of the worker, making possible the payment of wages well below the legal minimum. The flow of estate peasantry into independent commercial farming is limited to a select few, in specially fortunate circumstances, or with especial gifts or connections.

There is a widely generalised flow of adolescents and young adults to the towns and cities, and amongst traditional peasant families a spreading polivalence of livelihood : any possibility of retaining or obtaining access to land is grasped at, but is seldom sufficient to provide livelihood. It must be supported by work on estates and commercial farms either as share-tenant or labourer, in such conditions as may be offered. That is to say, with the displacement of the service-tenure system, and with the inadequate development of capitalist agriculture and industrial production in the society (hence a very limited number of permanent wage-earning positions available), more and more peasant families find themselves without any clearly defined position in the productive system, and livelihood is balanced uncertainly between various activities pursued by different members of the family.

Unfortunately, studies seldom include case materials about the livelihood situation of real families, but a limited number have been found from Brazil, Guatemala and Colombia, and are given below.

a. Two Bahia peasants, Felipe and Jovino

Felipe, of Camaçari, aged 25, has a wife but no children. He migrated from the *sertão* to the city of Salvador where he worked as a stonemason's mate until he tired of the work. He then took a job with an Italian colonist's family, and had been with them for five years. He had the right to a provision ground but without commercial crops. He was not registered officially as a worker, and was not therefore covered by insurance against accidents or illness. The family provided him with a hut made of wattle and daub with a tile roof and a beaten earth floor, divided into two rooms, without windows and without sanitation. Cooking was done on the ground. His salary was Cr$1,800 per week.

The family for which Felipe worked had arrived in Brazil 12 years before and had received a lot in the colony referred to above, with credit and equipment sufficient to move rapidly into commercial agriculture. The family contained three boys of working age. After six years the family was able to buy 43 hectares outside the colony, from the estate of a family whose descendants had been reduced to peasant status by fragmentation. On this land the three sons worked together, with Felipe, the labourer, planting coconuts and bananas, and producing vegetables for the Salvador market. They also contracted peasants to plant coconut trees and look after them until ready to bear, in return for the usufruct of the land between the trees for the cultivation of provisions. The bearing trees were delivered to the proprietor, and the peasant was then given a further piece of land on which the process was repeated. Casual labour was also hired when necessary from the local peasants.

The family enterprise had a tractor for the purchase of which a loan was made by the Bank of Brazil, and machinery had also been bought for a brick factory to be erected on the colony lands. A larger and more comfortable house had been built to replace that originally provided for the colonist.

The contrast between these two families is expressive of the economic differentiation between the new wage-earning labourers and the commercial farmers – more pronounced than that between traditional middling proprietors and their peasant tenants. Maria Azevedo also reports bewilderment and ambivalence in the new relation, since the worker still hankers for protectiveness and succour which the old landlords were expected to manifest, and resents the loss of freedom and status implied by the change, and she describes the attitudes of a tenant peasant turned tractor-driver as follows (1963:63):

> He is perplexed by the new systems of relations which arise, has ambivalent attitudes towards the patron: sometimes he finds him good, sometimes he feels abandoned by him and submitted to relations in which profit is considered rather than his own person. As regards the possibility of getting help, he shows himself half-conscious of his new condition: 'Nowadays everyone looks after himself'. He considers himself ill and claims 'I showed the patron these swollen feet of mine and he just didn't say a word'.
>
> Of the new roads appearing, the fish nursery and incubator in construction on the estate, and of the huge coconut plantation belonging to a large entrepreneur and managed technically according to rigorous controls, he says: 'He has this to show off to his friends' imagining it all the plaything of a rich kid, or at least pretending to imagine this.

In the meantime, the peasant tenant who cannot find steady work on an estate is forced daily nearer to starvation and destitution as lands acquire greater commercial value, for instance Jovino, who has never left the region:

He is about fifty and has no land of his own, so he has moved from estate to estate, now as share-tenant, now as cash-tenant, with casual labour as a stop gap. In the last two years he has had land from a woman proprietor who let him put up a hut there. Last year he rented a half task of land (2,200 square metres) for Cr$ 1,000, but it is poor land and he only got two sacks of charcoal out of it. Not allowed to plant anything but annuals, nor to keep animals, he sowed cassava and had one banana tree. His wife helps him a day or two each week. This year he got three quarters of a task and made ten sacks of charcoal out of it, and the land is better – this time the proprietress wants a quarter of the crop as rent, so when the plants are growing up he will divide the plot into four and the landowner can choose hers. She will also let him use her gear for making cassava flour. He can't plant vegetables because he has no money to buy manure, and the earth alone is too poor. The Arab shopkeeper who gives credit won't give it to Jovino – and the landowner? She neither. God gave Jovino a guardian angel (he says) to watch over his cassava and this is what he is going to stick to.

At certain seasons he reluctantly works for wages two or three days a week because the provision ground is not yielding. It is easy to get work in winter, but the summer is hard. The pay for weeding and cleaning the coconuts of an Italian colonist is only Cr$3,000 and this was not in cash but in the usufruct of 1,386 square metres for charcoal and ground provisions. Jovino finds this a fair deal. The Italian likes it since his weeding is done for nothing, and newly cleared land is returned to him for planting.

In addition to helping a bit at the provision ground, his wife also works by plaiting straw hats for local wear, but a single hat, which takes a day to make, only earns her Cr$ 60. The wearers are people like themselves, and could not pay at Cr$100. She also goes cutting coconuts and dende palm, which may bring in Cr$ 20 – 30 per day.

What does their labour buy them? The hut is a windowless construction of wattle and thatch on the bare earth, a bed and a table both topped with cut sticks (rods) and a bench of a plank on two logs. The stove is made in a customary manner out of modelled mud on the top of a stand. The landowner will not allow them to daub the walls as this would give the building a permanent status.

In addition to the clothes they wear, Jovino has a pair of trousers and his wife another dress. The bed has sheets of sacking, with the spare garments as additional cover. As for their social life, on Sundays they get a change by talking to another husband and wife like themselves on the estate. In case of sickness, there is no help at hand. If you are bad enough to need an operation you die, they say. The wife has a bad foot and nothing for it, and Jovino has an inflamed eye which he bathes in cold water and urine in the mornings. A fellow worker was ill for a week, and the proprietress paid for some medicine so that he wouldn't die for want of help.

Neighbours try to help one another by lending things, but it's a benighted place – not even any liquor to have a drink now and then. They haven't decent enough clothes to go visiting or to gatherings. And nowadays Jovino can't even get anyone to exchange a day's work with him.

In the morning they take coffee with cassava flour. At noon they eat cassava flour with water, and a bit of meat. At night they eat some cooked sweet cassava *(aipim)* and take it with coffee. He comments ruefully: 'In the morning it's hunger, at noon it's hunger, what does the night say?'

Other casual descriptions of peasants drawn into estates in different capacities are given below, since they show livelihood sequences and the barrenness of alternatives in a way in which numbers fail to do.

b. A Guatemalan peasant, Ramon Coj Choch[7]

San Andres Xecul is a village in the western plateau of Guatemala, some 14 miles from Totonicapan, capital of the department of that name. The municipality lies in a valley at some six thousand feet above sea-level, and is surrounded by mountains. A paved road running into the Panamerican Highway passes nearby without apparently touching the life of the village. Nearly all its 1,600 inhabitants depend directly or indirectly on agriculture, though a third of the family heads have no land of their own, and work as labourers in the lands of other peasants; and they, along with many others with insufficient lands, go down to the coffee estates on the Pacific slopes every year to work in the harvest as a way of adding to their earnings.

It is here that Ramon Coj Choch lives with his wife and four children. His property consists of two and a half acres which he inherited from his father who had three heirs and seven acres. Like his neighbours, Ramon has a proper title to his land, but it is in two separate lots, one on the slopes and the other on the tops of the range, the second being steep and stoney and hard to work. But providing for his family means tilling both parts continuously. He sows the usual corn, and some wheat where it is flat, perhaps half an acre. But in recent years his corn yield has fallen from 920 to 575 kilos per acre. Unremitting cultivation of the same soil seems to be the main reason for this, though the previous year's drought contributed.

Although he does not produce enough corn for the needs

of his family, he goes on growing wheat (wheat is for town consumption and not for peasant subsistence) because he can get good money for it: the mill pays him Q 5.80 per quintal. The corn grown on the remaining land of the first lot, intercropped with broad beans, and the much sparser corn-crop from the second lot, is not enough to supply his family needs, even less so because he has to sell one third of it for lack of storage. Corn is the staple of his daily diet, and he requires twelve kilos of it per week, so for two months of each year he has to buy it in the market when the price is up to Q 3 –5 per quintal. The broad beans and cucumbers interplanted between the corn-rows are for household consumption only. His other crops are green vegetables from his garden.

To work so small an amount of land only takes up 120 days per year, in spite of the labour he puts into conservation against erosion by terracing, which he was taught by an extensionist during the Arbanz regime. So when the harvest is through in November, he goes down to the coffee zone to work in the harvest as a labourer. For three months he goes from estate to estate, starting with the lowest, where the fruit ripens quickest, and finishing off in January and February in the higher cooler lands. Rather than take the lorry from one of the estates which is sent to fetch workers from the neighbouring villages, he prefers to go on foot. In this way he escapes the cost of the fare which would be deducted from his weekly wage. His wife stays at home minding the children and the property.

The few animals he has, five fowls and a pig, are not for consumption but serve as a savings bank. The eggs are sold in the market and the animals are only slaughtered in case of emergency or for a fiesta. Whenever there is less work to be done, he goes up to the mountain and exercises his right to cut pine-trees on the lands of the community. The sale of firewood also brings him in a small income.

All these productive activities yield an income worth about Q 400 in the year, half of which comes from the sale of his products.

Ramon has various other activities for which he receives no financial reward. He helped a neighbour with the terracing of his land and worked with his brother in improving the latter's house. He must also serve the community for a day or two every week. This year he is serving as community *Mayor (alcalde),* an office which involves helping the mayor of the municipality by going on errands and taking messages. He knows that next year he will serve as *fiscal,* or aid to the visiting priest, responsible for keeping the church keys and seeing that it is clean. So he participates fully in the religious and secular system of offices.

Coj Choch says that he is not making plans for the future. He hopes God will grant him the boon of going on living with his neighbours as at present. He is sceptical about official programmes because he does not believe that the authorities have any concern for the 'indigenous' population, so he thinks it's better to look after the defence of his own interests for himself (from ICAD, Guatemala, 1965).

c. *Three Colombian peasants, Hernan Garcia, Eugenio and Jose*[8]

In Colombia the number of rural heads of families without land probably still does not reach twenty per cent of the agricultural population but the number whose land is inadequate in extent and insufficient to provide a basis for a thriving enterprise probably reaches 60%. This situation produces a mass of souls who pass their lives alternating between three lines of productive conduct: building a frail bulwark of physical security by planting subsistence crops, especially yuca, corn, plantains, potatoes and perhaps a little sugar and coffee (sugar is taken as a beverage made by soaking loaf-sugar in water, *agua de panela);* working for a wage; and establishing their own enterprises by means of share-tenures or purchases of land. Many such peasants of this kind were met during the ICAD study, and some were interviewed about their careers. The following is the account given by Hernan Garcia.

Garcia was born in 1922 in the coffee-growing area of Antioquia. His parents were very small peasant proprietors, and he stayed at home helping them after completing his two-year schooling, which is all the country schools provide. He did his military service at nineteen years of age, and when he had finished he moved about earning his way by casual labour until he returned home at 22, to work again with his father. He then went to work on a small estate, where, as steward, he had supervisory responsibilities. He saved enough money to buy half an acre of land in a smallholders' neighbourhood, and there he has been able to build himself a house of wattle and daub *(bahareque)* with wooden floors, a tiled roof, two windows in the living-room, and a latrine made with the assistance of the Coffee Growers Federation. Thus, his material conditions are superior to those of the majority of Colombian peasants, though fairly typical of the zone in which he lives. While a steward he married, and has brought up his family of eight (so far) in the house described. At the time of the interview he was working on a large coffee estate, earning seven pesos a day and two stems of bananas per week. He added another 950 pesos to his earnings by doing contract work, and his wife earned 1,450 pesos in the coffee harvest. As a permanent labourer he has a right to paid holidays, family allowance and a number of other perquisites, none of which he receives. He says he has too much respect for the boss to take him up before the authorities to obtain his dues, and prefers to accept the arrangements which his boss decides. In any case, he says, he would need someone to represent him in making such a claim, and this would cost money too.

Garcia aspires to run his own farm, and two years before the interview he succeeded in obtaining a share-tenancy on some estate lands outside the coffee-growing zone. The terms of his arrangements with the estate stipulate that he may only grow annuals, that he must deliver the land when it is required by the proprietor (it is assumed that he will be able to harvest his crops or receive compensation for them in such a case) and that in return for the use of the land, the proprietor, who makes no contribution to the costs of operation should receive one third of the product. The interest of the case lies in the fact that Garcia, a share-tenant was not able to work the land himself, particularly since the land lay at a distance of several miles from his house, and confined himself to the role of entrepreneur. The gross product came out at 11,260 pesos of which the proprietor received 3,750, and the entrepreneur (Garcia) found himself with 3,250 after he had met the costs of production, mainly seed and the wages of the labourer whom he hired. Garcia also managed to get some subsistence crops out before rendering accounts to the owner.

This entrepreneurial activity gave Garcia an opportunity to improve his living conditions and develop his own productive potential. The year previously his family had received an income from all sources totalling 7,610 pesos, or 761 per head. Of this, 3,500 was spent on food, another 1,140 on improvements to the house, 300 on two pigs and 800 on a mule. But he had a debt of 300, and no cash savings whatsoever.

Unfortunately for Garcia, the proprietor of the estate where he had his share-tenancy wished to extend his rough grazing, and had decided to put an end to the arrangement.

Our peasant had very little hope of being able to find another lot. Thus his pretensions to entrepreneurship broke down over access to land. Purchase of anything larger than a house lot was well beyond what he could raise in capital. And a share-tenancy on a long lease was unheard of in the zone.

Even in looking after the health of the family, Garcia has the backing of the subsistence system. Last year he needed medical attention and got it free at the municipal hospital. Of the prescribed medicines, he could afford to buy only the cheaper ones, so the treatment was not successful. When unable to get medical help or to buy the prescriptions, he uses household remedies like *manzanilla* for stomach ache, *ruda* for indigestion, *toronjil* for the heart, *mejorana,* parsnip, etc., all of which he grows on his holding.

His children go to the urban school which is nearby, and he expects a municipal scholarship for the oldest boy who is bright.

In the same area another of the workers interviewed, Eugenio, 32 years of age, had six children whom he supported on his salary as a permanent estate worker, amounting to seven pesos per day, or 2,352 pesos per year, a weekly stem of bananas at a nominal price and a free house and garden lot. From the latter he was able to obtain a little yuca and corn for subsistence, and to raise some fowls, whose eggs brought him in 150 pesos giving a total of 3,050, or 340 pesos per head. With the 1,900 spent on food, the diet could not include milk, meat or eggs, and consisted mainly of corn, bananas and beans in various forms, with sugar-water and some coffee. The estate paid him all the statutory dues but, coincidental with the raising of the minimum wage, the estate labour force was being cut from sixty to forty and he had received notice to quit. What path would he follow next? And his nineteen work-mates and their families?

In the cotton growing area of Tolima, where cultivation is highly mechanised with the use of light aeroplanes for spraying the crops, two peasants were interviewed belonging to a group which had invaded an unused estate, on account of failure to obtain land for subsistence or wage-work. This is what one of them Jose, reported:

He went to work at nine as a houseboy in different parts of the *municipio,* in order to help his parents who were poor. At fifteen his father died, and as the oldest son he had to take charge of the household. He earned his living as an estate labourer.

He worked as a share-tenant until 'the presence of armed bands on the estate' compelled him to flee. He claimed compensation from the proprietor for his growing crops and other improvements, but all the proprietor would pay him was the value of the fence he had built. The proprietor burned down his house with his belongings in it, and his other improvements. With his wife and seven children he went to live with friends and the couple tried to earn a living as hucksters in the village market, but this brought them a very meagre living. He then began getting work as an occasional labourer, mainly in the cotton harvests, trying to live for the rest of the year on the money earned in the three-month harvest. They tried to borrow from friends, but it was always difficult to pay back and the friends gave up lending. His wife took in washing and also went picking up firewood and selling it from door to door.

NOTES

1. See Kay (1971) for arguments about the justification for using the term *manorial* in the present context.

2. H. Zemelman, in an internally circulated paper at ICIRA (the Chilean Institute for Training and Research in Agrarian Reform), Santiago, insists on the importance of urbanising as an essential part of land reform so as to open the social horizon, and dispel the submissiveness, dependence and routinism engendered within the Chilean estate.

3. The account of La Clemencia by Pablo Ramirez is taken from a report of his published by ICIRA in 1967 in which his main topic is the change of remuneration for estate labour from land and perquisites to cash wages. Both this study and the one which follows it were part of a wider research programme aimed at classifying and describing kinds of Chilean estate and was directed by Rafael Baraona, of the Institute's department of Rural Sociology, of which the writer was then head. I am grateful to both persons mentioned for the material used here.

4. We must also stress the fact that this collective of tenants, by virtue of its frontier situation, had been 'socially destructured' as Percy Cohen would say. He is right in asserting that in this new community the peasants were no longer subject to the external constraints (and correlative internal reserves) of their older tradition-bound communities of origin, and possessed a higher potential for social and cultural change, including aggressive self-assertion.

5. This study was done by a Brazilian sociologist, Gerardo Semenzato, and used in ICAD, Brazil. I have made use of his mimeographed report, and am grateful to him for permitting its use.

6. Maria Azevedo, like Semenzato, made her study of Camaçari through an arrangement with ICAD, Brazil. She has generously permitted me to use it.

7. Biographical data about the peasant Coj Choch appears in the ICAD report on Guatemala and has been translated into English by the author.

8. Reported in ICAD Colombia.

IV

Peasants and Revolution in Bolivia

The Bolivian Revolution of 1952 led to the brusque expulsion from their manorial estates of the whole class of landowners, freeing the service tenants from *de facto* serfdom, and making them individual owners of their tenancies. The power transference at the centre also installed a government emphatically rejecting most of those customary norms which had maintained a society based on serfdom, and by introducing universal suffrage made the peasantry, emerging from serfdom, the majority voter in the state.

On what did twentieth century serfdom rest? What part did the peasants have in breaking it? And what is the status of the peasantry in the altered society?

In order to discuss these questions some attention must be given to historical antecedents and geographical situation of the country.

Features of the pre-revolutionary agrian structure

The agrarian structure of the Altiplano of Upper Peru, which became a part of Bolivia, owes much to its great altitude, its landlocked isolation and the importance of its mining. From the mines there was a continual demand for labour, most of which was met by means of the *mita,* drawing on the reservoir contained in the Indian communities, whether these belonged to encomiendas or were directly tributary to the Crown (Parry, 1966:107). Agricultural supplies necessary for mining (leather, meat, tallow and pack animals) and for the urban populations which gathered around the mines had to be brought up from lower altitudes. Much of the Altiplano peasant's own subsistence, his potatoes and his quinoa, came from his own communities. This gives us a hint as to the absence in the colonial period of that drive towards individual landownership which led to the dislocation or encirclement of communities by private estates in other populous parts of the continent. Geographical factors severely limited the agricultural potentialities of the Altiplano and the possible rewards for entrepreneurship, and restricted the attractiveness of that cold landscape for the practice of lordship. Neither the native potatoes nor the barley introduced by the Spaniards produced at these altitudes have been the object of commercial demand from outside the area, while the cattle, sheep and pack animals also brought in by the Conquerors could be bred much more favourably in the valleys at lower altitudes. Thus, agricultural production has remained of local importance only, cut off from the breezes of international or even regional markets. Indeed, though the Spaniards introduced the mediterranean ox-plough (wooden with a crude iron point) which replaced the digging-stick, very little further general technological advance has been made since the sixteenth century (Carter 1964), and the level of surplus above family subsistence production has remained very low. [1]

Several writers have asserted that during the first decades of the Republic, most of the peasantry lived in 'communities'[2] and that less than one third were estate serfs (Urquidi, 1966: 177) and that three quarters of the cultivatable land was occupied by indigenas. The need for a reserve of mine labour was no longer pressing with the decline of mining (Jose Maria Dalence estimated the number of miners at less than 9000 in 1847 in Penaloza, 1946:282) thus doing away with one of the justifications for the protection of the indigenous community. However, during the course of the century, there was a powerful drive towards the incorporation of private landed properties, where possible on lands already occupied by peasants who could be reduced to personal serfdom by an estate owner.

The most spectacular assault began in 1866 when President Melgarejo, basing the legality of his position in earlier laws whereby ownership of community lands was vested in the Republic, declared a 60-day period within which the usufructuaries of the community lands could receive full dominion on payment of a stipulated sum of money, failing which these lands were to be put up to public auction. Most of the communards failed to take the necessary step of making the required payments during the very short period granted, and the law began to be put into effect. The sale of community lands implied either the acceptance of customary serfdom and a service-tenure arrangement on the lands formerly possessed, or eviction. As the new demands were pressed upon the communards, individual communities began to offer resistance, and later this resistance coagulated into patches of general rising. Between the middle of 1869 and the middle of 1870, punitive expeditions were sent out to various point on the Altiplano, and according to contemporary accounts, episodes of merciless slaughter and genocide followed, in which several thousands of peasants – men, women and children – perished. Santivanez (1871) reports the hunting of peasants as if they were animals, and the laying of sporting wagers amongst the soldiery about the number of kills each could make. By the end of the same year, however, a military rebellion had broken out and encouragement was given to a large band of communards from the Northern provinces, under their own general, to put themselves at the service of the revolutionary forces, on condition that they respected property and bowed to the commands of the 'gentry'. A force of 20,000 peasants was present at the defeat of Melgarejo and his flight from La Paz (Penaloza, 1946:289–297; Urquidi, 1966:173–4; Condarco, 1965:41–6).

What impelled Melgarejo's action? It is usual to attribute it to a need for raising revenue, by means of the fees paid by the peasants for the anticipated legalisation of their individual properties, or the price paid by the purchaser at the auction, and to note the justification given at the time, heard in so many similar situations before and since, namely, to stimulate agricultural progress by putting the land into the hands of more active entrepreneurs. It must also be assumed that a sufficiently vocal group of operators was actually pushing the project for what they might individually get out of it.

The period was a particularly bad one for the Bolivian economy. In the 1850's the quinine-gathering enterprises had been undermined by the price-cutting Colombian producers: there was very little manufacturing in the country since such older industries as glass, gunpowder, and soap-making, and the textile manufactories had not stood up to the competition of European goods. The price of silver continued to decline and the better mines were exhausted (Condarco, 1965:18). So there were plenty of idle gentry about with nothing better to do than to attach themselves to the political ambitions of some *caudillo* or to find a sinecure in the existing administration. Under such circumstances, many a frustrated entrepreneur or pretendant to gentility must have seen in the communities an attractive path towards latter-day lordship or profitable commerce. Certainly it is true that with the defeat of Melgarejo, although the sales of community lands were immediately declared null, the process of despoilation which had preceded his Presidency did not come to an end, but rather increased in force. And from the 1870's onwards, economic activity increased with the renewal of mining, (and an external demand not only for tin but also antimony, wolfram, copper, lead, zinc and bismuth), the building of the railways and the consequent growth of the town populations and mining camps and their food needs.

Under the 'Laws of Ex-Vinculation' (1874) the policy of turning the communards into small proprietors was persisted in, and administrative arrangements were made to carry out and legalise the sub-division of the communities. The commissions appointed for the task became catalysts of disorder and conflict, since in many places existing boundaries between communities, estates, towns and smallholdings were undefined, without formal legitimization, or already subject to latent dispute. As *de facto* and customary boundaries were thrown in doubt by the action of the commissions, violence blossomed as a means of affirming and defending land rights – estate against community and against neighbouring estate, community against community, and on the outskirts, the townsfolk picking up what they could by collusion with the members of the commission and with the public authorities. Fraudulent purchases from the new smallholders, ignorant of the significance of individual property, forcible seizure, trumped up sales by fictitious 'Indians' or by real co-heirs who had already emigrated, were some of the devices used, leading to the transference of a great deal of the community lands to the hands of traders, officials, estate owners – white and *mestizo* townsfolk for the most part (Penaloza, 1946: 297–304).

Rigoberto Paredes, himself said to be a descendant of *caciques,* who travelled frequently within the Department of La Paz in the exercise of his profession as lawyer during the last years of the nineteenth century, sums up the situation as follows, in his book *Tiahuanaco:*

> The legal abolition of the communities has done serious damage to the *indio.* Being accustomed to the collective form of cultivation, he lived perfectly peacefully and kept out of the hands of covetous land-grabbers. But as

> soon as he was transformed into a proprietor he became their victim. Not knowing the value of his landed property, and without guarantees of any kind, illiterate, he was relieved of his lands, usually by means of violent spoilage. And thus the great estates were formed, in which the *indio* is reduced to serfdom and lives nourishing an unquenchable hope one day to reclaim the rightful inheritance of his ancestors (1965:31).

Official views on the subject are well expressed in the following article which appeared in 'El Commercio', La Paz, April 1, 1895, and offer confirmation of the substance of Paredes' assertion:

> By the so-called laws of ex-vinculation, the communards have been granted absolute property rights to the lands they occupy. In the exercise of this right a great part of the *indios* have alienated their lands. Many have been deceived and have transferred their properties in return for miserable prices. But however they were persuaded, or whatever the means used by the purchasers, it is undeniable that once the legal transfer has been made, the seller has no alternative but to resign himself. But these have taken to violence, raising communities, cantons and even provinces in protest against the occupation of the lands and setting upon defenceless villages, unwary landlords and even the public forces of the line, in dense hordes!

As a result of these alterations to the agrarian structure during the second half of the nineteenth century, says Urquidi, 'a new layer of landowners has taken its place beside the traditional heirs of the Spanish colonists, this time consisting of business men, bankers and others who have likewise been enriched by the conditions created by imperialist penetration, but who have not pressed forward with an industrial or capitalistic agriculture but have rather consolidated the existing feudal regime' (Urquidi, 1966:178). This modified agrarian structure, with perhaps two thirds of the peasants incorporated in the estates in servile status and one third remaining in the communities, survived throughout the first half of the twentieth century.

On what was this anachronism based? We must answer that it was by the persistence of two related elements of the social structure and their manipulation as a system of social control for containing the strivings of the rural labouring people to enjoy the fruits of their labours. These two features are suggested in the following terms:

i. an 'estamental' division of society along economic-functional lines into two sectors, one of which we can call 'citizens' and the other 'peasants', one dominating and the other dominated and assigned to the performance of manual labour and services and especially agricultural production;

ii. the cellular dispersion of the peasantry into small and controllable landgroups whose nexus with the society was managed by members of the citizen sector.

In so far as these elements of the social structure were modified and weakened, so serfdom was threatened, and with the political overthrow of its primary beneficiaries it was, of course, abolished. The first of these two features was analysed in Chapter II, 8. We shall now consider the second.

The manorial estate

The second main prop of the pre-Revoluntionary system of subjection was the separation of the peasantry in discrete landgroups (both estates and communities) and the management of their relations with the rest of the society by a class of person highly conscious of the necessity of maintaining them in subjection and isolation. At the time of the revolution, perhaps two-thirds of the peasantry lived and worked in manorial estates.

In this system[3] the main labour force was based on a service-tenure arrangement, and a serf-like relation to the landlord. The full tenant was known as 'first person', owing four days labour per week and contributing his own oxen and plough, and an additional hand at sowing time. In return for this he received the use of a full glebe besides a lot of land for his house and garden. The 'second person', also the head of a family, was obligated for three days of the week and also had to bring his oxen and plough to the sowing. Sons living with service-tenants gave a day's work per week in non-agricultural tasks, such as making adobe bricks, cutting firewood, etc. It was common for a third category of family to live on the estate, with rights to a house and garden lot only, and owing two days labour per week to the estate.

In addition to these obligations to perform general agricultural labour, there were a number of specialised tasks requiring continuous attention. These were not, however, as in the more developed forms of estate, carried out by specialised workers receiving a higher level of compensation, but rotated in an obligatory manner among the service tenants, both first and second persons. Shepherds were appointed on a one-year basis, during which time they were relieved of their usual field duties. Each shepherd not only had to care for the sheep but was obliged to replace any which were lost or died from any cause whatsoever. Cattlemen and swineherds, on the other hand, had turns of eleven days only. Other jobs allotted in this way were the processing of potatoes for conservation, important because of the place of preserved potatoes in the subsistence system, and cheese-making.

In addition to those labours, which were considered as part of the service-tenure arrangements, the estate peasants were obliged to perform a series of labour duties or impositions not connected at all with the productive process. These are a clear survival of the servile obligations known as *'servicios personales'*, already forbidden by the Spanish Crown in the mid-sixteenth century, and once again by President Villaroel in 1945 ('El Consejo de Ministros: DECRETA – Articulo 1 – Quedan abolidos los servicios del 'pongueaje' y 'mitanaje' . . .') as well as on various occasions during the intervening four hundred years, and on none of these occasions with any lasting effects. The two duties referred to in Villaroel's decree are annual periods of general domestic service for men and women respectively, usually lasting about two weeks.

An interesting account of the service tenant as he pays his servile obligation in the Cochabamba region is given by Rafael Reyeros:

> The *pongo* must bring his own food, even though he has a right to the leftovers from the master's table. So when he goes to fulfil his obligation, he takes with him an earthenware or copper cooking pot, quite covered in soot, a faggot of kindling wood and a sack of dried llama-turds for fuel, and some supplies of food.
>
> The *pongo* is given a spot in the great house for his quarters, some alleyway near the mangers and pigsties, and here he builds a fire to prepare his soup, boil up his corn-grits or toast his corn. But like a watch-dog he must sleep in the lobby ready to open the door for the master's children and for the master himself if he is a night bird and likes to spend his time at the club or in a tavern.

> His work occupies him from dawn until far into the night, and amongst his labours are the following: to help in the kitchen, to look after the harness and mind the poultry. He must sweep out the rooms, the courtyards, clean the stables and pigsties and do the garden. The old-time colonial estate-house is a little world, a kind of Noah's ark with every kind of animal in it. The *pongo* is builder, messenger, nanny and chicha-brewer. He fills in the gaps in the phalanx of servants during the day. And at night he has other tasks to compose the dark rosary of his obligations, spinning, weaving, husking corn, 'mukeo' and of course, minding the doorway (Reyeros, 1949:141–2).

Another curious duty which was important in the Altiplano, where the estate owner was frequently a city trader, was that of *aljiri.* It required the collection and portage of agricultural produce from the estate to the city, where the owner kept his provision shop on the ground floor of his house. The peasant performing the annual *aljiri* duty was expected to carry the goods to town on the Friday or Saturday, remaining there as assistant in the shop during the following week, and returning to the estate the following weekend. Accounts describe traditional servile duties in great profusion and particularly in their local variants which between them seem to cover all the contingencies of economic and domestic life, and by their rejection of specialisation and division of labour seem to guarantee the persistence of the lowest possible level of technology and efficiency, and at the same time the most complete avoidance of the operating costs in money. Even corn-beer (Chicha) was prepared by the *mukeo* duty, consisting of interminable chewing bees, in which corn was masticated and spat into the pot and thus the bodily secretions of the service-tenants could be appropriated and used as fermenting agents (Reyeros 141–2).

One of the areas for which we have information is the Yungas, the name given to a system of valleys in the Department of La Paz, which run down the eastern slopes of the Cordillera through the various altitudes till they reach the Amazonian selva. They are areas of old settlement and were worked during Incaic times for coca. They have also been important as sources of quinine bark. Coffee and coca are their most important crops today.

The Yungas is an area which still has frontiers of virgin forest, though usually on steep slopes. Its labour force has been brought in or spontaneously attracted from the Altiplano during the course of the centuries, and there is still a tendency to scarcity of hands at certain times of the year. Debt-peonage has not been a main factor binding labour to the land, at least in recent years, and the peasant was voluntarily contracted as a service-tenant, with the usual servile obligations. Tenancies seem to have been generous in quantity and quality, commonly reaching four and five hectares, the limiting factor being the labour capacity of the service-tenant and family. In some cases it is reported that wages were paid, in contrast with the Altiplano, where no such cases were reported in the ICAD studies. Peasants were free to market the crops from their glebes, including the highly commercial ones, coca and coffee.

Nevertheless, the work regime was one of harsh subordination. Physical punishment was administered for the non-fulfilment of work obligations, and insults and beatings were common. A field worker from the ICAD team picked up the following description from an informant:

> So the patron would say to the headman (jilicata): 'This man is working badly – give him the lash!' – and calling his people together he would say – 'come, now, my son, down you get. Come along, headman, three lashes for this lad, three of the best!' So the headman would give him three strokes and if they were not hard enough then the patron himself would thrash the headman, saying: 'This is the way to thrash and this is how thou'llt thrash the workers, so that they feel it as thou art feeling it now . . . '.

The informant added that the headman was nevertheless a chosen and favoured person by the patron, 'a good Indian who carried out the patron's wishes'. Elsewhere it was said that a headman might make a point of buying a drink for the man he thrashed at the next fiesta, as it were to make amends. Thus, the violence of the repression seems to have a formal character about it, and to be subject to a mutual understanding.

Kathleen Barnes [4] working in five ex-estates near Coroico in the Yungas, tried to reconstruct the pre-revolutionary estate landgroup as a system of relations out of conversations by her Aymara-speaking interviewers with ex-service-tenants, with a special concern for their mental attitude to the repressive aspect of the system. She arrived at the conclusion that whilst there had been resentment and even resistance to abuses perpetrated by the patron or steward, there had been general acceptance of the system as such. She even cites two reported cases in which stewards were dismissed at the request of the headman for acting too softly in their treatment of the peasants. Does this mean that the headman, though a member of the peasant estament, and presumably bound to it by the usual ties of kinship, had simply allowed himself to be made a part of a repressive machine, along with the patron, the timekeeper, the steward and the local officials, all of whom belonged to the dominant estament? This is probably only true in a long-term structural sense that repression had become custom, and it should not therefore be concluded that a conflictive confrontation was a persistent element in the situation. The absence of a repressive military or police force of any size suggests that there was accommodation to the imposed norms, which were disturbed when abuses were committed, that is to say, when patron, steward or headman stepped out sharply beyond the limits of his expected role, and, for example, a common physical punishment became an outlet for personal cruelty. The peasant accommodated himself to the system and was reluctant to leave it because he could percieve no possibility of obtaining a better livelihood elsewhere in a society where members of his estament were either communards with usufructuary rights of their own or service-tenants on an estate. There were a few interstices within this rigid system, such as occasional labourer to a well-endowed tenant or a share-tenant charcoal-burner in the outlying parts of an estate, but conditions such as these would be considered as inferior. There was no hope of moving out of an estate into a community, and the peasant status set up obstacles to entry into a non-agricultural occupation. And freedom for the peasant to wander in this society with neither land-rights nor a patron behind him was no better than the freedom of the cockroach to walk about the fowl-yard.

Unfortunately there is an absence of studies of dominated landgroups in estamental societies which might help us to understand the motivations and potentialities of those who were delivered from traditional domination by the Bolivian Land Reform.

The word paternalism is frequently used to describe this state of affairs, but it is unacceptable and misleading since it belongs to the whole mechanism of rationalisation used by the dominant estament. Just as the word indio carries with it the connotation of racial inferiority, and implies that on account of the inadequacies and flaws of biological inheritance, the exploited must be regrettably denied the rights accorded to citizens, so 'paternal' implies the immature childishness of the peasants, justifying their subjection to the 'father', who, of course, acquires kudos from his dominant and exploitative role. The points of view of the situation as seen from above and from below are clearly distinguished in the following statements made by a member of the family of the patron, and an ex-service-tenant of the same estate, respectively:

> Patron: 'In my estate, we gave equal treatment to whites and to *indios.* All of the *'indios'* were well loved. When they needed something they would come and ask: 'Master, lend me the so-and-so and we gave them all they asked for. More than this, my father arranged their marriages. He would grab hold of a peasant and ask him whom he wanted to marry, and no matter whether the one he chose was widowed or single, my father would immediately make them marry. It was a splendid life – and see what it has come to now!'
>
> Peasant: 'Before, we were slaves because we were stupid, we didn't understand what was going on. We didn't have anybody to defend us and we were afraid to do anything for fear that the patron would beat us. We didn't know why we were beaten. We didn't know about our rights.' (Muratorio, 1966).

In addition to the lack of alternatives offered by the society, another quality of the estate is what has been variously referred to as closure, endocentrism, self-containment, and so on. This condition was accentuated by a kind of cellular confinement due to the fact that the patron and his people managed the nexus with society. Thus the steward exercised informal but effective administrative functions on behalf of the local authorities inside the estate, and cut off the peasant from open access to the society's judicial organs. Similarly, with the exception of the Yungas, the patrons managed the bulk of the market relations. Disputes between peasants were handled by the patron or steward and grievances against the latter were better forgotten since the local authorities cliqued with them. The servile duties which the communards owed to the priests and corregidores were by arrangement not required of the estate peasants. And religious observances were carried out within the framework of the ceremonies and festivals proper to the particular landgroup. Estate endogamy was a rule to which exceptions were few. Thus there were no institutional slots outside the estate which the inmates were expected to fill.

But closure goes beyond the external aspects of social organisation and in its most important sense refers to a mental and emotional orientation, an exclusive psychic involvement with the particular group and an adhesion to the particular place. The lands of the estate and the members of the landgroup become the unique context of the individual's life, disengagement from which would mean great personal loss. The daily struggle with nature to produce and conserve the products of the earth, to procreate and bring up children and maintain their health, to keep on the good side of the place spirits and to ward off ever-threatening evil, all these struggles must be fought with knowledge gained by experience in that particular locale, that hillside, that micro-climate, that odd congregation of elemental forces.

Social relations, too, involve a cumulative commitment, and for the individual they may be summed up in a set of many-stranded liens, based on kinship and ritual obligations and productive relations, each one of which involves claims on the future, debts, expectations. Regard comes with time as one fulfills the succession of ritual obligations (Carter, 1964:Ch. 4), and learns how to deal with that particular set of kin, with *those* neighbours, and how to defend oneself effectively from the demands of *that* patron and his steward. Disengagement, therefore, means the loss of accumulated lifesmanship. Moreover, if one learns to play the game according to the existing rules, then a certain vested interest grows up in the maintenance of the rules.

The system of manorial estates in the society represents a multi-cellular container in which the peasant could be put to work in permanent dispersion and isolation, prevented from aggregating into a social force with common aims and symbols and appropriate internal structuring.

The peasants' revolt of 1899

The pre-Revolutionary republican society, therefore, embodied a system of social control in which various elements played parts: the separation of the labour force from the civic activity, the bottling up or pigeon-holing in landgroups of limited dimensions, and the peasants' own inward-turning adhesion to the limited panorama of their landgroups as their exclusive patrimony. But before the revolution finally dismantled this system from the centre, it had already been threatened several times, and was subject to steady erosion. One such occasion was the peasants. rebellion of 1899, the antecedents and episodic sequence of which will illustrate the nature of the society, even though it is too remote to have direct causal links with the 1952 events. In this case peasant insurgence is forced by two sets of facts: one is the continuing struggle to defend community land rights from the encroachment of the townsfolk and the estate-owners, while the other is a 'breaking of the rules. of the estamental society by the liberal faction of the citizens' sector, first by exploiting the political support of the peasants and second by fomenting a peasant rising against the government of their political rivals.

In their political campaign of 1896, the Liberals, led by Pando, sought the support of the peasantry by appealing to such universalistic principles as justice, or rather, a single justice for peasant and citizen alike, rather than the ambivalent justice of that society. They also attracted the support of the peasants by their position of hostility to the government, represented for the peasant by corrupt and extortionate corregidores, tax collectors, judges and other petty officials who had abetted the encroachment on their lands. 'The 1896 liberal campaign found fertile soil for its politics in the prostration of the inhabitants of the Altiplano, and like the artisan, the peasant began to pin his hopes for liberation, his desires for a better life, upon the figure of the opposition *caudillo*, "Tata" Pando' (Condarco, 1965:57). *Viva Pando* became an insignia joining peasants together in united action beyond the confines of the landgroup. On May 6, as many as 1200 peasants were descried upon the heights above La Paz, filling the townsfolk with panic. When the authorities went to find out their mission, they announced that they had come to pay their respects to Pando. They were dispersed by the military, prisoners being taken and ill-treated. Another beating of the bounds took place, this time at the threshold of political participation (Condarco, 1965:55–59). After Pando's electoral failure the violence continued and various risings took place, mainly by communards.

But the breaking of the rules by a fraction of the ruling elite was to be carried a step further with the outbreak of the liberal revolution in 1898. A strong political faction in La Paz opposed the sovereignty of the national 'unitary' regime, centred on the capital Chuquisaca (Sucre), and forces were raised under General Pando in the area of La Paz to resist the arms of the constitutional government. As the constitutionalists began to march on La Paz from Oruro, lying some 150 miles to the south of it, aware of their military inferiority, and requiring respite to obtain arms and ammunition, they decided to call in the peasants as an auxiliary force. General Pando set up headquarters in Sicasica, between La Paz and Oruro, and proceeded to execute this policy.

The character of a breach of taboo hangs over this event. Later, General Pando and the liberals attempted to expunge it from memory, to claim rather that the liberal revolution had coincided in time with the spontaneous insurgence of the peasants. Our author himself qualifies it as 'a means which was and had been habitually vetoed and alien' (Condarco, 1965:472). A more journalistic author whom he cites describes it as 'resorting to the terrible and detestable extreme of raising *(sublevar)* the indigenous race' (ibid.:172). In terms of the values which held the citizen world together, such an act was anathema, an ultimate nightmare. The expressions of abhorrence are revealing. The society we are looking at, and which we have qualified as estamental, is based upon an unspoken agreement amongs the elite and the whole citizen order from which the elite is recruited, to maintain at all costs the procedures whereby the peasant estament is controlled and kept in subjection. The importance of this almost sacred tenet is made clear by the fact that rebellion against the constitutional order, serious though it is, is a lighter matter than the *decanting* of the peasantry. The compact to maintain the estamental order is the deep constitution of the whole social entity while the legal one serves only the citizens' sector.

Unfortunately evidence about the contact between liberals and peasants and the means used to enrol the support of the latter, is scanty. Pando wished to use the irregulars to harass the constitutionalist forces as they approached La Paz from the south. Therefore he set about raising the peasants who lived near this route, from the provinces of Sicasica, Inquisivi, Pacajes and Osmasuyos. It is reported that the liberal regime sent emissaries to various parts of the Altiplano calling on the peasantry to rise up, and warning them that the constitutionalist army would burn their crops, take their cattle and 'impose upon them the caprices of an abusive and discredited government'. Advertisements appeared in the revolutionary press at the time asking for donations of liquor and coca from supporters, for the purpose of rewarding the peasants. No doubt the Liberals exploited Pando's personal charisma with the peasants, and promised an end to abuses in the name of a future government. It is not known whether promises of restitution of lands were made, though we can take it that it was assumed that the peasant case would be given more consideration by the new government authorities in those communities with disputes pending. But though in the first days of the revolution the lack of arms and ammunition gave urgency to the campaign to raise the peasantry, there was an awareness of the danger involved and later a policy of confining their insurgence to certain areas, and dampening or repressing it where it was no longer necessary, was followed. Moreover, military firearms were not delivered to the bands, whose function was one of harassment and deprival of supplies rather than one of direct engagements. Weaponry consisted of the rustic implements of tillage like the flail or the plough-point set on a handle. Slings played an important part, with the occasional rifle or fowling piece. The forms of harassment included attacks on outlying units, massive encirclement of moving columns, cutting them off from supplies and making an end of stragglers, massive attacks on positions which might be carried by hand-to-hand fighting, and the intimidatory incantations of the *pututus,* or deep-sounding bamboo pipes.

The efficient use of the peasant bands as irregulars apparently required a single peasant leadership and it is not surprising that circumstances selected Pablo Zarate, known as Willka, who emerged as the strongest and most influential cacique in the Sicasica area, where for strategic reasons Pando established himself. Willka was an authority of the community composed of Imilla-imalla and Machacamarca and he seems to have become accepted as the highest peasant leader first in the Sicasica provincial capital, and later in all those regions to which the Liberals sent invitations with the exception of Umala which for some reason rejected him. And there is evidence of widespread support for the revolutionary cause to which they were summoned jointly by Pando and Willka.

Condarco seems to think that a single peasant leadership was considered necessary by Pando, not only to raise the bands, but to control them once raised. And it is hard to avoid the conclusion that the spread of Willka's authority was favoured and made possible by the fact that it could move within the circuits of Pando's own authority, receiving a kind of legitimation from the latter both amongst the citizen supporters of the Liberal cause and amongst the peasantry. And whether by agreement with Pando or by self-appointment, Willka assumed the title of General of a Division in the Federal Army and Commander-in-Chief of the Indigenous Army. This rank provided a means to autonomous peasant unity denied by the existing scheme of social organisation, and thus opened up new prospects for possible action and a new set of alternative forms of political or military action to be debated and resolved upon by the elders of the *ayllus* and the councils of the communities.

What actually ensued from the supposed messages sent out by Pando and Willka to the communities is difficult to determine, especially since at a certain point in the proceedings Willka began to summon the peasants on his own account and without the knowledge or approval of Pando, to an all-out war against the whole superordinate world of the citizens, to which the peasantry was subjected.

On the one hand, the communities in the path of the constitutionalist forces call out their men and execute tactics of harassment of the kind described above, as they did around Ayoayo (Condarco, 1965:223–239) or Huayllas (ibid.:311–314). But the encounters between peasant bands and military units had a special character. As *El Comercio* had commented in 1895 (April 1): 'With all his rights the peasant continues to be the inevitable and special victim of the military. Each march of an army brings him the same damage and terror as the most furious earthquake would'.

For instance, in the events around Corocoro, constitutionalist forces, requiring forage for their animals and food for the troops, despoiled estates and communities of their goods by violence. This, of course, arouses resistance, which is met by punishment, which may be followed by revenge, all of which is bound to have very important consequences in a civil war. And the tragic drama of Mohoza – referred to later – was born out of friction generated by similar marauding by one of Pando's detachments. Thus, the very presence of troops is liable to excite conflict with the peasantry *qua* peasantry.

But on the other hand, many of the incidents reported concern encounters between peasants and townsfolk. The town (or village) is the point of contact between the peasant estament and the rest of society, it is the cork in the bottle for the communities, the administrative centre where servile *postillonaje* had to be rendered, where taxes were paid, where commercial transactions were carried out. And even though the peasants supposedly are hunting down *'alonisistas'* or supporters of the constitutional government, their presence is a threat to the townsfolk as a group. The opportunity may be taken to pay off old scores. Once there is legitimacy for peasants to search the houses of citizens, the town's defences crumble. In Corocoro, various witnesses confirmed that the peasants threatened to kill 'all the townsfolk' *(vecinos),* still to the tune of 'Viva Pando'. In Mohoza, the peasants were inflamed by the news that the revolutionary troops, their supposed allies, had roughed up the local authorities and the townsfolk, and had taken cattle and provisions by force from the peasants, without payment.

When they encountered the squadron, consisting of 130 well-armed cavalrymen, a multitude of peasants surrounded them, and by their threatening behaviour forced them to face about and return to Mohoza for safety. The troops insisted on their friendship towards the peasants, but when they cheered Pando and the Revolution to prove their solidarity, the peasants treated them with cold hostility. 'We are lost, father,' says the commanding officer to the town priest, 'the peasants have risen; the war is not between factions but between races! We cheered Pando and the Federation and they answered 'Viva Willka!' (ibid.:283).

The obviously threatening behaviour of the peasants who closed in upon the town obliged the officer in command to attempt to extricate his troops from the town. But even as it withdrew, the squadron was enveloped by an ever-growing mass. The peasant leaders now adopted a stratagem. They persuaded the officers that they had mistaken the unit for constitutionalists, and that all they required now was a sign of good faith. They therefore requested the troop to return once again to Mohoza so that peasants and troops might fraternise. On the way back the commanding officer went even further in his apprehensive anxiety to forestall friction, and ordered his troop to deliver their arms to the peasants. This gesture was taken as a surrender, and from then on they were treated as prisoners, and were confined in the town church. During the night they were all slaughtered. The opportunity was also taken to assassinate a number of townsfolk, without reference to their political allegiance (ibid.:280).

Perhaps indeed from the point of view of the caciques and

elders of the community, there was little difference between Pando's and Willka's messages. Pando's revolution set the peasants against the government and consequently against the petty officials of the provincial and cantonal capitals, but in the experience of the peasantry, the rest of the townsfolk were accessories to the abuses and were the active practitioners of a consistent form of discrimination which excluded them from a dignified part in the society, and were the main operators of the system whereby their labour and their products were appropriated. And at the centre of the town was the seat of justice which had consistently failed to protect their basic land rights during the thirty preceding years, in fact had connived at and mediated their theft.

Pando also summoned the irregular bands formed by the men of the communities to harass the constitutional forces, but this served to legitimise resistance to any armed forces which demanded their cattle and crops and draught animals as of right. Under the system of domination in force, Willka's orders were simply a logical fulfillment of Pando's.

In the final stages, local revolts in response to Willka's summonses spring up, for example, Peñas (ibid.:359–365) and Sacaca (ibid.:371–374), which quite unequivocally aim at the overthrow of the dominant society and the restoration of estate lands to the communities.

Sometimes the peasants declare themselves enemies of the *whites* and *mestizos,* thus suggesting, as was said at the time, that a *war of races* had set in. But the enemy is also described as *estate-owners* (patrons) and *townsfolk (vecinos),* as the *Spaniards (los espanoles)* or those who speak Spanish and are at least partially descended from the conquerors and colonisers, and even as those who wear trousers *(pantalones)* or rather, those who don't wear the coarse homespuns of the peasants. Thus we must be on our guard in interpreting a tendency to slaughter non-peasants in terms of some stereotype of a 'race-war'. Indeed the society is so clearly dichotomised that each one of the attributes by which the enemy can be characterised, whether by 'blood' (supposed lineage), or by costume, or by language or by socio-economic function, traces out the same division between citizen and peasant estament.

In so far as the dominant group attempted to rationalise the system in terms of hereditary racial characteristics, then the equally rational, as well as visceral, reply was an uprising aimed at the liquidation of the dominant race. It is the believed 'racial' content of the estamental society which is used to rationalise the horrors of genocide, and to support ambivalent institutions and norms about human rights.

But if the critical relationship is *not* to be defined in terms of conflict between 'races', set at odds by differences of their 'blood' (their inherited characteristics), *nor* in terms of conflict between two *'razas'*, kept apart by the indelible imprint of two different cultures; if the critical relationship is the subjection of a labour force comprising 70–75% of the population and the forcible limitation of its access to the social product, then the transformation of the system requires not genocide but the demolition of the apparatus which secures the automatic assignment of individuals to one or other estament, and the delegitimation of the inherent discrimination, following a transfer of power to the hands of the hitherto dominated peasantry.

Using the evidence given at the trials which followed the rebellion, and some convincing circumstantial inference, Condarco is able to assert that Willka planned a general rising of the peasantry with the object of overthrowing the existing social system to which the peasantry was subjected. His plan was to mobilise the peasants to fight alongside Pando and defeat the existing government, using this period to organise and arm his people, then to turn upon the victors, and having once defeated them, to return the estate lands to the status of communities, which would form the prime unit of the new society. Other aims included the abolition of distinctions of dress between estaments, by the universal adoption of homespuns, and the taking over of the leading civic and ecclesiastical roles by those hitherto confined to peasanthood. Fortunately some descriptions of Willka in action have survived which provide clues to the way in which he perceived the society and went about altering it.

It is by no means certain that Willka was committed to race-war and genocide as the proper road to liberation of the peasants and restoration of the communities. In the rising at Peñas, in which the local cacique, the day after Pando's victory, set up an autonomous local government with Aymara peasant authorities, the extermination of non-peasants was the order of the day, and in most of the outbreaks, the same is true. However, it is most intriguing to discover that in the only situation reported in which Willka himself had direct command of the action, he adopted a policy which may show him to have had a more acute understanding of the social order and of the rules and conventions which made estamental subjection possible. Condarco, (1965:307) making use of oral statements made by many of the estate owners of Tapacari, tells us that:

> When Willka prepared the ambush to take the detachment carrying ammunition and supplies to Cochabamba, he demanded the cooperation and help of all the estates on both sides of the road to Cochabamba, announced severe penalties for remissness or incompetence, obliged the estate peasants to participate in the projected attack, visited estates and villages and forced the proprietors and townsfolk to wear peasant costume (traje indigena), organised rifle detachments, squads of slingmen and horsemen, and had slings set up on the summits overlooking the narrow passes through which the road to Cochabamba passed . . .

During this part of the campaign, he had his headquarters in Tambo de Iro, where he held court:

> There he received demonstrations of support and respect from all the people of the district *(comarco).* Serfs and gentry bowed before him. Men with light-coloured eyes, golden beards and pale skin put their pride in their pockets in the presence of this much-feared chief and came to his command-post to do him homage . . . picturesquely done up in native sandals in the peasant style (ibid.:107).

A further description of a military action written by the Battalion Commander of the Constitutionalists, states that the townsfolk of the neighbouring districts joined in the attack, forced to face the constitutionalist ranks dressed in rustic homespun clothes just like the peasants. They are qualified as 'disguised cholos' (ibid.:281).

It is true that at the time of this incident, the battle against the Constitutionalists had not been won, and that Willka at this stage had no declared intention of opening hostilities with the citizens' world as a whole, yet the significance of his policy should be carefully weighed. The regulation of dress in colonial society was a means of publicly manifesting the status of the *persona,* and so advertising the particular bundle of rights and duties with which he was endowed by birth or fortune. As such it served the purpose of social control in favour of the estamental order, and deliberate changes of dress either signified the passage of the individual from one status to another, or implied the alteration of the social order itself. The case just related is not unique, and has antecedents in the rebellion of Tupac Amaru. It is related that in the city of Oruro, in 1782, the commoners *(plebeyos)* rose up against the Spanish officials and merchants, killing most of them, and that the peasants moved in on the city under the influence of the larger movement of Tupac Amaru with the avowed intention of 'helping the *criollos*'. Lewin (1957:574) quotes the following passage from *The Fabulous Diary of the Vicar of Oruro:*

> So many were the Indians, and such the dominion they exercised over the city, that they ordered men and women to adopt their form of dress and to chew coca; and the townsfolk were so fearful and obedient that they did not rage against the order and for the few days following they put off their usual garments and wore those of the Indians, parading with deliberation in the streets to manifest their blind obedience. This was so general that the clergy and the monks were the only ones to refrain from imitating them.

How else can one interpret this than as a public symbolic act, putting aside the special privileges which the townsfolk were accustomed to enjoy at the expense of the peasants? And the further conclusion to which it leads is that the ethnic discrimination which the estamental order used in the economically most important arrangements (the subjection of the labour force) rested upon a power structure, and that even a momentary alteration of that structure leads immediately to the first steps in dismantling the mechanism of 'ethnic' separation.

The civil war itself was brought to an end by Pando's victory over the constitutional forces in which the decisive element was the participation of Willka's peasant irregulars on a large scale. Condarco believes that the early termination of hostilities prevented the maturing of Willka's plans. As it was, victory was followed immediately by a series of risings in various separate zones, in some cases in the belief that Pando's victory was a legitimate signal for taking back estate lands which had previously belonged to communities, and in others responding to Willka's call to an open struggle against whole citizens' estament. Units of victorious revolutionary army had little difficulty in putting down these risings.

The 1952 Revolution and the organisation of the peasantry

The Bolivian Revolution of April 1952 was a national event, decided within the urban industrial sector. Its immediate effects in the rural areas were radical since they replace the authorities established in the towns and villages which acted as capitals of provinces and cantons and consequently formed an essential part of the system of social control, by officials belonging to the new government of the National Revolutionary Movement (MNR). These new officials found themselves inevitably in opposition to the political forces with which the estate proprietors were aligned, though they were not necessarily protagonists of the sweeping changes which ensued.

The seriousness of the attack on the *ancien regime* was manifest in the legislation which quickly followed the taking of power. In May, the Ministry of Peasant Affairs was formed. The Villaroel (1943-1946) legislation on rural labour relations and peasants' rights was re-instated, and labour tribunals were set up to regulate the enforcement of the new conditions (Bonifaz, 1953). In July, universal adult suffrage was decreed. This delivered the majority vote to the peasantry, hitherto excluded by illiteracy, and obliged the politicians to take the peasant seriously as a voter for the first time. (Between the elections of 1951 and 1956, the votes cast rose from 120,000 to 960,000.) By November, the pressure of events had drawn from the government a declaration of intention to introduce radical agrarian reform in the near future, and a preparatory commission was formed.

In June of 1953, a Peasant Congress was held in Ucurena, at which a great variety of peasant organisations was present and on August 2 the Agrarian Reform was finally announced in the same village, in the province of Cochabamba. This law gave the peasants provisional possession of the estate lands they were occupying in tenure, pending the legal process which would decide the category of reform or expropriation to be applied to each individual estate. Meanwhile, the peasants were expected to organise a union on each estate to represent their interests in the process of expropriation, and campaigns to organise these intensified rapidly during the months following. Thus, between April 1952 and the end of 1953, a radical transformation of the structure of most Bolivian estates took place, though the completion of the expropriations and the confirmation of titles dragged out over many years.

In view of the closed and isolated character of the estate as a landgroup throughout most of the country, the agrarian transformation consisted of 5 – 6,000 discrete episodic sequences involving: the subtraction of the patron as individual and as role; the reconstitution of an internal administrative structure; and the building of a new *nexus* between landgroup and society, including market relations, and administrative and political links.

Events in each estate were precipitated by the news of the revolution, the changes in the local political set up, and the arrival of organisers at the estate itself. Who were these organisers? Perhaps the best lead to the answer, rather confused by regional differences, is to say that the organisers of the peasants came from amongst groups already marginal to the estamental system, and hostile to it, who had been mobilised by political movements within and on the edges of the new forces in power: miners, that is to say, persons of peasant stock detached from the land but not absorbed in the citizens' sector, townsfolk and students who were members of MNR and other left political groupings, and peasants who had been able to go through a partial personal emancipation through organised participation in political and union work, or through education in centres like Warisata.

But it was from Cochabamba that the strongest peasant impulses to revolutionary change merged. Unfortunately there is no adequate account of the social history of this department to help explain the fact that the estamental system had long been disintegrated there. Reyeros (1963:167), quoting cadastral lists for the year 1947 from the Departmental Treasury, gives the number of registered rural properties as 71,907, and for the province of Cliza 7,487. Although he then hedges by showing that it was common for a single proprietor to own a number of properties, nevertheless it is obvious that private ownership of property was widely disseminated. On the other hand, few juridical communities remained, and the proliferation or proprietorship appears to have been due mainly to the sale of estates. Enrique Sanchez de Lozada told the writer that on the day of the opening of the railway linking Cochabamba with the mining centres (circa 1914), the patrons arrived at the station to find the estate peasants and the free peasants had forestalled them, and were selling great quantities of produce to the buyers who had arrived from Oruro and the mining encampments. He remarked that many estate owners who had borrowed heavily from the banks in anticipation of improved commercial conditions following the opening of the railway, found themselves in difficulties as a result of the competition of the peasants and were forced to parcel out and sell the estates. He also mentioned the rubber boom of 1900–1918 and the 'golden market' for *alfalfa* to feed the mules for the supply routes passing through Cochabamba. Reyeros (1963:172) also draws attention to the large numbers of peasants who themselves worked as muleteers and traders between tropical Santa Cruz and the Altiplano and in the transporting of minerals from the mines to the Pacific Coast; as well as those who worked for spells in the Chilean mines.

A further sign of the commercial character of land-labour relations is the widespread resort to share-tenure arrangements *(compania),* albeit accompanied by servile obligations. (ibid.: 174).

Finally, the attempt to justify estamental discrimination and exclusion on the basis of the racial and ethnic difference is especially farfetched in Cochabamba, where already in mid-nineteenth century, the majority of the peasant population is referred to as *mestizo* (of mixed Spanish and native descent) although Quechua-speaking, though *indio* continued to be the name by which the peasant estament was known amongst the citizens up to 1952.

Thus a situation of great conflict existed in Cochabamba, where peasant could compete with patron for the market, yet at the same time, where servile duties continued to be enforced, where a class of small landowning peasants of mixed ethnic descent had established itself, yet estamental exclusion from participation in the citizens' world continued, where servitude chafed the more since the alternative of smallholding was visible to all. It was from this scene that the strongest revolutionary impulses emerged, and at a particular place in it, Ucurena, with specific antecedents in peasant union activities, that organisation and personnel were forged.

In 1936, the first post-Gran Chaco government, that of Colonel Toro, passed a law obliging 'municipal and religious entities' wishing to sell their properties, to give preference, in equal condition, to service-tenants in occupation of the lands who were able to organise themselves in an agricultural union. This law proposed to help a particular group of peasants who lived on the lands of a monastery in the province of Cliza,

Cochabamba and whose cause was supported by a number of influential professional people belonging to the growing numbers of those who rejected the estamental arrangements on which the society was based. A long struggle followed (well described by Dandler-Hanhart, 1967) from 1936 to 1943, when finally 216 service-tenants had been transformed into proprietors of small 2½ acre plots. Soon after this struggle was initiated, a school was established at a new settlement which took the name of Ucurena, and this served as a centre from which a network of sectional schools was organised in the neighbouring localities and estates in a development similar to that of Warisata. The school and its staff supported and worked with the peasant union. By 1946, the Ucurena school served as a centre of 41 sectional schools in the rural areas of the province of Cliza, with 62 teachers and 2,100 pupils. Such was the power of the school-union combination that in 1946 their pressure secured the appointment of a peasant as corregidor. A further linking of this centre of peasant emancipation with the society was the associating of peasant and school leadership with the Left Revolutionary Party (PIR) and the consequent alliance in political outlook with citizens of the provincial and departmental capitals. In 1947 a candidate for this party was elected, but in 1949 conflict with the government became intense and a sharp campaign of oppression led to the imprisonment of a number of leaders (Dandler-Hanhart, 1967:Ch. III). Thus, Ucurena and the province of Cliza around it provided what has been described as a 'revolutionary hearth' or 'focus' with experienced leadership and a network of organisations which could mobilise the peasants not only by landgroups but *en masse* and a peasantry with revolutionary thoughts (in terms of the existing social situation) and clear short-term revolutionary objectives, namely, the taking of the land by those who worked it. It comes about, therefore, that although Ucurena did not participate in the takeover on April 9, 1952, its success was the signal for insurgency directed at the Cochabamba estates and beyond, organised by the peasant leadership under Jose Rojas, and carried out by peasants politically mobilised in the area, and students.

The other main centre of diffusion of the revolution to the estates was the Ministry of Peasant Affairs. Unlike Ucurena, it was not a revolutionary peasant *foco,* but the Minister assembled his team with the help of members of the miners' unions. We may safely assume that it was from these two centres that the great majority of the estates were organised, though other contenders were in the field. Leons (1965) reports that the Trotskyist Workers' Revolutionary Party (POR) organised the union on one of the estates in the Nor Yungas and persuaded the peasants to prepare for an armed uprising. The plot was discovered and the leading peasants imprisoned. Delgado (1968) asserts, however, that POR made strong headway in many estates until MNR announced its intention of carrying out an Agrarian Reform.

No doubt there were other cases like that of the peasant turned policeman, from an estate beside Titicaca who returned home when the Revolution took place and organised a union with his own people, not omitting, of course, to obtain a glebe for himself in the adjudication.

Delgado reports that the unions on all 20 of the estates about which he gathered data in the Canton of Ancoraimes were formed between July and December, 1953. On at least some of these estates the peasants had already shown impatience earlier, and one had sent a delegation to the Ministry of Peasant Affairs, where an official had told them to return to the estate and await the commission which would supervise the setting up of their union correctly. This conduct suggests concern by the Ministry to manage the situation at the risk of dampening revolutionary zeal. The formation of a union was an essential step for the peasants of an estate if they wished to benefit directly from the Land Reform since the union was the recognised corporate body for dealing with the government authorities administering the reform and with the patron. The head man of the union was known as Secretary General and he receives his office by annual election. He was assisted by about a dozen Secretaries with specific responsibilities, i.e. 'relations', justice, finance, agriculture, livestock, roads, sports, education and health. There was always a recording secretary and other posts which varied, such as secretary for propaganda, messenger, member-at-large, etc. The remaining members of the landgroup were incorporated automatically in the union in such a way that the landgroup *became* the union for formal purposes. There was no opting out.

Once elected, the Secretary General wielded formidable authority. He settled internal disputes, even intra-familial conflicts. He could intervene in questions concerning usufructuary rights and on occasions had been known to take land away from peasants who were not cultivating their glebes. He was usually known as 'the General' or even 'don General'. 'I am like the patron so long as I am the General' said one of them (Delgado, 1968:418). 'The Secretary General dictates, the people obey', says Carter (1964:58). As regards punishments, there is a good deal of variety, from those areas where these are admonishments, fines and community tasks, to others in which whippings, imprisonment and expulsion are occasionally used (Leons, 1965:47). Peinado (1971) reported that a Cochabamba union had to deal with a peasant who, having a gleaning right, harvested three untouched furrows of potatoes. The general ordered him to work for three days on his own (the General's) lands as a punishment, and was told that for a further offence he would be taken to Ucurena for corporal punishment. Of the other secretaries, two or three might be active people, but seldom more, and even these were not likely to act out of delegated authority but to serve more as assistants.

These were frequently rather young since few of the older heads could read, but authority seemed to have been freely vested in them by the peasants of the landgroup. It was also usual for difficult and critical decisions relating to the landgroups' affairs to be referred to general meetings of the members.

The 'General' also attended meetings and rallies in the name of the union, and would have to impose a levy on the members to defray his expenses. He 'represented' his landgroup in the locality, in the administrative area formed by the canton. Yet though he defends the claims of the landgroup in competition with others to the best of his ability, and though he tries to ward off impositions, yet his position is more that of a receiver of orders from above than a proposer. Thus, his position rests upon the consent of his fellow landgroup members and the legitimation given to his incumbency by the union hierarchy, the 'authorities' of the local town and ultimately the government. And so long as *el general* was needed for calling out the men of the landgroup as an armed band or as a segment of a street demonstration or a political rally, so long as the government and the peasantry concurred in the priority given to the defeat of the reaction, the *'rosca'*, the Falangist Party, the proprietary interest, etc., he exercised power outside the landgroup. But when once the government's position was assured, and a new army was built up, the general and his people withdrew into the landgroup.

In the Yungas a tradition of peasant organisation already existed. Enrique Callisaya had participated in the Villaroel

Peasant Congress in 1945 and had suffered police persecution, threats of death and imprisonment since, but had continued to go from estate to estate, legitimately organising schools and so preparing habits of organisation. On the day the revolution succeeded, a provincial committee for peasant organisation was set up and Callisaya was asked to direct it. He declined in favour of his son, giving as his excuse his age and fatigue. The new committee sent out messages to the estates calling on the peasants to send 'respected elders' to meetings. Horns *(pututus)* were wound on all sides, and an atmosphere of excitement reigned. The leaders were cautious, advising the peasants to form unions and to work only for wages, but to stay on the estates and to refrain from violence to the patrons. In the interregnum that followed, the excitement continued. A group of local peasant leaders accompanied by one of the townsfolk sympathetic to the cause visited the estates and organised the unions, while proprietors and their stewards stayed in the town and kept away from the estates. Mass meetings were held, radios brought the latest news from the capital, the families of the proprietary classes waited for the counter-revolution, and the peasants strolled around the *plaza* in the evenings vaunting their new status while their representatives the new peasant officials took over posts in the local administration and established themselves in the town hall (Barnes, 1965).

In the Chulumani sector of the Yungas, however, there already existed a group of MNR townsfolk hostile to the landowners who were much larger city-based operators than those of Coroico. The commission which visited the estates and promoted the organisation of the unions were townsfolk, including local traders, truck drivers, officials, middling mestizo landowners, and also miners and others from outside. Thus, in this case, there seems to be an additional motivation, and some of the participants in the movement were small operators (townsfolk), more concerned with putting an end to local dominance by a powerful clique of entrepreneurial magnates (Barnes).

The revolutionary process for each one of the thousands of estates moved in stages. The peasant-patron relation was first exposed to the political changes made by the Revolution, implying essentially the delegitimation of the patron's time-encrusted domination. In the new situation, this relation was restructured according to the existing degree of conflict and the political pressures which made themselves felt in the locality. Next the landgroup is remodelled without the patron and given the form of a union *(sindicato)* and thereby provided with an internal administration and also tied to the new institutional structure of the society. This stage reaches a certain stability when the union has successfully presented the peasant case to the land reform authorities, and the final adjudication and confirmation of the individual titles has been completed.

In the more populous areas (the Northern Altiplano, Cochabamba and the Yungas) where political activity and consciousness were greater, and where there was more rapid penetration of the landgroup by the agents of the new order, most patrons with their families and stewards seem to have been obliged to give up residence on their estates well before the Land Reform was passed. But the degree of rupture may be seen in the maintenance or otherwise of communication or interaction between patrons and peasants. Delgado classifies 23 estates about which he had information in this way. In only three estates, all belonging to the same patron, was there complete rupture. In one of these there had been a long history of conflict, including the attendance of six peasants at the 1945 Peasant Congress and the gaoling of several in the same year, on orders of the patron, for attempting to set up a school at their own expense on the estate. From the time of the revolution onwards, the peasants have refused all dealings with the patron and his heir, meeting their physical presence on the estate with threats of violence, and taking over for their own use the lands which were adjudicated to the patron.

In eight more of the estates, contractual arrangements relating to the use of patron's land continued for a time, both in the name of the union and in the name of individuals who became share-tenants of these lands and who were bound to loyalty to the patron by godparenthood *(compadrazgo)*. However, external political pressures upon the landgroup and internal pressures against the accommodating individuals led to the abandonment of the share-tenancy agreements in respect of the land which remained to the patron, and in most cases the peasants cultivating these lands continued to do so for their own sole benefit.

In the remaining 11 cases, only one of which Delgado studied closely, arrangements existed between peasants and patron for use of the land adjudicated to the patron, or else the purchase of the land by the peasant.

In the remoter areas the process passed more slowly and smoothly, in the Cochabamba region the confrontation was from the start more violent, and the ousting of the patrons more rapid. A revealing glimpse of the situation is given by Luis Antezana (1955:50–51) whose description of an adjudicatory hearing in the Cochabamba area reveals either a revolutionary consciousness on the part of the peasants or else great imagination by the author.

> The lawyer representing the *latifundista* begins to speak, supporting his case with articles from the Agrarian Reform Law. After a bit, his words degenerate into rhetoric, which is interrupted with some difficulty by a peasant, who gives him a warning. Taking up other points, once again the lawyer falls into rhetoric. This time he is threatened; 'We have no lawyers', say the peasants, 'we defend ourselves with the truth. Any more of this rhetoric and we'll chuck you in the ditch'. Sometimes they even let off shots in the air to put an end to the talk and the twisting.
> The hearings take place before a representative of the Land Reform Service, and the proprietor and three peasant authorities take part. Here is an example of some dialogue: 'The patrons' says the peasant, 'used to beat us and made us work with blows or with a pistol'.
> 'That's a lie', says the patron's wife.
> 'Its you who is lying. I would have you know that we peasants don't lie'.
> The peasants go on with the list of abuses of the *latifundistas* and the patron's wife says: 'Quietly, my son, quietly. Where's your respect! Don't shout.'
> And the peasant replies: 'That's enough of your "quietly". Now's the time for us to tell of all the things you did to us, so we're not going to be quiet. And if we want to shout, we'll shout. I'm telling you now that you used to beat me; and that's enough of the "my son", too. You must call me "comrade"'.
> And so the peasant tells of the abuses of which he was victim for all those who are standing around to hear.
> Another peasant says: 'Master *(niño)* George . . .' and is interrupted noisily by the crowd which explains that there are no more *masters* nor patrons now, and that all are equal.

Some changes effected by the Revolution

The landgroup continues to be the essential and viable unit

of rural life, and in general continues to have the same physical perimeters as before the Agrarian Reform.

Before the Revolution, the peasantry occupied and used for their own agriculture 60–85% of the land of most estates, though of course the demesne lands frequently included those of better quality. In case of the estates declared 'middle-sized properties', most of the demesne lands continued to belong to the patrons. These lands may have been subsequently bought by the former service-tenants of the estate, after a period of share-renting or even cash-renting, but in those cases where the patron has returned to cultivate them directly, the existence of a separate more extensive productive unit with greater capital resources and a labour deficiency can be expected to have an important effect on the adjacent peasant economies and consequently on the structure of the land-group. But patrons retaining land have only recently enjoyed conditions enabling them to work it, and there is little data available at the moment.

Where the demesne land passed to the peasantry, there has been an increase in the size of individual peasant holdings and in undivided lands available for pasture, but as the number of holdings has increased as a result of including amongst the beneficiary families some which hitherto were simply dependent parts of larger families, or returned migrants, the average increase has been restricted and insignificant.

Two other persistent features of the land tenure situation are unequal distribution and fragmentation. As already noted, the estate tenancies were stratified. It is not surprising that those families which enjoyed advantage in this respect, being the strongest, saw no good reason to introduce a principle of equality and sacrifice their advantage. Carter (1964:76) reports a ratio of 1:5 between the small and large parcels of land adjudicated. Even the redistribution of demesne lands has often followed the existing pattern, with the larger parcels going to those who already have most. As regards the complicated archaic system of land allocation (ibid.:65–69) no attempt to rationalise it is reported. But without technical innovations requiring such rationalisation, the issue has not yet become important.

Soil erosion may have accelerated since the reform (Preston, 1969:11–14). Certainly there neither was nor is any conservation control and the greater freedom of access to land enjoyed by the peasants seems to have led to over-grazing and a shortening of the fallow period for arable land. Hitherto a very high infant mortality rate and a low life expectancy held the population to a low rate of natural increase in spite of what was apparently a high rate of fertility (Whitehead, 1968). If, however, it is true that the physique of recruits to the army has recently shown marked improvement, then the general causes of such improvement in better nutrition may also decrease the mortality rate fairly soon, and put new pressures on the landgroup by bringing about a relative shrinkage in resources available per family.

Has the 'closed', self-contained, 'endo-centric' quality of the landgroup been retained? Carter (1964:86) thinks that in the Altiplano estates he looked at, the break with the patron had enfeebled the articulation of the landgroup with the society. 'They continue to be agricultural, sedentary, subsistence oriented, and are almost wholly reliant upon the accumulation of local food-stores . . . the peasant concern is still almost invariably with the local and not with supra-community phenomena . . . and tragedy in a neighbouring community is looked on with complete indifference'.

Barnes stresses the harsh limitations imposed by nature on the Yungas landgroups and the persistently low level of technology, and the resultant adhesion to a way of life in which magic and witchcraft are essential means and in which ritual celebrations *(fiestas)* continue being ends absorbing the wretched surpluses obtained. Nevertheless there is plenty of evidence about the relative decline of the role of the sponsorship of the traditional fiestas as the exclusive golden road to the pinnacles of community esteem for the individual; and complementary to this, the increasing importance of literacy and ability to conduct oneself with townsfolk. Thus the young now compete with the old. Prestige also is bestowed on those who possess certain objects that money can buy, such as bicycles, transistor radios, two-storey houses, glass windows, and those who can buy their friends beers in the village. All these characteristics point away from closure and suggest that a very important opening up of the landgroup is taking place, which implies a recognition not only of the dependence of the local group on town people and urban procedures but also that the peasant now has a greater stake in the larger society. He is no longer categorically relegated to rusticity. Indeed, it is in the remaking of the nexus between landgroup and society that the changes effected by the Revolution are most striking.

Under the *ancien regime* the peasants of each estate were

'bottled up' in their individual landgroups. We shall now discuss new institutional forms, especially the market, the peasant union and the new towns, providing new links, new canals of interaction between landgroup and the larger society.

a. Market nexus

With the exception, already discussed, of the comparatively free marketing permitted to the service-tenants of the Yungas estates, the proprietors kept commercialisation of estate products in their own hands. Indeed in the Northern Altiplano their central function seems to have been that of shopkeeper. Of the 51 estates studied retrospectively by Clark, 'all the proprietors had homes in La Paz' and 'all but five had *aljerías'*, that is to say, wholesale-retail stores, usually on the ground floor of their town houses, in which they sold the produce of their own estates. Most of them had some other line of business or a profession as well. The service duty of *aljiri* covered the packing, transport and advertisement of the goods, (the latter consisting of calling on the regular customers to tell them of their arrival) produced by the peasants on the lands of the proprietor, and also the delivery of a certain quota of eggs and fuel (dried llama dung) from their own animals to the patron. Indeed, to make more certain of the exclusion of the peasant from the market, in some cases there were specific prohibitions against peasants selling elaborated goods of their own manufacture, such as brooms and blankets, knowing that there was a market demand for them.

There was, however, a certain level at which the peasants were permitted access to the markets of the neighbouring towns, namely to exchange or sell small amounts of staples such as barley and potatoes in order to acquire necessities such as coalpots, cloth, hats, salt, coca, alcohol, sugar and matches. But the mainstream of produce from the estates to the city did not correspond to a flow of manufactured goods to the country, and the rural population met its consumption requirements with its own labour. Thus the peasant in his own right did not confront the city as a producer, but simply as a servant or porter of his master's goods, even though he was the sole producer.

The withdrawal of the proprietors and stewards from the estates during 1952 and 1953 broke this market mechanism and goods became scarce in the capital. But new connections soon emerged as enterprising citizens sent or drove lorries into the country, meeting the peasants by the roadside or at cross-roads and buying their produce directly.

On the basis of fact-finding in three markets, Preston (1969: 7) gives a composite description of the process of formation:

> The growth of the market was probably the result of the people from one or several communities (including both former estates and freeholding communities) getting together to arrange for some lorries to come to a certain place convenient for all concerned where people would be on hand with goods to sell. It must be realized that lorries often travel along only vaguely defined routes, whether empty or with merchants on board aiming to pick up enough passengers and freight to make a profit on the journey. If there are merchants with the vehicle who may only be going to collect 100 kg. of potatoes at some point 200 miles from La Paz, then both the driver of the vehicle and the merchants are going to be on the lookout for some more trade. Thus half a dozen families on the roadside with goods to sell can stop several lorries with their attendant merchants to sell produce to them, and thus haphazardly a market occurs. Maybe after several weeks of activity at this level, there can be an agreement between lorry drivers, merchants and peasants to meet and to sell goods regularly. Maybe too at this stage the peasants may suggest that if the lorries collect at a central point for several agricultural communities that are some distance away from the main road, then perhaps more people will bring items to sell. After a storm, part of the track may become impassable and the drivers will only agree to come if the local people build up the bad bits of road and thus, casually and maybe over several years, an all-weather road comes into existence. Drawn by the good cargoes on some lorries from a new market, or through word of mouth, other drivers and merchants are attracted and thus the market grows in size. Somewhere along this scale merchants will come bringing manufactured goods to sell at the market and thus it grows in scope.

So a network of new markets sprang up at points from which neither La Paz nor a railway station could easily be reached without motor transport. These spontaneous markets were legalised, and their existence encouraged by peasants inclined to specialise in commerce. One of the results was the growth of a trading sector amongst the peasantry in direct competition with the townsfolk (*cholos* and mestizos) who previously held commercial activities in their hands. Another was the growth of new towns around the market, in which the new Bolivian society was able to grow unsegregated, and in which peasants became authorities and notables.

b. Administrative nexus

The estate peasant had also been excluded from civic status. On the estate itself, the authority of the patron was delegated to his steward, who added to it whatsoever elements of power he could muster on his own account, by means of godparenthood, favouritism and bullying. Society permitted him to settle most disputes by the usual estate methods, including fines and labour impositions, invective, beatings and imprisonment. In more serious cases such as killing, then the police and the judge of the canton were called in. And if an *acta* had to be signed in settlement of a dispute, 'binding over' the disputants on pain of a fine to keep the peace, this had to be done before the corregidor. This officer, however, if he were not himself an estate steward, shared the same class of loyalties, and would be expected to accept the word of the steward of the estate about anything which went on there, and he would certainly not be expected to entertain complaints made by peasants against stewards or patrons (Leons, 1965:125–132). 'The steward, the corregidor and the town police were informal and formal components of a single authority system'.

The Revolution broke this occlusion which held the peasant beyond the civic pale and replaced it by a several-stranded nexus. If he now wishes to go beyond the elected authority of his landgroup (the general) in case of a dispute or grievance, he can seek his rights particularly in two hierarchies:

i. the officers of the national government as before (judge and *corregidor*) with the difference that they no longer have a commitment to the ambivalence of estamental justice, and indeed may themselves be peasants, and

ii. the peasant union hierarchy, particularly the cantonal representative or Sub-Central, also serves as an adjudicator of disputes and officer of customary justice far beyond the statutory limits of his office. He is assisted by a number of 'secretaries' including a Secretary of Justice and a Secretary for Conflicts, described as a 'sort of bodyguard' (ibid.:154).

c. Urban accretions to landgroups

The formation of new towns provides an opportunity to look at some of the structural changes going on, though of course it is probable that where new towns have been created, the forces for change have more intensity than elsewhere. Leons' study (1965) of Arapata gives us a valuable sounding. In 1950 it consisted of a few houses built by the roadside in the Yungas, occupied by a few families of townsfolk trading in peasant coca. Its population was 24 souls. It occupied a precarious interstice between two estates on the lands left beside the road when this was cut out from one of the estates at the time of its construction in the early forties, being deeply resented by the patron who did not wish to see the growth of any potential rivalry to his autarchy so near at hand – (a very mediaeval situation!). After the Revolution, peasants from the two adjacent ex-estates, and outsiders, began to acquire more lands along the roadside from the new owners, and to build there, so that by 1965 the number of inhabitants reached 751, or about 180 families.

The new town became a centre for marketing, administration, services, communications, social gatherings and ceremonies, catering for eight ex-estate landgroups, and especially the two out of which it had been carved. A good idea of its function is given by the following list of occupations, omitting those of peasant agriculturalist:

37 traders or dealers buying peasant produce for resale.
39 shopkeepers selling produce and manufactured articles to the peasants. This number includes 9 peasants of the adjacent landgroups whose lands were not sufficient to occupy them and who tried to supplement livelihood by running small stores.
13 masons, 10 agricultural labourers, 7 tailors, 6 restaurant-keepers, 5 owners of public ovens, 4 barbers, 4 teachers, 3 carpenters, 3 hatmakers, 2 midwives and one of each of the following – registrar, notary, dentist, medical dispenser, ice-cream maker, tinsmith, mechanic, shoemaker, lamp repairer and smith.

The majority of these were peasants from the adjacent landgroups while a few were townsfolk from the provincial capital Coroico, which has declined as a commercial centre. But an important proportion of the active population consisted of communards from the Altiplano, numbering 57, who, it is thought, probably left their communities for the insufficiency of their family lands.

d. Social ascension

The Revolution delegitimised the estamental system and, by means of unionisation and the arming of the peasants, was able to punish discriminatory conduct and replace discriminatory institutions. But it was not able to join up that which had been put asunder, nor to homogenise cultural practices, nor produce immediate bilingualism, nor wholly to transform the stereotyped perceptions of society held by its members. What it could do was to initiate progress, or to redirect it. 'Beating the bounds' was put an end to. No longer would the peasant youth get beaten up for attempting to attend evening classes to learn Spanish. On the contrary, every encouragement was given to the building of schools. Peasants appeared in high office, encouraging the raising of aspirations.

But while this lifted the imposed handicaps from peasanthood, it did not lead to a revaluation of peasant sub-culture nor to a re-sorting of social ranking. The peasantry remained the lowest class, even though peasant birth did not prevent an individual from rising to a better life, and a higher social rank. This is how one new citizen sees his own situation:

> Before, the *campesino* was deceived. My father was a *campesino* and that's how I know . . . I had a truck that my father bought me so that I would no longer be a *campesino* like him. With that truck I made trips to La Paz to sell various products. Little by little, the people didn't look at me any more as the son of a *campesino,* but told me I was good and generous. Afterwards I bought a house in town and then I was not considered a peasant any more. Even though I later sold my truck, nobody looks at me like an Indian now. Now there are no longer any marked differences . . . There is only hate between Indian and Cholos, but with time it is going to disappear and things will be better (Muratorio, 1966).

The estamental identification and concomitant treatment passes with the change of occupation, the change of residence and the possession of so obvious a status symbol as a lorry. The young man enters the citizens' world. Then the remark about *cholos.* Does this mean that he is still identified as an ex-'Indian' and exposed to cholo hostility, or that as a new cholo his relations with 'campesinos' have become difficult? Whichever way he felt the pinch, his remark draws attention to problems of status identification and relations in the new society.

When I asked an ex-estate headman of the Altiplano what a *cholo* was, he replied 'a person who is different from us – they dress better, are cleaner, *have words*; we too can get to be like that now . . . we hope they will continue to exist and be different and respected . . .'.

His son, who attended secondary school, and hoped to become a teacher, identified himself as a cholo, saying that a peasant could become a cholo but not a *vecino.* The latter are 'better', have more intelligence, live better, dress better. By 'cholo' is meant a distinct sector of the population to be found in most (but not all) towns and cities, consisting of peasants and descendants of peasants who have left their landgroups and live in the city by labour crafts and commerce. They are Spanish speaking, belonging to the citizens' estament, within which they move restrictedly, suffering social discrimination and exhibiting strong solidarity. The phenomenon obviously requires an historical explanation, which no one has yet successfully been able to provide.

Thus a clear expectation of social ascension exists, and requires of the peasant-aspirant ease in the Spanish language, urban occupation and residence and the relinquishment of other overt features of peasant sub-culture. The placement of the ex-peasant in the town society in relation to the cholo has yet to be revealed.

What does seem probable is the persistance of a peasant subculture and landgroup solidarity in those areas where the winds of commerce are feeble and where no trend to internal urbanisation is manifest. The very feasibility of social ascension for selected individuals and the conditions which this requires make such persistence more likely for those who remain.

e. Peasant power

In post-1952 Bolivia, the peasantry had importance politically because its vote was decisive in elections. But this does not mean that the peasants exercised democratically based power. It meant that the apparatus of the peasant union became a part of the apparatus of integration and control, and was used in order to attempt to deliver the peasant vote to ruling parties and to their nominees. The peasantry did indeed wield real power for a number of years, but this circumstance belongs to the revolutionary episode, and has passed. Put at its crudest, real power lasted until the government was able to build up military power of its own, and ceased having to rely on peasant manpower for direct action.

In the early stages of the Revolution, the peasants held extensive local and regional power by virtue of a unity of aim between landgroups: that of taking possession of the estates and escaping from the restrictions imposed by their estamental status. They succeeded in developing their own leadership, made themselves masters of the estates and in some cases ended by dominating towns and large regions, and forcing the nomination of officials from amongst themselves or those friendly to them. But it was the fact that they were armed and officially legitimated as a militia that gave them strength. For in spite of the laws which were passed, reforming their condition, the only real guarantee of these conquests against the inertia of ancient discriminatory custom was their power to coerce with violence and the threat of violence, in a country where the rule of law had never been established.

Nevertheless, there are inherent limitations on the capacities of peasants to hold national power. As members of landgroups they are mainly concerned with local problems – their particular legal process of expropriation, the building of the school, the water supply, the road, and so on. Marketing problems and fear of the return of the patron may raise interest to the level of the local urban centre, but this is about where it stops. A coherent policy of intervention in public affairs at a national level is not likely to be motivated by grassroots interests. A further cause of disunity is that where there is a market economy, those who have most voice are those who have most success economically, and these have private interests which set them off from the rest, such as monopoly provision of some service, concern with commercialisation of the products of others rather than production, or the purchase of cheap labour of others rather than the sale, at the best price possible, of their own.

In the meantime, the middle and upper reaches of the union structure had become an important part of the new social system, and the interests thus created developed their own dynamic. One of the characteristics of the new system was what has been described by J. Medina Echeverria (Naciones Unidas, 1958) as *prebendalismo.* This Spanish usage refers to a situation in which the licit and illicit perquisites of office become the major concern of the officeholder, to the detriment of the performance of the office. It corresponds to a certain stage in the evolution of large-scale politico-bureaucratic structures. Thus, the office of *encomendero* in the sixteenth century was conceived of as legitimately prebendal in the sense that his services as local administrator were rewarded by what he was able to extract from his *encomendados* in tribute. Later he was replaced in his administrative duties by a colonial official, i.e. a corregidor. The latter soon became illicitly prebendal, using his office to corner lucrative privilege. It is structurally comparable with subsistence agriculture where the overall market system is too weak to ensure the distribution of consumer goods by money-purchase, and where the bulk of what is consumed must be obtained by the consumer's own productive effort. This subsistence principle was aptly imaged by Councillor Raymond Quevedo of Trinidad, famous as a calypso singer, Atilla the Hun, when he sung a justification for the taking of presents by officials and politicians in the words: 'de donkey mus' graze where he tether.'

The victory of the Revolution, and especially the explosive growth of trade unionism, opened up extensive pastures of petty office to hitherto unprivileged strata. Says Antonio Garcia, a Colombian observer, who was later United Nations consultant in Bolivia, and was intimate with many leaders of the revolution: 'From 1952–1956, a policy of massive trade-union promotion held sway motivated by prebendalism and the possibilities of rewarding union leadership and political services by distributing access to lucrative facilities, such as import licenses and special price and customs concessions.' (For instance, he quotes a Customs report of 1958 showing that two miners' unions and one railwaymen's union were granted 42% of the duty-free allocation of sewing machines, which totalled 6,168, while the miners' union of the famous Catavi mine was granted the complete allocation of duty-free bicycles.) 'As there was no existing mechanism for economic and social planning, the distribution of privileges did not lead to greater social justice but to a cancerous process of corruption and the hypertrophy of trade union bureaucracy (1970: 606). He also quotes a report from the Ministry of Labour to the effect that there were 51,000 union officials for the 150,000 members of non-peasant unions, organised in 5,000 branches, that is to say, one official for three members. Thus the strongest motor force became the individual self-seeking of the middle and upper ranks of the trade union movement, which found expression in a policy of continuously expanding benefits and an indifference to increased productivity which the success of the revolution required.

During these years, the number of peasant union members is said to have reached 600,000 (ibid.:608) and initially its organisation feasted on self-sacrifice and revolutionary fervour. The organisers received no recompense except those who were officials of a Ministry. But the absence of a leadership unified around a clear doctrine and an articulated programme, and the contagious spread of the norms of self-enrichment, altered the motivation of those into whose hands power and control over facilities were thrust. And while the 6,000 land-group revolutions went their way according to the discrete circumstances of each, peasant unionism in its middle reaches was damaged by internal fractional strife, territorial brawls and raqueteering. Canelas (1966:202), whom we quote with some reserve, includes amongst the various perquisites which a peasant union chief was able to exploit: the actual pillage of estate property in furniture, installations and stock, collection of municipal dues, the charging of fees in connection with land transactions, benefits from lands worked collectively by union members, usufruct of desmesne lands in dispute with government machinery, use of union transport for commercialisation of estate products, sale of arms allocated for distribution and even the manufacture of cocaine.

Both Canelas and Garcia mention the linkage of individual *caciques* (chieftains) with particular factions within the government resulting in the disaggregation of the peasant movement as such, and actual conflict between territorial groupings under rival *caciques.* In other words, internal conflict and competition within the new ruling elite finds expression in struggles between the realms of neghbouring union *caciques.* Garcia also mentions the damaging influence of the inclination of the government to use the structure of the peasant unions almost as a party machine as the industrial unions moved further into opposition.

Unfortunately the term *cacique* is not as precise as one could desire. I use it here for the individual who accumulates personal power beyond the normative blueprints of the formal institutions concerned and actually takes over their functions. *Caciquismo* makes its appearance typically in a societal condition where hierarchically ranked vertical organisations purporting to work according to bureaucratic rules are introduced, but the conditions for their proper performance do not exist. Although the pre-emption of powers by the cacique leads to the suspension of many rules of the institution, he must nevertheless satisfy the needs of some of those on whose behalf the institution exists.

The union hierarchy operated at six levels – the national, the departmental, the provincial, the canton, the sub-canton and the landgroup. As we have pointed out, at the level of the landgroup, leadership generally operated in a peculiar democratic-traditional manner, but above this level, the national leaders of the union organisation were recruited by the elites of the official party and the administration, and they in their turn nominated the intermediate leadership, or exerted pressures in favour of their candidates (Delgado, 1968:423). These intermediate-level leaders, especially the 'centrals' with authority over a province (98 in number) and the 10 departmental federations, composed the sector from which the most powerful caciques arose.

The mapping of the whole complex hierarchy of the peasant unions as a structure in action would look very different from the formal *organograma* which so often hangs on the walls of the headquarter offices of organisations. The really important caciques, counting among them such names as Sinforoso Rivas, Jose Rojas, Toribio Salas and Ignasio Calisaya, became national figures with territorially based power. The careers of many men of this kind are almost legendary and unfortunately cannot be described here. But it is important to recognise that *caciquismo* is indeed a system.

The role of cacique rests upon certain implicit compacts defining his relations with those above him and those below him. Those above him, the leading figures in the unions, the ministries and the party, etc. may be referred to as the *providers,* that is to say, those who could make and enforce decisions affecting the allocation of national resources, and facilities, whether by legislation, administrative decision, or by nominations to office, etc. The cacique is linked both institutionally and particularistically to individuals in the ranks of the providers, on the basis of friendship or alliance, and to these national figures he owes the support of his realm, which may take the form of votes or contingents for marches or demonstrations or of armed bands. But support must imply consent to their policies except where these might damage the position of the cacique himself or the benefits which should accrue to his realm. In return he will receive the 'franchise' of his own realm, that is to say, his friends will see to it that his operations in his own territory are as far as possible not interfered with. He will also receive access rights to facilities, a share in the port-barrel, and he may expect to get prior attention for the solicitations and petitions of the landgroups, citizens' committees and so on, within his realm. The fullness of all these benefits will depend on the weight of the support of his following and on his own bargaining position.

To his own rank and file, organised in landgroups with their 'Generals' he provides, or seems to provide, a means of obtaining from the government the services and facilities which they require in connection with local needs, such as a teacher for the school, roads and bridges, the legalisation of titles, help in resolving the boundary dispute, and so on. These may be secured from regional authorities, but in special cases he may short-circuit bureaucratic channels and go right to the top for a decision. He is also expected to keep up a continuous defence of the new rights and dignity of the members of the formerly subjected estament. In return for this, he expects and obtains the obedience of the general in extra-landgroup questions while refraining from interfering in intra-landgroup concerns. He can, of course, expect the same kind of political support for himself and his friends above as we already enumerated. Once he loses his friends in the government elite, he can no longer serve the peasants, who will be obliged to transfer their patronage if not their loyalty to a new cacique, able to re-open the circuits of communication and supply with the providers.

Indeed, when once the governing elite holds military power and controls the facilities required by the peasants, the compact sustaining *caciquism* may be described in the following simple terms: political compliance is offered to those above and required of those below, in exchange for facilities and franchise received from above and passed on, in reduced scale, to those below.

NOTES

1. Delgado gives figures from various sources to show that the service tenants occupied on the average 4/5ths of the land of the Altiplano haciendas, and that their farms sufficed for little more than family subsistence. This implies a very low level of surplus for the estate as a whole. See also Dion (1950).

2. The *comunidad* is a legally recognised landgroup in which formal possession of the land is vested in the collectivity, though in fact actual possession, with rights of inheritance, is held by the individual families. It has evolved out of the *ayllu,* or kingroup encountered by the Spanish conquerors, and given legal standing under the Spanish colonial regime.

3. There is now no single system, of course. What is described is based on Barnes, Delgado, Reyeros, Carter and others. It refers mainly to the Altiplano and the Yungas, and to a lesser extent to the Cochabamba region.

4. The interpretation of the agrarian reform was made possible by an invitation from Tom Carroll of the Inter-American Committee for Agricultural Development to spend two periods of one month in Bolivia as consultant to the Land Tenure study being done there. I am much indebted to members of the study team, led by Ron Clark and including Oscar Delgado, Kathleen Barnes and Marcelo Peinado for their ideas and observations, and also very grateful for being permitted to see their drafts and reports during 1967 and 1968. This paper was completed before the author took up work with the United Nations Research Institute for Social Development.

V

Peasant Organisation

The organisation of associations explicitly serving the interests of peasants across an extensive agricultural region takes various forms and expresses different social conjunctures. It is relevant to the present discussion since it reveals conflicts and hence the motors of change. In particular it reveals the way in which peasantries seek some sort of terms with the urban industrial society and with the aspirations of those who represent it. It is part of the process of incorporation of the locality-bound landgroup and represents an attempt to defend interests based on productive status, landgroup status and societal status.

The most elemental form of peasant organisation is the communal landgroup itself with its own representative leadership and its legitimate collective land rights and fiscal duties. These are permanent general purpose organisations which are activated from time to time for the defence of the landgroup. The Bolivian peasants' revolt of 1899 was organised through the existing leadership of the communal landgroups of the area affected. Willka's revolt could be considered as resulting indirectly from the expansion of the industrial urban sector which took place as the world demand for minerals grew during the second half of the nineteenth century. Certainly it did not result from the intrusion of a developed capitalist agriculture in the midst of rudimentary self-provisioning traditional agriculture. However, in neighbouring Peru, a society with similar estamental arrangements, a number of examples have been presented in which landgroup takes militant action in defence of group – and individual – interests, apparently resulting from anomalies and contradictions intensified by the ups and downs of a commercial agriculture dependent on world markets.

Cases of unsuccessful action (Tocroyoc, 1921) **and successful action** (La Convencion, 1962) **against estamental handicap and for entrepreneurial freedom in the Cuzco area of Peru**

The background to this episode is analysed by Jean Piel (1967), and goes roughly as follows:

The War of 1914–1918 and the opening of the Panama Canal in 1918 created a voracious demand for wool, and exports reached unusual heights in 1917 and 1918, falling again to one quarter of the peak-period volume in 1921. This sudden decline in mercantility affected the different economically defined groups in different forms. Whereas the technically advanced capitalist sheep farms of the Central Andes, established during the first decade of the century, increased productivity and attained a dominating position in the market, the pre-industrial service-tenure estates of the Cuzco area were unable to intensify productivity, and increased their production only by the usurpation of the lands of *communidades*. When the market declined, their policy was a typical retreat to low levels of subsistence and market production but they sought to maintain power in the landed society by the consolidation of lands acquired. The communards having experienced some commercial successes during the boom, sufficient to transform them into a monetised economy, aspired to recover their usurped lands and to escape from the commercial monopoly exercised by the townsfolk of the district capital. No doubt the various classes of intermediaries in whose orbit the townsfolk moved were also put under pressure by the shrinkage of commercial activities. Setting the episode in perspective, Piel observes that Domingo Huarca, leader of the community, was himself rich in money and livestock, and aspired to a commercial role. Under open rather than estamental social conditions, he might have moved on to join the townsfolk in the benefits of trade for those who have accumulated capital. As it was, we observe the spectacle of the would-be entrepreneurial capitalist subjected to the handicaps, servile duties and abuses of his ascribed status.

Tocroyoc, a pastoral Andean community near Cuzco, Peru, and its leader Domingo Huarca, petitioned the government in Lima in 1921 for the redress of certain grievances. They sought relief from obligatory labour-duties in building roads and administrative buildings for the local authorities and also from an obligation to provide the labour to the neighbouring estates. They reclaimed pasture rights usurped by the estates, which had extended their herds during the Great War. And finally, they claimed the right to hold their own market, a right hitherto legally monopolised by the nearby market town and its mestizo traders.

The government authorities responded to the petition by forbidding all meetings in the community. When it was reported that the communards of Tocroyoc continued to hold clandestine meetings in the mountains, they were declared collectively to be 'in rebellion'. They responded by invading the market-town, demonstrating in the streets and driving out or killing thc local authorities. They then proceeded to exercise their rights by holding markets in Tocroyoc, and pasturing their flocks on the disputed pastures. In due course, the provincial authorities sent an armed detachment to Tocroyoc on a market day which opened fire on the peasants and suppressed their movement. The leader Domingo Huarco was killed, and his body exposed on the church tower for a month as a deterrent.

As members of the landgroup, they had suffered loss of communal usufruct rights to pasture their flocks; as persons born to the 'indio' estament, society thrust upon them discriminatory labour duties; and as producers of a marketable commodity (sheep), they found themselves excluded (by extra-mercantile factors) from direct access to the market: recourse to law provided no relief and in the absence of intermediaries, dialogue could not be initiated. The logic of the situation led to violent repression. Piel, who did the Tocroyoc research in the archives and in the field, refers to similar episodes affecting eight other provinces in the Cuzco area between 1921 and 1925.

In more recent cases of peasant organisation, the starkness of the juxtaposition of peasant and superordinate society is missing, and some at least of the goals of organisation are obtained with the help of an important sector of the urban society, equally opposed to the peasants' enemies, and especially to the existing proprietary interest. This is an additional element in the case which follows:

The Convention Valley in Peru is like the Yungas of Bolivia, a valley leading down from the Altiplano (near Cuzco) into the Amazon basin and containing important tropical lands at altitudes from 2,500–5,000 feet. Until 1880, the whole area consisted of great autarchic estates, with no interstitial urban development, and no independent landgroups whatsoever. Quillabamba was founded on estate lands left in inheritance for the express purpose of providing an independent dwelling place for 'the multitude of indigent families and honourable merchants , who were forced to lodge in improvised huts on one or other estate. In 1928 the railway reached the head of the valley at Machu Picchu and in 1933 a penetration road reached the provincial capital of Quillabamba, but economic growth was hindered by a lethal maleria epidemic. This disease was eradicated in 1940, and population of 27,243 rose to 61,901 between then and 1960 (Craig, 1969).

The estates occupied the flatter valley lands and cultivated sugar-cane, cacao and tea, using service-tenants attracted from the Altiplano by the generous lands allowed to them on the hillsides. The great leap forward must be attributed primarily to the cultivating of a new crop (coffee) by the service-tenants, its sevenfold expansion as the price rose from a 100 base in 1945 to 1,221 in 1954.

The landlords were late in adopting coffee, being organised for the crops given above, but when they too began to plant, heavier demands were made on tenant labour just at the time when the tenants could contemplate exceptional incomes from their own holdings and labour. The tenants extended their enterprises as market conditions improved by taking on sub-service-tenants or wage labour, using the additional labour force to pay their obligations to the landlord. The unions, though they had some antecedents in 1930, got going effectively only after the Odira dictatorship in 1956. In 1961 the Departmental Federation of Peasants and Communards of Cuzco was formed, having 214 sections, and by April 1962, the official abolition of service-tenures was secured, that is, the tenures were put on a cash basis. Initially the individual unions, assisted by Cuzco lawyers, politically motivated students and urban worker unions, prepared petitions and lists of grievances for presentation through the Labour Office. The success obtained in the abolition of service-tenures led on to more ambitious claims, and estates were invaded and symbolically occupied, and the landlords took to their heels. By October 1962, 70 estates had been occupied, and the government promptly declared a Land Reform for the area, enabling tenants and sub-tenants to become owners of their lands, which were to be paid for through the government.

In revising the grievances contained in the 33 union claims filed at the Labour Office in Cuzco between 1952 and 1962 and analysed by Craig and also the principal claims advanced during the general strike of the peasants, 1961–62

(Hobsbawm, 1967:387), one remarks that the plaintiffs appear in three different roles: as estate peasants, complaining of abuse of custom, as emergent citizens rejecting estamental impositions and as capitalists demanding entrepreneurial freedom and unhindered access to the market. It is typical that estate peasants should not complain of the 'system' but of arbitrary breaches of unwritten understandings and of the capricious demands by a bad patron. These are the complaints of injured dependents. Hobsbawm also reports fury at the landlord who failed to follow the custom of educating his own illegitimate children.

However it is from the second role that the hatred and the fire is derived, and above all the unity which held together peasants of these latently antagonistic productive statuses. This is expressed in the rejection not of the labour rent, but of the labour-duty insisted on as a tribute to lordship, and comparable with *pongueaje* in Bolivia and *cambão* in Brazil.

Unfortunately none of our informants analyse the way the whole peasant group was structured in relation to the estamental or ethnic distinction of the society, and they are referred to as 'Indians', 'Mestizos' and 'Cholos' by different writers. (The observations made by the participants in the discussion following Hobsbawm's paper (1967:395–407) show great semantic and conceptual confusion.) However, judging from other situations in Peru, it may be assumed that in the process of leaving their native communities, estates and villages, the emigre peasants of La Convencion had shuffled off some of the handicaps and restrictions of their former residence-bound status. And the high degree of tension, the hatred of the patrons expressed by the tenants (Hobsbawm, ibid.) is due to the incongruity between the patron's view of his tenants (as indios) and their own view of themselves, as no longer submitting to this handicapping classification.

Yet is is impossible to deny that the core of the conflict was the contradiction between the customary structure of the service-tenure of the landed society which the landlord tried to uphold, and the entrepreneurial freedom which the market and the whole ethos of the capitalistic national society required. The most important demands were for negotiated fixed-term cash-tenancies in place of arbitrary one-sided verbal service-tenure arrangements, the freedom of access to the market for the producer, and his right to benefit from his own capital accumulation which took the form of lands cleared and trees planted. Perhaps more attention should be given to the activities and influence of the group of coffee traders which grew up rapidly and provided the tenants with their market link in replacement of the landlord's monopoly. It is certainly true that the commercial interest supported the peasants' claims, as is manifest in the Cuzco Chamber of Commerce's call for the execution of the Land Reform and the urgent adoption of the measures necessary for the total abolition of anachronistic systems of agricultural exploitation.

It seems, then, that in both the foregoing cases the revolutionary impulse was born out of the aspirations of the most successful producers to enjoy full entrepreneurial freedom, and of all those who had suffered the injustices of the decaying estamental system, to put an end to ascribed handicap.

Birth of the peasant leagues, northeast Brazil: a structural breakthrough analysed

The analysis which follows is in contrast with the Bolivian and Peruvian examples because of the absence of the estamental element. Apart from this, the same elements of the situation are to be observed, namely the push towards a market economy, the decay of the estate as an economic unit and as a system of social control and the role of urban allies opposed to the established proprietary interest.

Between 1960 and 1964, peasant movements in the northeast of Brazil burst out on the national stage in a style which threatened landed interests and traditional power. How can we explain these movements? Why at this particular time and place, and what is their socio-historical significance?

Some account has already been given of the transformation of a marginal area on the edge of the sugar belt in the Recôncavo. But the penetration of Camaçari by industrial methods of agricultural production does not provide many elements for the explanation of the agrarian movement in northeast Brazil, with the possible exception of the increasing desperation of the peasant as his accustomed institutional means of securing livelihood and of realising his values become ineffective.

Brazilian society has been built on the great estate, and the foci of political power throughout the colonial and monarchical regimes were set within the estates rather than in regional cities. Local administration was essentially the writ of the lords within their estates and the rural social order was a net-like structure of lordships whose relations alternated between conflict and accommodation. 'The role of the city was marginal, dependent on the rural environment. Social control was in the hands of the powerful families, owning vast *sesmarias* lands and slaves, and possessing prestige. The city was only an entrepot where they went to get what they needed, the little that their sugar mills *(engenhos)* did not produce' (Rios in Hanke, 1969:333). Thus the rural man, if not a slave, had to obtain access to the land for subsistence by means of a relation of dependence to a lord, who concentrated and controlled all available facilities. So the lord cannot in any important operational sense be considered a *nexus* man through whom the rural family related to a society, although in a certain theoretical sense this was the case. The lord was the apex of an autarchic or self-contained sub-realm. This dependence had a certain finality. It is in these terms that the various rural statuses must be understood.

But the lord did not necessarily need the labour of those who came to him seeking a place to live and labour for their subsistence and the essential facilities and security. The *'agregado'* and the *'morador'* were tenants at will who paid no rent but put themselves at the disposal of the lord as his loyal followers. They cultivated the lands which he allowed them, raised their animals and carried on small-scale commerce in local markets. They could be called upon for occasional labour services, or to join his fighting bands, or his colonisation or mining projects. (Pereira de Queiroz-Diegues, Jr., 1967). But in conditions of incipient mercantility and labour shortage, his status tended towards share-tenure and cash-tenure.

This does not imply a complete absence of interstitial occupied lands, but that which fell between the realms of the lords in the early period lacked elementary security against slave traders *(bandeirantes)* and frontier hazards and scarcities of all kinds. From the eighteenth century onwards the areas of smallholding appear to have increased but were situated in remoter zones of sparse population, and characterised by great rusticity.

The year 1888 may be taken as a pivotal point since it is the date of the abolition of slavery, followed by the end of the monarchy and the liberalisation of the society. Social trends suffer a sudden turn. Industry makes rapid strides before the end of the century is reached, and coffee production and export in the south, using migrant wage labour, proceeds to become the dynamic and predominant element in the national economy. Towns grow rapidly (Brandao Lopes, 1968).

A slow and agonising process of decay and change took place in the north east which is relevant to the fate of the peasantry, into whose ranks a proportion of the ex-slaves began to enter (Lins do Rego, 1966). The most important variables in this process are probably the changing demand for sugar, the industrialisation of the sugar-manufacturing process and, independently of sugar, the persistent growth of the population. For if in the earlier part of the period, proprietors were obliged to offer attractions to the would-be labourer, including a reasonable extension of land, and the possibility of using that land as he wished, when once the threshold leading to a labour surplus had been passed, the raison d'etre for 'generosity' faded away, and labour could be had in return for hungry survival.

As regards the demand for sugarcane, of course the peasant enjoyed a livelihood of greater amplitude when the demand slumped, since more land was available for the less lucrative production of a wide variety of crops for the internal market and also for subsistence.

Correia de Andrade asserts that the years 1945–55 were marked by an increasing pressure exerted by the industrial sugar mills on the land, on account of the technical modernisation of the mills after the War and high prices. Appetites for use of sugar lands increased, and the typical tenants who occupied lands suitable for sugar cultivation, and who combined sugar, cotton or other commercial products with their own subsistence crops, began to come under pressure from the proprietors. In some cases these were the sugar mills themselves, bent on increasing and rationalising production. In other cases they were proprietors who had withdrawn from direct production when market conditions were bad, and who lived in the cities collecting rents in cash and kind for the usufruct of their lands. Both sectors desired to profit by planting cane under improved market and technical conditions.

In some cases the tenants were expelled, with or without indemnity. Other tenants were obliged to destroy crops other than sugar and become tenant mono-cultivators. Thus, considerable numbers of tenants who had developed independent entrepreneurship, producing for the market, but with the security of a humble but varied core of subsistence, saw their livelihood prospects threatened. The emergence of the peasant leagues in 1955 is a manifest reaction of this sector to the threat. We shall now attempt to show the structural and circumstantial conditions which made possible the formation of these organisations.

The estate of Galileia, in the Municipality of Vitoria de Santo Antao, had been a sugar plantation whose old-fashioned mill went out of operation in the 1930's when sugar prices were low, and it was parcelled out to cash-tenants for the production of fruit and cereals for the town market (Correia de Andrade, 1964:245–246). Thus it became a 'multifarm' estate, that is to say, it ceased to contain a demesne farm (see page 77 of this work) and its 500 hectares was occupied entirely by tenants, supervised by a steward whose duty it was to collect the rent, and organise a few days of collective labour each year to maintain the ditches and roads and other services of the estate (Juliao, 1968:86).

This labour service known as *cambão* (meaning a 'cornstalk') came to have great symbolic importance in the organisation of the tenants in general. It was remembered as having been a form of homage to lordship paid by tenants holding lands on the traditional *engenho* (sugar estate).

As the pressure of the proprietors on the tenants increased, *cambão* was demanded on an increasing scale by those proprietors who had kept up or re-instated a demesne farm, and became increasingly objectionable since the tenants were obliged to perform what they considered to be the most degrading tasks of field labour. However, in Galileia no attempt was made to insert a demesne farm. The cash-tenants were in a substantially better position and each family disposed of some three hectares. But they were actually conscious of the threat to the situation by the continual tightening of the economic conditions of their tenure by the proprietor. They knew that, in some estates, peasants were being ruthlessly evicted. Correia de Andrade (1964:246) reports:

> We were personally present at the eradication of old orchards and coffee fields under the impulse of the merciless thirst for land for cane in the Pernambucan municipalities of Vicencia and Amaraji.

Some of the ways in which conditions of tenure on the estates were unilaterally tightened in the region are described by Juliao (1968:85–88): the annual raising of cash rents on the Feast of the Conception, the appointed day for payments, giving as excuse the rising cost of living, the size of the tenancy or a specially good harvest; the curtailment of the size of tenancies by putting in additional tenants on the same land; the exact measurement of lands, and the imposition of a rate per hectare; prohibition of the planting of permanent crops, and the restriction of usufruct to common subsistence provisions like corn, beans and cassava; and they began charging additional rent for each head of cattle kept on the land, even for the horse, as necessary for his marketing as for his self-esteem, and raised like the other animals on pastures nurtured by the peasant's own labour.

Just exactly which of these forms of rack-renting were practised on the 'Galileia' is not clear, but what is certain is that the tenants, under the leadership of the steward himself, formed a sort of benefit society known as the 'Agricultural Society of the Planters of Pernambuco', and invited their proprietor to become its President. Although he accepted at first, he later withdrew under pressure from his son, who then attempted to expel the peasants resident on the estate.

Huizer (1969:107–112) who made some enquiries in the area, states that 'the main purpose of the society was to establish through contributions in cash and in kind a small fund which could be used to help the peasants to avoid eviction because of failure to pay their debts to the landlord'. He was also told that rents charged rose to 40 or 50% of the commercial value of the land. So it is not surprising that another of the ideas current amongst the society's members was that of accumulating money to purchase estate lands outright. Juliao, however, does not give these as the society's central concern. He says (1968:107):

> The members of the Society were trying to raise funds amongst themselves in order to employ a school mistress to teach their children to read and write. They also wanted to form a market-gardeners' cooperative for the purpose of obtaining credit for seeds, manure and tools, and were to solicit the enjoyment of those rights which the constitution affords to those who form agricultural cooperatives, and to the countryman in general.

No question, he says, of land reform or of the renting of lands or of minimum wages was raised, or indeed of anything likely to upset the landowners and sugar manufacturers, in spite of the fact that these matters were already being embodied in Bills and presidential messages . . . in higher spheres. Why this discrepancy? Probably Juliao is talking about public objectives agreed to by the Society *after* conferring with him. That is to say, it was his advice to them, accepted by them, that the structural questions of land tenure and contractual relations with the proprietor should not be given prominence at first. Huizer also draws attention to the fact that the steward of the estate who led the peasants was the ageing Jose dos

Prazeres, a veteran revolutionary who attempted to reach Mexico in 1910 to advance the anarcho-syndicalist cause, and who had participated in the communist peasant leagues of the mid-forties.

He was one of the leaders of the movement, and later in 1955 was elected President of the Agricultural Society of the Planters of Pernambuco, by which time it already included numerous other local branches. It looks, therefore, as if the Society was indeed formed to stabilise land rights of tenants, but under the experienced and sophisticated leadership of dos Prazeres and after contact with Juliao, this essential purpose was tactically cloaked. What is certain is that Juliao became involved in the movement after the patron had counter-attacked by attempting to expel the peasants. They encountered Juliao in their search for a lawyer to advise them on the defence of tenaure.

There seems to have been a favourable conjuncture for the birth of this new peasant movement in Galileia. It was a homogeneous landgroup consisting of peasants with a set of unifying concerns. They were free from immediate domination and manipulation by the proprietor, who was an absentee. The formal head of the estate and representative of the proprietor was an experienced revolutionary committed to the peasant cause, Jose dos Prazeres. Moreover, Galileia was only 60 kilometres from Pernambuco, to which it had been recently linked by a new road, a fact which not only meant a relative intensity of communication with the state capital and main city of the whole region, but also a growing market for vegetables. They had the prospect of managing their own commercial relations with the city and of developing entrepreneurially. Most of the men were literate and registered voters, and this gave them a certain civic weight in relation to the local political bosses. Their interest in schooling may be also related to their expectations of being able to deal with town people and central institutions with greater skill and confidence.

In January 1955 the events in Galileia opened a door. A second Liga was formed on an estate belonging to Juliao's brother and others followed rapidly so that by September of the same year (1955) it was possible to hold the First State Congress of the Society. The head office was set up in the state capital, and very quickly became linked to the political struggles and strivings of the region. Organised support was received from the left, especially from the urban trade unions, the radical students and aspirants to political office in city and state. They also received support of commercial and industrial groups in conflict with the proprietary interest (Hewitt in Landsberger, 1969).

The Galileia events provided an institutional instrument which was soon to be recognised by the peasantry as a means of escaping from the whole apparatus of social control which had been built up to retain a subjected labour force or tenantry for agriculture after the liquidation of slavery. It is not without reason that Juliao confers on Galileia the title of 'mother cell of the peasant leagues' since the formation of the 'society' and the building of a new kind of political nexus with the opposition in the state capital are the first moves in an episodic sequence with revolutionary implications in which the peasantry is a main actor.

We shall try to look more systematically at the social process which followed in the train of changes within this 'mother cell'.

i. This particular landgroup (Galileia estate) which was submitted to rack-renting was already undergoing a qualitative change from the traditional estate pattern of domination in which vertical asymetrical relations prevailed, to a horizontally linked common interest group. Unlike the typical smallholder group, the holdings were comparatively homogeneous in size, so that land itself did not constitute a framework of inequality and dependence among the tenants.

Secondly, the patron had withdrawn to the city and become a rentier, and the whole cluster of liens which patrons are accustomed to hold in their hands had been whittled down to the payment of the cash rent. The new role of the proprietor also left the nexus functions to be performed by some other means: that is, the market link, relation to the politico-administrative systems, and so on. As regards the rack-renting, all were attained in equal fashion, unlike the common estate style in which the patron or his agent transacts with each family particularly, favouring some and treating others harshly so that he remains overtly and palpably the source of advantage and appointer of destinies, and can command the loyalty and submission of each individually.

The one indispensable ingredient of the situation which is not structural but circumstantial is the 'deus ex-machina', Jose dos Prazeres, who instead of enacting the role of faithful steward by maintaining the patterns of domination and exaction to his own advantage, chose to follow his progressive beliefs, and while remaining a correct steward, initiated the tenants into democratic collective action when the economic pressure of the landlord became too heavy.

ii. As soon as the qualitative structural change in the land-group expressed itself in the 'mutual benefit society', the more class conscious landed proprietors of the district saw the danger to the system of social control, and the patron was persuaded to counter-attack by attempting expulsion. But in fact the system had already withered unperceived: neither agents of terror, nor divisive distribution of favours, nor ignorance nor accommodation to 'paternalism' could prevent the tenants from searching out the means of access to the law, and claiming their citizenship and its rights against the patrons' illegal exercise of power.

iii. The third stage is a convergence of interests between the peasants and the political opposition to the proprietary class. This alliance was sufficient to ensure that the courts sustained the legitimate rights of the tenants. On the other hand, it opened new prospects for the opposition, the 'counter-elite', whose various elements were quick to assess the potential importance of a whole class of new political allies.

iv. From now on the initiative comes from the state capital, and its success requires the confection of a new institutional instrument likely to have an immediate appeal to a sector of the peasantry as a means of securing usufruct of land by just and stable agreements, and freedom to control their own labour. The creation of this alliance, and the establishment of its communications centre in the state capital quickly began to dissolve the frozen isolation in which most of the estate landgroups had been kept, and which was so essential as part of the system of social control. The image and the message of the new movement are perceived at the state capital from the distant estates.

The news of this new recipe for action, this new institutional means is carried away by peasants who visit the city, by student agitators who penetrate the estates, by parliamentary debates, and even when the Press is silent, by the traditional country balladeers (*violeiros:* Morais, 1967) who carry the news wherever they go in song. Now, in spite of the harassment of the proprietors and their *capangas* (or armed estate guards), it is hard to stop the peasants forming unions and utilising the Civil Code to defend themselves against eviction even when they refuse to pay service rent. As the political situation becomes more conflictive and the government itself takes the peasants' part, their demands include possession of the land itself — a radical land reform.

The argument sustained, therefore, is that in the particular case of Galileia, a structural change took place which led to a breakthrough, triggering a wider episodic sequence. While there is no place here for an analysis of the political state of the 'counter-elite', the conscience stricken gentry and the working class organisations of the state of Pernambuco, whose alliance with the peasants was essential to the explosive growth of the movement, something has to be said about the suitability of the new organisation to the needs of the peasantry.

Most of the groups to which the movement was made to appeal had not gone through the structural changes of Galileia though as tenants they were in a better position than the landless labourers to put up a fight; Julião puts the matter succinctly when he describes the aims of the movement as democracy, and then poses the question 'What is meant by democracy for the peasant?' And answering it he says:

> I will explain it to you. It means taking away the soldier from your door. Disarming the *capanga.* because your problem must be resolved by Justice. Never by the police, much less the *capanga* . . . it means putting an end to the *cambão* which was born of slavery and even now contrives to weigh down on you. It means doing away with 'halves' and 'thirds' or giving to the landowner a rent of a half or a third of the harvest that you have sown and tilled.

And he includes payment in estate scrip, the 10–12 hour day, and rack-renting.

The demand is for the use of money for wages and rent payments, contractual relations subject to civil law in place of arbitrariness and coercion, and reasonable terms in such relations. Once again, we find the peasant demanding the 'normal' practices of capitalist society. Does this mean that the peasant leagues constituted an attack on vestiges of a feudal society? Though this might be argued in the Andean countries, a closer look at the tenants' position in Brazil offers quite a different picture.

If the estate as a functioning hierarchical landgroup with strong patriarchal or paternalist traits was able to persist in places until recently (e.g. the plantations in the Reconcavo studied by Hutchinson, 1957) there is certainly little sign that the many farms studied and described in the northeast in the

ICAD reports attained this quality. Indeed, after reading these full, ably-written studies (only in Minas Gerais does a certain complacency reign), one is impressed first by the excessive and irregular variety of land-labour relations in force, and the absence of the kind of clear institutionalisation therefore which appears in the Andean countries, and acquires the attribute *traditional* after a generation' stability. What becomes clear is that avoidance of institutionalisation, or norms, or customary rules is precisely the method of exploitation adopted when one side monopolises all the advantages, and wishes to exploit each individual case to the maximum.

By way of example, the situation of a cash-tenant family living in a *'rua'* is recounted below by the tenant's wife from Sape, Paraiba, and given by Carneiro (ICAD, Brazil, 1966:223).

> One of our neighbours has already made 4 trips to locate a plot but did not find anything and here we are already in mid-March. Two other neighbours also have found nothing. All the workers in the street who have a plot pay rent at the end of the year . . . They are all small, less than 1.2 hectares . . . all are obliged to plant cotton which is obligated to the owner. With the cotton they plant corn or beans. In order to plant yucca or something else which is not cotton, they ask for advance payment and the poor cannot pay in advance. *The price of the rental agreements which are always for one year is never arranged beforehand. If the crop is good, the owner charges more; if it's bad, less.* Last year, my husband paid 3,000 cruzeiros rent. This year he is already afraid of what he will have to pay . . . [Last year] the corn did poorly because although he planted it in May when it rained sufficiently, the corn reached only 2 feet feet . . . It was a windy location, bad for corn. The owner from whom he rented the plot, planted the same corn, but in a more moist soil and without wind and harvested the nicest corn in the world. The cotton just was enough to pay for the rent. Not a dime was left for my husband. He did not buy a single shirt; it was I who bought – otherwise he would have remained naked. What helps my husband is that I am a midwife which earns me about 5,000 to 6,000 cruzeiros a month, 1,000 for each birth. However the people owe me 10 deliveries for 2 months. I cannot do anything about it. But the worst period for us was 1961 and 1962 when no one got a plot.

This case speaks for itself. The peasant has reached the end of his tether, the end of peasanthood. Each year he must fight anew for the opportunity of being exploited in this cruel form, that is , to produce a crop of cotton for the landowner in return not for wages but for the right to plant a corn patch for his family's subsistence in the waste lands of the estate. The last straw is indeed the *cambão,* or tribute labour, which made the patron's corn flourish.

The family quoted manifests in acute form the situation of the class to which the peasant leagues appealed. Without security of any kind, they were called upon to bear the risks of entrepreneurship in the commercial system without access to the profits or even the enjoyment of wages. This particular family had already gone far in the process of proletarianisation. Indeed it has already escaped our definitions of peasant by going to live in a *rua,* thus belonging to an interstitial residential group (rather than a landgroup) similar in kind to the Uruguayan *rancherio.* And no doubt if wage-labour were readily available these families would be in the process of accommodating themselves to a proletarian condition. But the only alternatives are: access to land, migration or destitution, or as frequently occurs, migration for the man and destitution for his family. So peasant aspirations for land survive objective proletarianisation.

A characterisation of the prevailing system in which the peasant leagues grew up and spread out show it as one of unfettered commercial exploitation of family labour by manipulation of the minimal concession of subsistence rights, and one in which proprietors were divesting themselves as fast as possible of their earlier paternatlist obligations to a more permanent labour force. And cambao, whatever its origins, owed its viability to the excessive contractual inferiority of the peasants, excluded from ownership of the land and heavily in excess of the existing demand for labour.

The peasant leagues movement spread rapidly during the years 1955–1960, appealing especially to tenants and smallholders. Under the Civil Code the tenant had a right to retain the usufruct of his land in the case of a dispute with the landowner, and this gave him a bargaining position which the landless man lacked. However, the advances secured by the leagues, and the radicalisation of political life amongst the middle strata and professionals led to an extension of the movement to the sugar-estate workers, not only those who received land but those without it. The Roman Catholic

Church and the Communist Party entered the struggle on a large scale, aiming more especially at the wage-earners as such. In 1963 the Rural Labour Statute was introduced, as a sort of bill of rights for the countryman, and this was followed by a rush campaign, organised by the government, to achieve the massive organisation of the rural labour force, as a basis for its political power for its hoped for electoral successes. The 1963 statute made legal recognition of a new union effective from the moment the request was filed, and thus gave security to the peasant organiser from dismissal by the landowner. In November of that year, a strike of 200,000 peasants was used to insist on the fulfilment of the new regulations regarding conditions of labour, remuneration, and so on.

Thus the organised peasants came to be major actors in a fateful episodic sequence which led to the coup d'etat of 1964. Of the agrarian situation in the northeast as she was able to see it two years later, Cynthia Hewitt (in Landsberger, 1969:398) wrote:

> The coup was followed by acts of vengeance on the part of the large landowners against the peasants . . . and the end of observance by many patrons of the legal gains won . . . in the preceding two years. Very few sugar plantations are now paying the stipulated minimum wage, and some are paying their workers in *vales* or IOUs.

The government-built unions and the *Ligas* were repressed, though some of the Catholic unions were allowed to continue, after replacement of many leaders by men chosen by the regional labour delegate of the federal government.

The organisation of the peasantry from above, Venezuela

The contemporary situation of the Venezuelan peasantry gets its special character from the circumstance of the precipitous growth of the petroleum industry out of a landed society in decay. The especially poor condition of the archaic agrarian economy around 1930 owed much to the rupture of the trade links for the staple products, especially cacao and coffee, with Germany in the course of the First World War. A low level of mercantility and a low density of population in relation to productive land made possible the persistence of an extensive sector of subsistence agriculture in shifting provision grounds known as *conucos* (comparable to the *roça* in Brazil), sometimes on the lands of cattle *latifundia,* with or without knowledge or permission of the nominal owners. Estates used service-tenants' labour, or let out their lands to share-tenants, or, in the case of high levels of mercantility, they employed wage-labourers, to whom they also gave the usufruct of provision grounds. Family farming based on land-ownership was not widespread.

The vertiginous growth of the oil industry made possible a gross domestic product growth rate of 8% per annum between 1936 and 1958. Although the amount of manpower employed in this industry was not great (only 2% of the population) its bounding exports led to a rapid process of urbanisation. Building construction and energy sectors were growing at the rate of 20% per annum during the fifties, and within a few decades, the population changed from an essentially rural one to a two-thirds urban one, the flow townwards being tilted by the unusual disproportion between the level of *value-added* per employed person in the non-agricultural and agricultural sectors – a ratio of 8:1 (Ahumada in Conven, 1966:25–59).

Thus, exceptional conditions of what we have called 'penetration' of the rural society by the urban-industrial nucleus existed in its three main forms: i) in respect of market for labour and demand for agricultural products; ii) in respect of the growth of mass-communications of which Mathiason (in Conven, 1966:203) comments that the Venezuelan peasant must be 'the most media-exposed of all near-subsistence agricultural workers in the world', and iii) in respect of institutional penetration, first of all through the opening of rural schools and health centres and later through the implantation of a whole new set of political, economic and welfare institutions in and around the land reform and the formation of peasant unions.

It is this third form of penetration, and its results, which is of most interest to us. The process was initiated by the political movement which began to flow in the years following the death of Gomez the dictator in 1935. It expressed the personal and ideological aspirations of the growing middle sectors for an open society based on clear rules regulating the exercise of power in which their own talents and achievements would give them participation (Ahumada, 1966). An important part of this movement was a platform of 'redemption' of the peasantry, and their mobilisation in unions as a political force related to the slogan 'masses without intellectual chiefs and the intellectual chiefs without masses' (Powell, 1966:4). In 1945 a military coup brought Acción Democratica to power, and it was followed by a three year period in which a radical transformation of the rural power structure appears to have taken place, initiated by a series of juridical and organisational steps by the new government. In particular, usufruct of idle estate lands following the Renting of Rural Properties Decree of March 6, 1947, Agrarian Commissions were created for each state with powers to oblige and control the renting of the unused parts of estates to peasants requiring land. This enabling legislation gave great importance and power to the Peasant Unions whose organisation was promoted by the political parties, and according to Powell (ibid.:13), by 1948 the union leader had displaced the landlord as the primary figure in the control of, and influence over, the social, economic and political forces which affected the lives and fortunes of the Campesino masses.

Powell may be overstating his case here, but the rural power wielded by the new government must not be underestimated. However, two other factors had contributed to the weakening of the old proprietary class as a whole: the attacks made by Gomez on the military power of regional *caudillos,* and the dynamism of industrial growth and development, which was by this time emptying landownership of financial and prestige attraction. The Perez Jimenez dictatorship delegitimised the peasant union movement, freezing funds for peasant credits and dismantling the machinery for arranging the obligatory leasing of idle estate lands, and declaring null and void existing contractual leases which had come into existence as a result of the 1947 Decree. Government lands were sold off cheap to the Dictator's circle of friends. Peasants on government-leased lands declined from 73,000 in 1948 to 3,759 in 1958. Migration to the cities increased and there was bitter disgust amongst the peasantry.

With the fall of the Perez Jimenez government, a few years of almost explosive change took place. The new democratic government consisted of the very leaders who had initiated the rural transformation of the 1945–1948 period, and they were able to convoke the old peasant leaders and rapidly to remake their movement. The peasantry, aware of the new possibilities of the economic situation yet embittered by the forced regressions of the Perez Jimenez period, was ripe for change. The Land Reform, which was passed soon after the return of democratic government, made it possible for peasants (the majority of whom were subsistence squatters and occasional labourers) to apply for land from the government, priority being given to collective requests.

The following figures, taken by Powell from various issues of *Memoria* of the Ministry of Labour, give some indication of the growth of the movement:

Year	Number of unions	Membership	
1936	3	482	
1945	77	6,279	
1948	515	43,302	
1949	19	?	) Pérez Jimènez
1958	130	4,586	) Dictatorship
1959	782	39,090	
1961	2,197	109,698	
1965	3,476	171,299	

Who were the new leaders? Powell (ibid.:22) reports that 86% of a sample taken in 1965–66 gave *farming* as their primary occupation, and 84% said that their fathers had been *campesinos.* Unfortunately this term does not tell us enough about the peasant's role in the productive process, the degree and exclusivity of his integration in the landgroup, his reference groups and aspirations, and his urban experience, to form a clear idea of his motivation and the coincidence of his interests with those whom he represents and serves.

Ramon Pugh (1969) analyses the CENDES/CIDA study done at about the same time, and draws some important conclusions. Most (i.e. 54%) of the local union leaders in 1966 had already been party-political militants before 1948, another 12% having been recruited during the Perez Jimenez dictatorship (1949–57) and a further 25% were recruited in 1958–59 on their participation in the reorganisation of the political parties and their pre-electoral work. Only 8% postdate this period. This seems to show that their primary orientation was a political one, and that it was in this capacity that they organised groups of peasants into unions to apply for and later to occupy lands under the provisions of the land reform. An appreciable proportion of the peasant leaders recruited up to 1948 (nearly 40%) were traders or shopkeepers. This suggests a certain strategy in the political mobilisation of the peasantry, involving the recruitment of political activists from those who already had followings in the traditional landgroups or amongst the interstitial transient *conuqueros.* Pugh (ibid.:14) points to pre-existing structures by which the subsistence *conuqueros* of a particular zone were dependent upon a trader (often a peasant like themselves, but with urban commercial relations) who tended to appear where and when mercantility grew – who would advance loans for seed and living expenses charged against that part of the harvest which was surplus to subsistence. It was to this emerging sector scattered through the rural areas to which the party's organisers addressed themselves, and these were not slow to appreciate the advantages to be gained from political activity. As we have seen in Chile, a coupling between the commercial nexus and the new political nexus took place in the person of the trader in the peasant setting.

The local leader also tended to 'monarchy' over the local situation, at the level of settlement or union as a result of a conscious policy emanating from the political party, by means of the acquisition of key roles in the local organisations. In the sample used (CENDES/CIDA) the secretary generals of the unions held the following offices:

59% were members of the local directive committee of a political party (Accion Democratica and to a lesser extent COPEI).
35% were members of the administrative committee of the settlement.
31% were traders.
27% were employed by National Agrarian Institute or other public agency.
18% were members of the community development committee.
6% were municipal councillors.

Alberto Aguirre (Pugh, 1969:44–56) is presented as an example of a union Secretary General. His father significantly lived at the junction of two roads and kept a shop there, at no great distance from the municipal capital, a town of some 7,000 inhabitants. He owned 10 hectares of land and produced corn and carrots, that is, he was a commercial producer.

Alberto Aguirre completed his primary school, and then went to work in a shop in the state capital for three years. At 18, on the death of his mother, he returned to help his father. He already had some savings so he went into partnership with a Portuguese to cultivate 10 hectares of tobacco, a crop requiring much skill both to grow and to sell advantageously.

His political career grew out of a friendship with a trader who was the Party's local representative, and during 1959 and 1960 he left his tobacco growing enterprise to his father and became immersed in the organisation of the local party activities. 'In these years my eyes and ears belonged only to the party,' he says. He and his friends were successful, and their party (Accion Democratica) won the municipal elections easily, Alberto becoming a councillor. The growth of his responsibilities in the party required that he should have a permanent clientele (Pugh, 1969:49) and it was the land reform which made this possible. Says he:

> One day in February 1960, after we had talked to most of the peasants in the area, we in the party decided that it was time to start a peasant union, in order to have the people better under control and to give a bit of life to the place . . . .

Within a fortnight, Alberto was appointed Co-operative officer with a salary of Bs.900, or three times the median income of the peasant (given as between Bs.200 and 399 by Mathiason, 1967). A peasant committee was formed to request the local implementation of the land reform. Negotiations took place between the National Agrarian Institute, the party, and the Municipality, which was willing to make 2,000 hectares available for a settlement, and in all of these entities Alberto had an official position. Once the negotiations were successfully concluded, he was elected President of the new peasant union, and took up the task of establishing the settlement. Thus, by 22 years of age, he had become a local leader of formidable power and undoubted ascendancy over the peasants who joined the new settlement and over the many more outside it.

Alberto had of course ceased to be a peasant in our sense of the word. No landgroup of origin circumscribes his decisions, and probably never did, perhaps not even those of his father. Subsistence agriculture offers no security for the kinds of career he wants. His friendships, reference groups and much of his culture are already urban. Yet his origins make him no stranger to the peasantry, and he is the kind of person they have looked to in the past to relate them both to market and society. And his rise to prominence, his social and political ascent, certainly cannot be explained without taking into account the drawing-off (and upwards) of alternative contenders from amongst the older established townsfolk by the vortex of urban growth swirling in the wake of industrial expansion. But we must also give full importance to the impact with which the Land Reform broke upon the scene.

By 1964, government spending on large scale development programmes in agriculture associated with the Agrarian Reform amounted to $182,000,000 (Mathiason in Conven, 1966: 202–3) or 11.3% of the total government budget, and the settlement of which Alberto was general secretary benefited to the extent of Bs.933,000 during 1961–1965.

From the point of view of the peasants the years of the most spectacular expectations were 1960–1962, that is to say, the first three years of the land reform, during which petitions for land involving 97,000 peasants were received by National Agrarian Institute, or 70% of the total received. The organisation of unions was already acquiring momentum in the two succeeding years, and by 1965 the rate of formation of unions and of settlement was falling off rapidly (Pugh, 1969:5–7).

Thus the peasant union movement came to have a very specific character attributable to the conjuncture of socio-economic and cultural factors at the time of its birth. The peasant leaders, originally recruited for political purposes from an emergent entrepreneurial sector from the margins of townsfolk and peasantry, became the essential link between the national institutions set up to promote improved agriculture and rural life, and the peasantry. That is to say, the secretary generals became essential links in the remade social order. Their official position in the union formalised their ascendancy over the peasant membership and was combined with other bureaucratic and commercial roles, while by using their political positions they were able to put the necessary pressures upon the various agencies through which the agrarian reform beneficiaries, their clients, were to receive supplies and services, i.e. the National Agrarian Institute, the Extension Service, the Road Programmes, the Rural Housing Programmes, the Credit Programmes, and so on. (Pugh, 1969; Powell, 1966:36–37).

It is interesting to contrast the views of Powell and Pugh (American and Venezuelan respectively) in their evaluation of the union organisation in relation to Venezuela's socio-economic development. Powell sees that the execution of the land reform required the mobilising of the peasantry in an organisation tightly linked to the political protagonists of the land reform. He also cites similar forms of peasant organisation in Mexican and Bolivian land reforms, and attributes to them 'the incorporation of the peasant in the process of political participation' and hence probably a pre-requisite, in the long run, for stable national development. He sees the organisation as providing a 'self-sustaining and dynamic problem-solving process' in which local criticism and demands for expansion of programmes do influence the political managers who are sensitive to the need for maintaining their local election bases.

Pugh's analysis leads him to quite a different conclusion, namely, that no such 'democratic' transactions have grown up within the organisation, but rather a deepening rift between those who manage the machine, allied with a minority of local beneficiaries, leaders and 'nexus men', and the majority of still 'traditional' peasants who are managed by the highly 'paternalistic' organs of the system. Thus, those who are supposed to represent the peasantry have interests in his continued submission and dependence. Does Pugh succeed in explaining this process of differentiation? He analyses those producers who have substantially improved their incomes since becoming members of the settlements, and finds that generally they have town experience, usually in some functions involving commerce, they have some political experience and are active members of one of the parties, and they also have schooling. They are people who are able to perceive and grasp the possibilities of new situations, and take advantage of them. It is probable that they have some personal abilities superior to the average, and are able to manipulate certain conjunctures and resources which are available to the many, but are only exploited by a few whose personal characteristics or situation in the economic, political and social structure gives them special opportunities. And so, in competition with other peasants, these are able to bring to their productive activity and to their land, which may be no more than of average size, certain special qualities which enable them to exploit the situational possibilities, to get more credit, to learn new techniques more quickly, to manage their commercialisation more successfully, and to establish and manage contractual relations with others. They are those who, by the circumstances of their social situation, find themselves looking out on a social scene in which various alternatives are possible, even expectable, for people of their status – and a certain cultivatable talent for using available possibilities. The different kinds of learning situation implicit in the available roles are mutually complementary. Living near the town facilitates a better schooling which widens livelihood perspectives which stimulate political activism which makes for friendship with commercial people which leads to retail dealing, and so on, all of which provide socialisation for entrepreneurship. The more facilities you have, the more you can attain, or 'to him that hath shall be given'. The spread of an 'entrepreneurial spirit' is a function of the existence of these various roles, implying learning, and an absence of factors restricting entry to these roles.

The dispersion of entrepreneurial capacity and access to 'facilities' manifests itself in the settlement structure. The 'progressive' peasants, along with the Secretary General, come to manage the nexus between the bulk of the member families and the socio-economic system, holding offices and roles in political organisations, credit societies, agencies distributing inputs and technical assistance, welfare and education, as well as trading in consumer goods and products, and owning transport and other services. This may look like the democratic grass-roots structure of popular representation to be found in certain industrially developed countries. But Pugh insists that it is not, and that it becomes a structure of domination as a result of the sheer inertia of a social structure characterised by a pattern of ascribed status domination, and that the elaborate machinery of land reform and rural development, by failing to protect the traditional peasant in obtaining a fair share of the facilities and in commercialisation, actually fosters discrimination. Thus, the state, and the dominant political apparatus provides an umbrella under which a small group of progressive farmers and nexus-people takes control of the situation and the lion's share of facilities.

The collective ethos of the members of this leading group is the mutual protection of individual economic expansion, and is opposed not only to cooperative mechanisms, but to policies defending the equitable distribution of facilities. Control is maintained by the *cacique*-like position acquired by the Secretary General of the union, and by what Pugh calls 'paternalism' of the credit and assistance agencies whose experts take every kind of entrepreneurial decision out of the hands of the 'traditional' peasant. The latter has no opportunity to get an understanding of the technical and bureaucratic complexities involved, and is driven to permanent personal dependence on the *cacique*. Thus, structures of domination persist, though entry to the dominant 'progressive' nexus group is democratised. However, no effective political control by the rank and file exists, and the few ideologies of democratic participation, cooperation, and so on, have little effect on the modernising yet predatory currents released by the exuberant injection of credit and facilities transferred from the industrial sector.

In this case the peasant organisation is the expression of the forces of incorporation emanating from the centre; it is the form given to a new system of political and commercial manipulation, in which benefits accrue mainly to the growing middle strata whose livelihood depends on the individual's ability to profit from nexus functions.

VI

Peasant Destinies

Though the great estate has dominated the agrarian structure, smallholders are now the most numerous sector of the rural population in most countries, with the notable exception of Brazil. They owe their origins to three types of circumstance: to official land grants (colonial grants of lands to recognised communities, grants to immigrant colonists, land reform grants, and so on, to spontaneous settlement, and to the dismemberment of estates by inheritance, sale or squatting. One of the inevitable consequences is that physical perimeters of landgroups tended to be set, and in many cases give a quasi-legal-administrative status at the time of foundation, and on the basis of the existing number of nuclear families. In the absence of out-migration and epidemics, therefore, natural increase and the cultural rule of equal inheritance by all the children has led to rapid fragmentation, the older landgroups manifesting the most excessive cases of *minifundio* and the highest density of population. This density itself has produced an overuse of the existing land, loss of vegetable cover, leaching, and various kinds of erosion, and so has accelerated the decline of the resource-ratio. The great estates have not suffered in this way since lands have been held as part of a monopoly system already described, and seldom fully used.

The landed society and the struggle for resources, Otavalo, Ecuador[1]

Before looking at encounters between landgroups and the forces of incorporation, we shall scrutinise a zone of varied pre-industrial production and busy internal exchange, in which industrially manufactured goods and improved agriculture have had little effect as yet and which remained largely outside the market for industrially made goods. This does not imply stagnation but a dynamic process of attrition as the peasantry desperately looks for new livelihood opportunities and passes into the later stages of resource-ratio decline. Their possibilities for manoeuvre are sharply restricted by the persistence of an estamental cleavage which excludes them from the upper occupational openings, and which historically has made possible peculiar institutional forms of appropriation of their labour and produce by a class of 'townsfolk'. The zone referred to is the canton of Otavalo, Ecuador, lying near the equator at approximately 8,000 feet.

The social map may be described simply as follows: the canton has an urban capital (Otavalo) with some ribbon growth running out from the urban 'squared' nucleus, which may be described as suburban, and beyond that the canton is divided into ten parishes which are administrative units in which government is represented by a *teniente politico.* Two of these parishes are centred on the city of Otavalo, and one which is more remote and sparsely populated has not been taken into consideration. The remaining seven parishes have village centres. The nine parishes considered include some 80 landgroups, of which 19 are estates and 61 *parcialidades,* or settlements of smallholders.

TABLE 5

OTAVALO: NUMBER OF FAMILIES ACCORDING TO TYPES OF SETTLEMENT AND ETHNIC STATUS

	Total	blanco	indio	indios as % of total
Otavalo city	1,580	1,450	130	8
Suburbs	782	636	146	19
6 Parish centres	735	641	94	13
Smallholders landgroups	5,400	219	5,181	96
Estate landgroups	356	36	320	90
TOTAL	8,853	2,882	5,871	
%	100%	36%	64%	

Source: author's census, 1960.

The estamental structure is quantified in the following tables, which show the coincidence of ethnic status (accompanied by sub-cultural differences in respect of language, dress and so on) rural-urban residence and occupation. The commonly used terms for the two estaments are *indio* or *indigena* on the one hand, and *blanco* on the other. Both categories consist of a biological melange of both European and American stock, with a stronger proportion of the latter in the estament called *indio* (Salz 1955).

TABLE 6

OTAVALO: POPULATION OVER SIX ACCORDING TO LINGUISTIC CUSTOM

Mother tongue	Monolingual	Bilingual	Total
Spanish	Spanish – 10,308 29%	Spanish and Quechua – 2,175 5.8%	12,483 34.8%
Quechua	Quechua – 20,928 55.5%	Quechua and Spanish – 3,662 9.7%	24,590 65.2%

Source: National census, 1950.

Tables 5 and 6 show that a little less than two-thirds of the total population belong to the *indio* estament, which corresponds closely to those whose mother tongue is Quechua. Exceptions to this coincidence include some house-girls or *hijas de crianza,* children of poor *indio* parents sold or given to *blancos* and brought up as child servants. Obliged to wear *indio* dress as a mentor of status, their socialisation is subculturally *blanco,* and they speak only Spanish. Other more numerous exceptions are ex-*indios* who have deliberately changed status, usually on the occasion of a move from one place to another, or on demobilisation from the public forces, and children of *indio* peasants who have moved to the town. The teacher in one of the suburban schools known for his progressive assimilationist views, held a haircutting session on the first school day each year, and encouraged *indio* boys to get parental permission to have their pigtails cut off and thus have a fair chance of growing up as *blancos.*

TABLE 7

OTAVALO: OCCUPATION OF FAMILY HEADS BY ETHNIC STATUS
as % of total family heads

(100 = 8,856)

	Occupations	indios	blancos	Total
urban sector	Professionals 'white collar' workers	0.0	6.28	6.28
	Commerce	1.53	8.19	9.72
	Crafts and trades	1.76	12.73	14.49
	Agriculture	0.03	0.91	.94
	Urban wage-earners	0.55	3.02	3.57
	Sub-total	3.87	31.13	35.00
rural sector	Resident estate proprietors	0.0	0.11	0.11
	Supervisory or technical staff	0.11	0.30	0.41
	Estate service-tenants	0.0	3.50	3.50
	Agriculture and rural crafts, commerce, minor services	58.50	2.48	50.98
	Sub-total	62.12	2.88	65.00
	Total	65.99	34.01	100.00

Source: author's census, 1960.

The coincidence of indio/*blanco* cut with the rural/urban and the occupational cuts is closer than the figures suggest if we take into account the changing status of the members of the Araque landgroup, many of whom were in some contexts thought of as *blancos* or referred to as mestizos, though of indio descent. They account for a large part of the 219 *blancos* living in *parcialidades,* (Table 5) and the 2.48% blancos in agriculture, etc. (Table 7).

In the urban sector, professionals and white-collar workers include not only doctors, teachers, priests and office personnel but also all kinds of employees whose tasks are not manual. The category 'commerce' reaches down to the humblest hawker.

The indios in commerce in the urban-sector, like those in crafts, are connected with wool, woollen textiles, pigs and pork-butchering. Along with the urban wage earners they constitute 3.8% of the population which, though indio cannot be defined peasant and in this sense escapes from the estamental division of society. But a closer examination of the apparent anomaly of the situation tends to reinforce the validity of the concept. Various indios living in Otavalo said that they maintained a footing in their landgroups, receiving small amounts of produce from the usufructuaries (usually kin) of the fragments of land which remained their own property, participating in festivals and exchanges of favours and presents.

Very few modern skills are represented in the crafts and trades of the urban sector. Of the 183 tradesmen from five of the parish centres, all are traditional with the exception of seven, who are chauffeurs, mechanics and electricians. The traditional craftsmen include carpenters, smiths, rope makers, tapia and adobe builders, makers of tin utensils from thrown-away tins, sandal makers, locksmiths, shoemakers, tailors, felt-hat makers, etc. Craft work of the *indios* is concentrated especially in weaving, spinning, dyeing and mat-making.

At the time of the study, calculation made on the basis of the map of the canton prepared by the Instituto Militar-Geografico, and the author's survey, showed that the 62 smallholders' landgroups could be classified according to the average amount of land available for each family as shown in Table 8.

Araque, in which the average extension of land per family was 6.3 hectares, was the only landgroup which had broken out of estamental containment. Unfortunately no careful study of the history of the last few generations of this group had been made. Araque stands beside the lake, on the road out of San Pablo (largest of the parish centres). It has a sub-urban appearance, many of its houses being built on either side of the road, in contrast with all the other landgroups whose houses kept their distance from the road. Its middle-aged and young spoke Spanish and wore the clothes of blancos. Its old talk in Quechua, and the older women wear homespuns, unlike blancos. Two hints have been contributed

TABLE 8

CLASSIFICATION OF OTAVALO LANDGROUPS
by average of land per family

Size class	No. of landgroups	Example
Less than ½ hectare	10	PEGUCHE
½ – 1 hectare	14	CARABUELA
1 – 2 hectares	19	TOCAGON
2 – 4 hectares	13	VAGABUNDO
More than 4 hectares	6	ARAQUE

to an explanation. The group enjoys much more extensive lands than most (see above), and these are said to have been used for pasturage of pack animals passing San Pablo and going to Otavalo by the north side of the lake, and linked with long-distance trade routes. This provided an entree to the trade of *arriero* or mule-train merchant. The opportunity of learning alternative roles to agriculture and crafts and the cultural requirements of blanco status, had been taken. Moreover, it had been possible to leave behind ascribed land-bound status since estamental handicaps have local particularity, and would not be applied automatically by townsfolk or blancos outside the locality where the *arrieros* plied their trade.

In contrast, the people of Peguche had been reduced to an average of 0.26 hectares per family and had long sought livelihood outside agriculture. Many of them worked as hands in a textile factory built on the road beside their parcialidad. But for most, domestic textile manufacture was the most important of their resources. The confection of earthenware vessels had, at an earlier period, been practised on a large scale (Parsons, 1945) but manufactured table and cooking ware had reduced demand. The people of Peguche are weavers of *ponchos* which had been sold locally but had caught the taste of the national and international market, and a widespread potential demand was discovered. Commercialisation in this case was not developed by the townsfolk of Otavalo. The men of Quinchuqui, the neighbouring parcialidad, were almost as land-poor as the Peguche people, averaging no more than 0.77 hectares (of which a large part is hillside) per family, and finding livelihood as travelling butchers, buying, slaughtering and cutting-up pigs for sale in the town markets. Perceiving the existence of a high class market for handwoven woollen goods, they began buying textiles from the Peguche people, for sale in the capital, and later in foreign countries, reaching Rio de Janeiro, Santiago, and New York, where their striking peasant dress and pigtails gave a distinctive brand to their wares. Younger men of Peguche and other parcialidades became travelling merchants, and in this way a new sector emerged, maintaining indio sub-culture, but gradually emancipating itself from estamental discrimination. The new trade, once established, attracted technical improvements, and varied design, but remained firmly in the hands of the indios (new style). Undoubtedly the grasping of this market opening, and the modification of weaving styles and designs to meet the needs of the market had a transforming effect on the land groups concerned, and led to the development of welfare and improved education. But the differentiation between the craft weavers, and the new merchant class was all too obvious to see in the Otavalo market – when the weavers with their week's production confronted the merchants, both groups *indios,* the weavers old, shabby, dour, persistent, the merchants young, energetic, decisive and cleanly and expensively dressed.

While the people of Peguche recognise the limitations of their land base as offering them little more than residence with small garden plots, in Carabuela there is sufficient land, (an average of 0.82 hectares per family) to keep alive an aspiration to self-sufficiency (and the relative freedom which accompanies it) through subsistence agriculture, and the struggle to retain and obtain land is acute, producing a generalised anxiety and distrust, both internally and in relation to the social environment.

There is an institutional ambivalence over inheritance, since an old custom permits a father to pass on his property to the oldest and youngest sons jointly for disposal, while the law enjoins equal inheritance amongst all the children. Landed property is also used as a pledge on loans, frequently leading to judicial auctions. Encroachments by townsfolk who buy properties are resisted by systematic nocturnal theft of crops. Turnover is high as heirs try to consolidate their holdings in the interests of security rather than efficiency. Robbery, removal of boundary stones and the use of magic for both encroachment and defence were common.

The unremitting demand for usufruct causes a number of very poor households to become praedial dependents (known as *yanaperos*) of one of the neighbouring estates, each man giving two days labour per week in return for rights to graze cattle along the grass verges of the estate roads, and to collect firewood in the gullies. Assumed rights of lordship are also used to extort labour from the freeholders: each family is required to provide the estate with one day's labour per fortnight or per month, supposedly for use of thoroughfare on the estate roads since these are the only means of access to the public road, as well as for the right to take water from the stream which, though it passes through the estate, does not rise within it. The estate owner and his servants attempt to enforce this corvee on all families in the landgroup by the ancient device of taking forfeits (garments, pots and pans, etc.) from remiss households, which could be redeemed only by labour.

Livelihood gained from agriculture was supplemented from three other major sources: the weaving of ponchos, the practice of magic and the sale of labour in distant estates.

The weaving of a poncho required a week's work by the weaver, with some family help. The wool was bought in the Saturday market, washed and dried out on Monday, shaken out, beaten, carded and teazed on Tuesday, spun and washed again on Wednesday, dyed and dried on Thursday, woven, carded and sown on the Friday, and offered for sale in the market on Saturday, most of the money received being used for the purchase of next week's wool. Raw materials cost S/.145 and the selling price was about S/.170, leaving perhaps S/.25 as the cash reward for the week's work, reckoned as eight man/days. No wonder the weavers looked ragged and sullen in their confrontation with the young, well-dressed exuberant *indio* merchants. (In 1959 18 Sucres = $1 US).

From the following details it will be seen that the lands were inadequate for subsistence. The position of a family with the average landholding (0.8 hectares) isshown in the table below.

The provisions produced on this land amounted to 6 quintals of corn and barley and insignificant quantitites of potatoes, beans and quinoa. (In Pupuya, Chile, 20 quintals of wheat was regarded as an adequate family harvest, allowing for about 1 kilo of bread per head per day.) Eighty % of the expenditure on food went to buy dietary components which the land would not produce (salt, fat, sugar, meat, seasoning) but 20%

TABLE 9

A FAMILY'S INCOME AND EXPENDITURE

(One year)

Net income	Sucres	Household expenditure	Sucres
Weaving	1,200	Clothes	580
Magic	732	Food	961
Provisions (imputed cash value)	(200)	Other expenses	380
Cash total	1,932		1,921

went to the purchase of additional carbohydrates. No sales of any sort were made from the holding.

It would be a mistake to miss the significance of the practice of magic, and the connection of the townsfolk with it. Although the indios had succeeded in preventing the occupation of their lands by blancos, a family had recently managed to install itself in 1959, and another followed. The first was able to 'promote' a forgotten saint with miraculous attributes and to organise a *fiesta* around it, persuading indios to become patrons *(priostes)* of the celebrations, for the purpose of profiting by the sale of liquor to the devout pilgrims and local participants. The role of the blancos in magic was that of using their outside connections to find clients for the magician, and at the same time promoting the magical properties of liquor, and so ensuring likewise that the lion's share of the fees came back to them. The role of the blancos in the promotion of the 'indigenous' propensity to excessive drinking, 'traditional' religious festivities and magical practices was observed in detail by field workers in the case of Carabuela. Other detailed and also more general observations in the canton support the view that indio sub-culture is not to be explained by cultural persistence but rather as an expression of the socio-economic relations characteristic of the societal whole.

The external pressures upon the peasants were exercised by two distinct classes, the estate owners and the townsfolk. The estates had in the past encroached upon the lands (according to report). In the present, they found means of appropriating labour, using the devices of enforced praedial dependence and imposed lordship. The townsfolk, (blancos) exercised the familiar nexus functions in relation to the purveyance of consumer goods, and of raw material inputs for magic and weaving, though the sale of the woven product had been taken over by the indio merchants. They maintained a continual pressure on the land, which was used as a pledge for indebtedness, and encouraged legal action in the case of disputes from which they also profited.

The role of the practice of magic is seen here clearly as a recourse brought into existence by the sheer necessity of the exhaustion of productive potentialities. Forty-five of the land-group families contained practitioners, whose clients were found in the surrounding regions. Magicians' fees earned by the head of the family studied amounted to S/.2,000, but expenses, including S/.1,000 for liquor, and the rest on eggs, candles, cigarettes and guinea pigs, and so on, left a profit of S/.730 only.

It is obvious that the peasants of Carabuela were under two quite different kinds of pressure. The declining resource-ratio drew them away from agriculture, but had called forth a response in institutional change. The viability of the custom of leaving the property to the oldest and youngest instead of its division amongst all led to the drastic but necessary expulsion of the disinherited, to seek livelihood outside. Birth control was also practised by the induction of abortion, but the methods were not revealed, and no local population statistics could be analysed.

The most extreme case of deterioration was found in the landgroup of Tocagon in the parish of San Rafael, in which the average amount of land available per family was 1.87 hectares, a large part of which was unfit for agriculture and in commons, and where the process of fragmentation had gone further than in any other place.

The family of Melchor Peña offers a good example of this process of fragmentation. Melchor's grandparents were owners of 10 lots of land, three of which belonged to the grand-mother, and seven to the grandfather. The total holding amounted to between one-quarter and one-third of an hectare.

The grandparents had three daughters, one of whom was Melchor's mother. One of his aunts had two lots of land settled upon her by the grandmother, but she died at the age of 13 and the lands were then sold. The other aunt received one half of each of four of the grandfather's lots and one from the grandmother. Both grandparents were anxious about the fate of the lands left to this aunt since the husband was a heavy spender in liquor *(chicha, guarapo* and *aguardiente),* and had been forced to sell his properties to pay off his debts before he married. The couple died young without issue and all the lands were sold to pay debts.

Melchor's mother was the grandfather's favourite, and received from him one half of each of four lots of land and the whole of three others, a total of 1.933 square metres. Melchor's father brought with him 4 lots of land, totalling 790 square metres. Melchor was one of a family of seven children, having three brothers and three sisters. Four died without issue, and the parents' lots were each divided in three parts between those who survived, each receiving 11 lots with a total of 989

TABLE 10

ORIGINS OF PROPERTY OF MELCHOR AND HIS WIFE

	M^2	
1.	83	Wife's property, being the fifth part of a lot of land owned by her father
2.	64	
3.	256	These seven lots are each a one-third share of the lots which belonged to his mother. These in turn were made up of half shares of four, and the whole of three lots owned by his grandfather.
4.	130	
5.	28	
6.	61	
7.	60	
8.	45	
9.	105	
10.	80	These four lots are each one-third shares of four lots which belonged to his father.
11.	80	
12.	80	
13.	105	Acquired from his brother.
14.	60	
15.	756	Lots adjoining the wife's property, brought successively in *mancomuna* in the process of consolidating the land around the house.
16.	140	
17.	210	
18.	84	
Total	2,427	

square metres. Melchor acquired two further lots from his brother in an unspecified form, his wife received one lot from her parents, and between them they were able to buy four lots. Thus their total holding consisted of 17 lots, 12 belonging to Melchor, one to his wife and four possessed jointly (in *mancomuna).*

The purchases of land made by Melchor and his wife were all adjacent to the small parcel inherited by his wife. Thus he was able to accumulate around his house in contiguous form five of his lots, with a total of 1,273 square metres. The plan shows the position of these lots in relation to one another and in relation to a single area of land enclosed by the old boundaries. This total formed a single property various generations ago. It now contains 17 lots of land.

The remaining half of Melchor's lands, comprising 13 lots, are to be found in 11 separate places, since in two cases he was able to effect exchanges resulting in a consolidation of adjacent lands. Visits to the sites of these lots showed a situation similar to that observed where he had his house: the time-worn boundaries of a single holding of 3,000–5,000 square metres, and which probably belonged to one of his ancestors at 3–4 generations remove, which land was now divided between 20–35 owners, one of whom was Melchor.

Of Melchor's nine children, all died in infancy or childhood save one married daughter, who lives in the house with Melchor and his wife, her husband and her two children.

The number of families living in Tocagon according to the 1962 census was 228, with an average of 4.4 members each. The table below shows the insignificance of agriculture for livelihood. Other sources of income were contract labour, weaving, confection of sleeping mats and rope making.

Access to flags *(tortora),* growing on the margin of the San Pablo lake in estate lands, had been obtained by a contract for the payment of a service-rent *(yanaperia)* of nine days per month per person by a group of 45 peasants, and in addition an annual cash-rent of S/.2,000. A single family could produce 6–8 per day, obtaining from S/.3–5.5 per mat.

Rope making was done by women, using the sisal plant, and weaving by men using the Spanish loom as in Peguche. Those men who could not establish themselves in any of these activities sought wage work from contractors, going to labour mainly on the coast, in seasonal stints, and earning up to S/.20 per day.

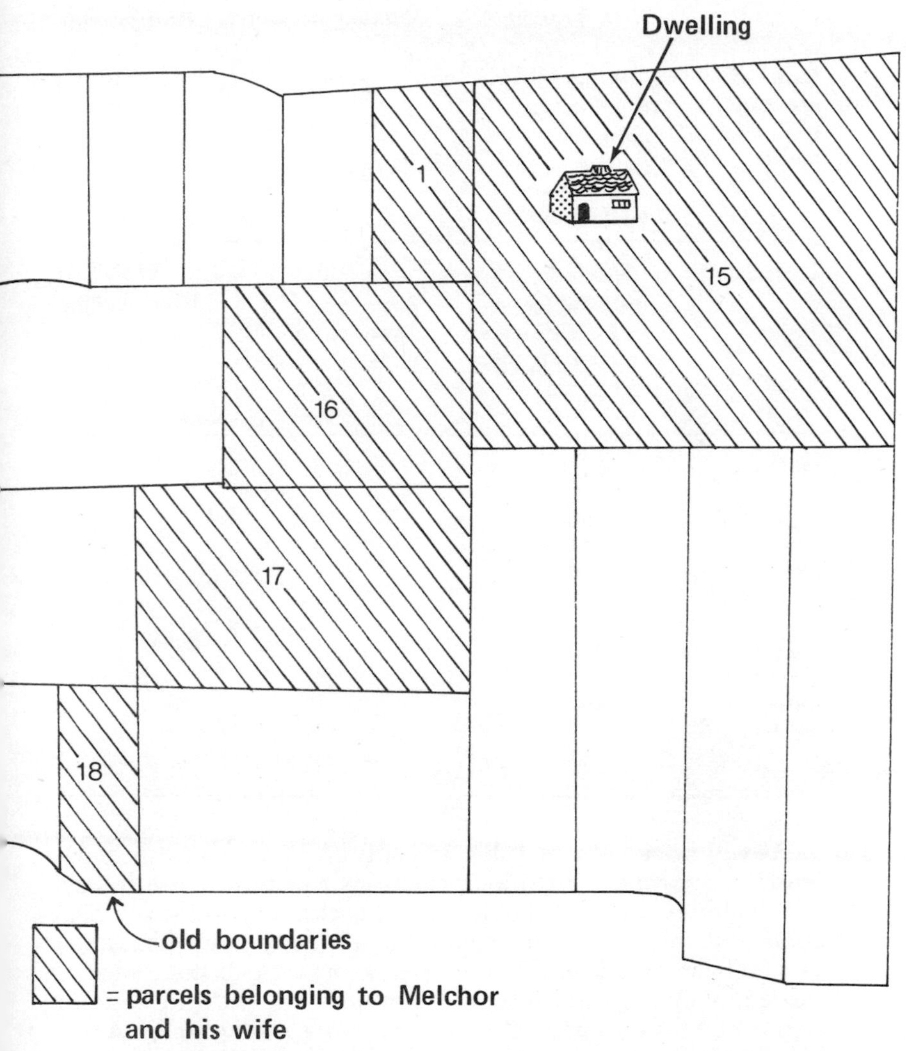
MELCHOR'S PROPERTY
Dwelling
1
15
16
17
18
old boundaries
= parcels belonging to Melchor and his wife

Fig. 1

TABLE 11

PEASANT LIVELIHOOD AT THREE LEVELS, TOCAGON, OTAVALO

Income	*'Rich' peasant*	*Middling peasant*	*Poor peasant*
Value of provisions from own lands	S/.432 (6 quintals of corn, barley, potato, 2 quintals of mixed grain)	S/.64	S/.48
Cash income	S/.5,500 for manufacture and sale of mats, and trade in them	S/.1,025 Rope making: S/.850 Weaving: S/.175	S/.800 Rope making
	S/.5,932	S/.1,089	S/.848
Outlay	S/.	S/.	S/.
Food	340	419	241
Clothes	947	110	150
'Normal' liquor	700	576	264
Religious obligation	982	—	—
Family fiestas	390	200	135
Charity	222	20	35
Other	800	—	—
	4,381	1,325	825

As will be seen from Table 11, only the 'rich' peasant had land enough which provided provisions contributing seriously to livelihood, and to keeping down his cash expenditure on food. But social obligations had fallen heavily upon him, and he had been drawn into large expenditures. In all the budgets, more money is spent on liquor than on food, without counting liquor bought in *fiestas.* Rough cane spirit and home-brewed beer made from grain *(chicha)* were the least harmful. But cheaper brews were made from anything fermentable, with additives of excrement and putrifying animal flesh to speed the fermentation, and bones from the graveyard to promote sales. Drunkenness cloaked despair, and the results were apparent in the vital statistics. Taking the births and deaths for the four years 1959, 1960, 1961 and 1962, the following figures emerged:

TABLE 12

RATIO OF BIRTHS TO DEATHS IN FIVE PARISHES OF OTAVALO, 1959–1962

Parish	*indios*	*blancos*
San Pablo	1.76	3.04
San Rafael (including Tocagon)	0.9	1.43
Quichinche	0.88	1.87
Peguche	1.21	1.6
Espejo	1.21	1.95

The peasants of San Rafael had a declining population. There was no opportunity to analyse in detail the immediate cause, but the situation was not obscure. According to the 1962 census, San Rafael as a whole had a population of 3,138 with 44% men and 56% women. Nine hundred and ninety lived in Tocagon. The birthrate, 3.25%, was not exceptional but the deathrate reached 3.5%. This was partly accounted for by an infant mortality rate of 326 per 1,000 births. Both the sex ratio, caused by the absence of a considerable proportion of the men of working age, and general intoxication and malnutrition undoubtedly raised the death rate. But most probably infanticide, or deliberate population control, was the most important cause. Several different informants reported to the field worker Eloy Robalino that unmarried women and wives whose husbands were absent put an end to the lives of newborn children, whom they could not hope to sustain, by rolling on them or drowning them in the lake, or asphixiating them in some other form, and that it was agreed that three children was the maximum a woman should have, whether legitimate or illegitimate.

In addition to the adoption of infanticide, as an answer to overwhelming poverty and the disintegration of families, great importance was given to the tradition of charity, or *huaccha caray,* an obligation on all to share a portion of their livelihood at the church door twice a week with the indigent.

The consequences of penetration

But equally and more dramatic in its effects is the smallholding peasant's encounter with the expanding urban-industrial complex, and the transformations and dissolutions of the landgroups which follow from it. Passage into the new kinds of society, which involves the incorporation of the rural producer in complicated bureaucratised technically improved systems of production, elaboration, transport and commerce, whether capitalist or socialist, is radical, discriminatory and painful. In so far as the process is considered 'development', we are reminded that this word means distress and conflict for the peasant or perhaps his relegation to some marginal limbo without even subsistence lands.

The treatment of this theme will be explanatory and illustrative, and use is made of a general conceptual scheme, introduced piecemeal and put together in the concluding pages (Chapter VII).

Importance has been given hitherto to the intensification of mercantility at certain periods and places, associated with the export market for minerals, sugar, hides, coffee, cacao, wheat, cotton, quinine, bananas and a number of other products in demand in the industrialised temperate countries. As the Camaçari study is supposed to exemplify, recent decades have ushered in a new stage in which a general intensification of mercantility reaches most rural zones, especially as a result of the growth of national markets, the relative decrease in the proportion of the population devoted to agricultural production and the continuing expansion of the already industrialised countries. The expansion of the market for agricultural products, and of the national market in particular, forms the central prong of a triple movement of penetration by an 'incorporative impulse' radiating from national and regional urban centres, through nexus towns into the country and the landgroups. The pressure itself, the content of the penetration, and the structures which it uses and creates, are to be analysed in the context of the relationship of dependence of the Latin American countries upon the great metropolitan industrial-political-systems. The other two aspects of this penetration are the intensification of communications, especially by the spread of roads and motor transport, and of the radio; and institutional penetration, that is, by national and international organisations and their expansion into even the remoter areas. Schools, peasant organisations, political agencies and committees, community development and extension agencies, credit programmes and health centres, answering two linked pressures from the centre: the exuberant pressure of the bureaucratic expansion of the institutions, fomented by the recently launched middle sectors and 'townsfolk', and the recruitment of the peasantry in really, or potentially, political organisations, either by the government or by the competing parties.

a. Itapecerica, Sao Paulo, Brazil

This drastic character of the immediate juxtaposition of the landed society and the industrial core is modelled in the following encounter between a zone of peasant occupation and the rapidly growing São Paulo since the 1930's.

According to Perreira de Queiroz, (1967:287–298) the existence of a smallholding peasantry in Brazil must be explained functionally in relation to the rigid structure of the dominant sector of commercial monoculture. So long as the areas devoted to commercial monoculture were flanked, even remotely, by 'open resource' zones, the harshness, distance and inequality of the relations between landlords and entrepreneurs on the one hand and their labour force on the other escaped a desperate and explosive finality by offering an alternative of subsistence lands for those who were self-reliant and could accept a truly rustic though independent life on one of these frontier zones. The peasant smallholders *(sitiantes)* of the Sertão de Itapecerica (São Paulo) are presented as one such group. In the early decades of the present century they were able to achieve comfortable family subsistence by rudimentary extensive hoe agriculture (growing corn, cassava, beans and sweet potatoes, along with pig raising). Situated at 33 kilometres from São Paulo, and owning their own means of transport (donkeys) they were able to dispose of surplus production by selling it directly in the city of São Paulo and in market towns nearer at hand, and to buy their necessities (cloth, gunpowder for hunting, salt, wine and cane-liquor) with what they received for the product. Their economic independence made possible a rustic, typically *caipira* social life including religious festivals, visits, cooperative labour, pilgrimages, and even independent participation in municipal politics.

But as the rhythm of the industrial-urban growth of São Paulo accelerated, the balance of their relation was upset. The city's demand for food brought into existence a belt of intensive cultivation by immigrants (Spaniards, Portuguese, Japanese, etc.) while the domestic and industrial demand for charcoal offered an easy option to agricultural production. The simultaneous spreading out of road and rail transport facilities gave rise to an intermediate merchant group, taking transport to the market out of the peasants' hands and interrupting the relations which they had maintained with the city. A new (and familiar) pattern of relations imposed itself, in which the polyvalent nexus operator took over the more complicated entrepreneurship from the producers, and by management of outflow of the product, inflow of consumer goods, and of transport, reduced the producer to dependence, imposing prices in such a way as to leave only a subsistence margin.

As the resource-ratio declined by population growth and intensified extractive methods, the peasants, frustrated in their attempts to enter the commercial circuit as beneficiaries, regressed to shifting self-provisioning agriculture without surpluses, using charcoal burning as a cash crop (c.f. Azevedo, 1963:110–115), while an increasing number found themselves without the land necessary for this, and were obliged to become share-tenants of the more fortunate.

The destruction of the landgroups is consummated by the building in 1960 of a highway right through their lands which at once raised their value. Many peasants now began to sell out parcels to meet their cash needs while continuing their self-provisioning agriculture (CNRS, 1967:291).

Thus the homogeneous landgroups suffered a traumatic process of differentiation; some few families became merchants, gradually adopting urban living patterns and dissociating themselves socially from their ex-neighbours. Others, who followed the retreating forest frontier as charcoal burners, became physically dissociated from the population nucleus, working now as share-tenants receiving their rations from the weekly lorry that collected the charcoal, living in wattle and daub huts, in rags and with a minimum of social contact, social isolates, already loosed from the chains of kinship. The remainder is described as consisting of families which try to live by roadside commerce, or as intermediaries in the sale of lands, or as a last resort, accepting casual wage work. The answer given is that independence had been a prime value for this peasantry, and the delicate balance at one stage achieved between the extensive resources available for self-provision, and the open option on the city market had made this state possible. They have now accepted a situation economically inferior to that of industrial wage earner, but prefer the independence of casual employment to permanent factory submission. Even as workers, after emigration, they look for the possibility of setting up on their own account and let themselves be encouraged by the few visible cases of social ascension. Failure is blamed on bad luck.

The sharpness of the change of fortune suffered by the peasant who lived so near to Sao Paulo, one of the great sources of development, is symbolised by the author's comparison of the offerings for auction at a bazaar in the 1920's: a cow or mule, a fowling-piece, or three acres of land, with quantities offered in a recent sale, for instance, 6 eggs, ½ kilo of beans, 3 ears of green corn, and so on.

The breakdown and disintegration of these *caipira* landgroups – bewildering defeats for most of their members – is lent a dramatic character by the overwhelming force of the expansion of São Paulo in its triumphant march of expansion.

b. Santa Maria Chiquimula, Guatemala

Jean-Loup Herbert, in his report on Santa Maria Chiquimula in Totonicapan, Guatemala (1969), makes a very valuable contribution to understanding the dynamic quality of the smallholding landgroup and its social inventiveness when pressed to desperation by loss of the land base.

He was able to show that this particular people distinguished themselves in withstanding the Conquest, and that perhaps for this reason, they were granted a very restricted land area by the Spaniards. And in the four centuries which have followed the Conquest, the records show a continuous succession of court actions and violence around their attempts to defend their rights to the lands granted them by the Spanish conquerors (a reduced part of those they had formerly held) against the colonial and republican powers and the greed of neighbours and townsfolk, whose advantage was consecrated by the estamental system.

As early as 1778 the native authorities are quoted as writing in a petition that the land they possess is 'not even sufficient for half of the tributaries of the township, and the remainder are obliged to go to other townships to rent lands for cultivating their *milpas,* providing for their families, paying the royal tributes and other impositions'. Since that time the resource-ratio has continued to decline, and domestic crafts for export have been developed. Using the earth from their own fields the poorest peasants manufactured earthenware articles on a large scale and transported them long distances to the markets of the coast on their backs. The spinning and weaving of garments of peasant wear from the wool of the local flocks also played an important part, and 650 weavers were noted in the 1893 census. But both domestic weaving and the manufacture and sale of earthenware pots have been effectively liquidated in the last decades, by the competition of industry-made garments and utensils. Industries using locally produced wood, such as sawmills, producing pine boards; the making of handles for agricultural implements and even the cutting and sale of firewood, are dying out with the exhaustion of the raw material. The lime kilns are now monopolised by five producers all of whom use wage labour. And only 50 weavers remain, supplying a local demand for women's garments, now that all men's clothes are machine-made.

Santa Maria de Chiquimula is no longer a landgroup dependent on agricultural production in its own lands. Present population density reaches 210 persons per square km. and 60% of the farms are of less than 1½ hectares. Herbert calculates that at the present level of technology and of natural conditions 4 hectares are necessary to make possible an agricultural livelihood. The contemporary holding produces dry and broad beans, squash and wheat, and has an average of 8–12 sheep and some fowls, and a cow or two on the larger holdings. But the common diet consists of tortillas (made of cornflour and flavoured with chilis), and coffee with sugar-cane syrup, three times a day. Herbs, meat on the bone, beans and eggs, being commercialised, are consumed only under exceptional circumstances. Thus the *milpa* is quite divorced from subsistence, and no longer very important as a source of raw materials from which livelihood can be gained. Wheat is still sold in some quantity to the mills or else made into the traditional loaves (*shecas*) sold in the fairs of the region, and already mentioned in the 1700's. But the staple food is corn (for tortillas), which is brought weekly by lorry and on muleback and sold in the marketplace.

About half of the adult population make their living as traders outside the municipality, operating a number of well established circuits linking the mountain regions with the coastal areas and looking to establish themselves permanently as shop-keepers at some fixed point on the circuit. These traders keep their *milpas,* and pay some poorer peasant to work on them. In this way they keep up their membership of, and participate in, their group of origin.

A further very important source of livelihood, developed as craft production decayed, is the making of trousers, which occupies some 500 families. This involves the purchase of sewing machines, usually from Japan, and of industrially produced cloth, bought from the national capital. Since most of the tailors are poor, they received the consignments of cloth on credit each week from a merchant or lorry owner, under whose control they are liable to fall. Herbert also reports typical mercantile capitalist development in the grouping of workers together under a single entrepreneur, who purchases the machines and installs a rational division of labour amongst a group of workers, including paid vendors.

Clearly our peasants are peasants no longer, and the totality of this group now manifests strong tendencies to economic differentiation between those who dispose of capital and can use it, and those who have neither capital nor access to land and who must therefore find employment. To the first of these groups belong the traders, proprietors of less than 0.7 hectares, owners of lorries, mules, kilns, mills, more than twelve sheep and the few surviving owners of woodlands, while the rest are reduced to wage earning tailors, salesmen, woodcutters, day labourers, or shoe-blacks. Our peasant society is transformed into a residential group with strong ties of ethnic solidarity built up by centuries of estamental discrimination and external siege, as well as a body of local common interests, and at the same time, a growing differentiation of interest derived from their opposing productive statuses.

c. *Tenza, Colombia*

By way of comparison, a milder version of the same encounter is presented in which a more viable adaptation is arrived at by a peasantry not submitted to estamental handicap.

Tenza is one of a group of rural municipalities which lie spread like a rumpled handkerchief on the eastern slopes of the Andes, going down towards the Orinoco Plains, an annex to the Bogota Altiplano, to which it was linked by motor transport during the 1930's. Its soils were once rich and its production varied by virtue of its altitude ranging from 1,300 metres to 2,400 metres. Its natural products included sheep and cattle, corn, sugar-cane, wheat, cotton, chick-peas, parsnip, jonquils and sisal, not to mention various kinds of fruit. Perhaps it was the fact that it offered comfortable and varied subsistence but no highly profitable export-crop which led to the steady fragmentation of once larger holdings, and reduced estates to small family farms.

Before the motor transport link was forged, Tenza participated in an extensive 'rural complex' or pre-industrial exchange network. Within the individual landgroups there was division of labour. And in the census of 1905, only 529 family heads were smallholding agricultural produces while 296 were artisans and craft-workers and there were still 112 families of labourers. Professionals and merchants amounted to only 18. Manufacture included the making of loaf-sugar, the spinning, weaving and dyeing of cotton and woollen goods, the confection of hats from cane-leaf and bamboo, of *alpargatas* from sisal, of cargo saddles and harness for mules, of corn-beer and sugar-cane beer. Since manufacture was based on local products and transport was by farm animals, most peasant families were able to perform the function of salesman on their own account. One informant reported as follows:

> My mother used to trade between Tenza and Guateque from 1910 to 1930, and I always went with her along with an ox for carrying the wool. We used to take hats of wicker and cane-leaf as well. We would bring back rock-salt *(sal vigua)* – the local supply came from a salt spring and was inadequate – sugar-loaf and animal-fat *(gordana)*, and later manufactured fabrics (*casemires* and *bayetillas*) and special orders of goods. We set out at about two in the morning or sometimes at dawn, and the trip took about five hours. The wool we sold either to Guateque weavers or else to buyers who came with mules from Bogota. When business was done at midday we used to have our dinner in some cane-beer tavern *(guaraperia)* for five cents, including 2 plates of corn-soup *(mute)* and a main course of meat, potatoes, parsnips and rice, and a calabash full of *guarapo*.

Some commercial routes reached quite distant zones such as the Orinoco basin and Tolima.

The first effect of the road was to bring in the lorries of the sellers of manufactured articles, especially those of dress. Sandal or *alpargatas* made of sisal with handwoven dyed cotton bands, were replaced by short boots, tennis shoes and more recently the 'Croydon' boot, rubber soled with fabric uppers, and the poorer peasants took up sandals made from old rubber tyres and brought from the towns. The market for local hats also disappeared as factory-made felt and cloth hats were put on sale, being cheaper and more durable. The women also took up the men's trilby-type hat, which they wear to this day. But it was not only the penetration of Tenza but the linking up and penetration of many other rural areas by manufactured goods, especially textiles, which undermined the crafts of Tenza. It was reported to us that early in the century there were as many as fifty looms in the neighbourhoods and in the village centre of Tenza, all of which productive activity disappeared under competition with factory-made cotton-cloth and linen.

The decay of craft manufacture intensified the demands made on the land, on the one hand for an exportable surplus to meet increasing money needs and on the other because many additional families turned to the land for their subsistence, and this in turn accelerated the deterioration of the soils. This is inferred from the following observations and reports: loss of all forest cover, some of which had survived until a few decades back; recent expansion of areas bare of topsoil; decrease in pasture lands maintained by larger landowners, with the process of fragmentation; present prevalence of 'clean' crops which leave soil open to the leaching and sterilizing effects of sun and rain; present cultivation of steep hillsides; the absence of any systematic manuring, and the abandonment of wheat cultivation on account of declining yields. In addition, fruit-crops, including peach, chirimoya and citrus had become subject to uncontrolled diseases.

With the dissolution of the 'rural complex' and the domination of the whole region by the city of Bogota (population approximately 2 million) both as a market for agricultural produce and as the main supplier of manufactured goods of all kinds, it has been necessary for the peasants of Tenza to adapt their economic activity to the new situation in which, though dominated by the industrial economy, they cannot find security. While the old landed economy provided security in the variety of elementary productive activities available and the manifold petty mutualities belonging to this cultural form, under this present regime of production there is no division of labour and each family must come to terms with the dominant city-based market system. Much more money is needed now, and fashions and habits demand urban consumer goods. To meet the new situation, Tenzans developed the one craft for which there was a significant city demand – basket-making, using as raw material a locally growing jonquil. This craft is carried on by all members of the family, especially the women and children, and accounts for one quarter of all exports. The largest single item is eggs, and together, eggs and baskets (the former sold all the year round, the latter for seven months of the year) provide for daily cash needs, while the sale of animals looks after occasional expenses. Agriculture contributes little to the market, except indirectly by the production of corn for the fowls. The bulk of its produce is consumed: plantain, potatoes, chick-peas, cassava, corn, broad beans and squashes. In addition, each family aims to produce some sugar-cane which is ground to make cane juice, coarse loaf-sugar and cane-beer, all for domestic consumption.

TABLE 13

PERCENTAGE DISTRIBUTION OF TOTAL EXPORTS FROM TENZA – 1962

Fowls and eggs		34%	Cattle and animal products		30%
eggs	30		oxen	15	
fowls	4		pigs	15	
Cottage crafts		33%	Agriculture		3%
baskets	24		green peas, beans and chick peas		
ropes and sacks	2				
mats and pack saddles	6				
miniatures	1				

The other interesting adaptation was the planting of Guatemala (fodder) grass and the extended capacity of those with less land to keep cattle, important both as product and as draught animals. The grass was planted in a 1–1½ metre strip around the perimenter of the holding, and took the place of, or was added to, sisal, now less in demand, as a boundary.

Land and livelihood are tightly linked together, the amount

of land used by the family determined the level of living. About one sixth of the families had no land of their own, but were able to take land in rent from those who had more than their family labour could profitably use, for a moderate money payment of about 5% of its value. But, as the following table shows, there was a great difference in the extent of land each family was able to use.

TABLE 14

TENZA – FARM FEATURES AND LIVELIHOOD LEVELS

		1	2	3	4	5	6
	Townsfolk	5 +	3 – 5	2 – 3	1 – 2	½ – 1	–½
				hectares			
Average size of holding	5.9	8.4	3.9	2.5	1.5	0.7	0.3
No. in each category	11	8	22	22	31	32	18
Hectares in annual crops	0.3	1.9	1.8	1.6	0.8	0.4	0.2
Hectares in natural pasture	2.45	3.58	0.44	0.29	0.15	0.07	0.06
Average number of oxen or cows	7.1	5.1	3.0	2.5	1.6	0.9	0.6
Average number of pigs	0,8	1.7	1.5	1.5	1.2	0.7	0.7
Days sold	–	14	3	32	5	29	34
Days bought	52	119	175	62	34	16	12
Average number of fowls	19	28	19	21	12	11	8
Pasture as % of holding	64	45	13	14	12	14	19
Pasture per cow in square metres	5300	7400	1700	1400	1100	1150	1100

Those peasants who have access to 2–5 hectares represent a 'normal' level of livelihood. They cultivate up to 2 hectares in annuals, maintain a cane-patch, have an extension of natural pasture from a quarter of a hectare upwards according to total size of holding, a fodder grass boundary, a yoke of

TABLE 15

MATERIAL AND CULTURAL STANDARDS ACCORDING TO FARM SIZE

	Townsfolk	Tenure classes 1	2	3	4	5	6
		5 +	3 – 5	2 – 3	1 – 2	½ – 1	–½
		hectares					
No. in each category	11	8	22	22	31	32	18
Lbs. of meat per annum	177	169	151	149	102	73	39
No. of rooms in house	6.4	4.1	3.0	2.4	2.0	1.7	1.4
Wore shoes on Sundays	100	75	59	45	25	28	22
Pesos – Men's clothes per annum	228	124	164	199	136	160	105
Pesos – Women's clothes per annum	509	150	196	262	155	150	83
Own radio – %	81	37	27	27	16	12	5
Own clock – %	72	37	50	36	22	9	16
Sons and daughters left home	2.27	2.62	1.13	1.77	1.61	0.5	0.5
Years in school	2.9	1.6	1.1	0.6	0.6	0.8	0.6
Knowledge score	7.2	6.0	5.8	6.3	5.0	4.3	4.4
Desired agricultural future for sons – %.	27	25	77	40	58	32	22

oxen, a tethered cow or two, a few hobbled pigs and 15–20 fowls. For this group, life is an intricate, systematic and fairly successful adaptation to circumstances of nature, and to the market. But the majority of the families (56%) have farms of less than 2 hectares, and the lower the level of essential resources the more the agricultural system is likely to break down in the disfunctions of poverty. That is to say, emergencies continually arise which must be met by making inroads into the system itself; for instance, crops are sold green, or loans at exorbitant interest are sought when the money runs out, time is wasted going from one market to the other looking for the best price, animals are sold to repay a loan for which land is guarantee, oxen must be hired for ploughing, land must be taken in rent, when the corn crop gives out corn must be purchased in the market at a high price, money must be earned in day labour just when time is needed on the holding.

In addition to fodder grass, concentrates, purges and block salt had been adopted by about one third of the families for maintaining their cattle and poultry which, with the baskets, made up the bulk of commodities exported.

Improvements had also been made in the breed of pigs and of fowls. Within the comparatively recent past, the peasants had acquired and bred New Hampshires, purchasing them as chicks in one of the local market towns. Similarly, the old stock of creole pigs had in the last few years been completely replaced by Duroc-Jerseys, first by breeding with a hog belonging to peasants in a neighbouring municipality, and later by use of services at the government station. So the Tenza peasants showed no reluctance to innovate spontaneously when presented with reasonable alternatives. But it would not be unfair on them to speak of *defensive innovation* rather than a breakthrough into 'modern' farming or entrepreneurship for which their declining resources hardly fitted them.

In addition to changes in their productive system, the people of Tenza manifest three interesting elements in their adaptation to their economic conditions, which are:

i. their church-dominated quietism;
ii. the pattern of migration which prevented an increase of population, and
iii. changes in the relation between landgroups and townsfolk.

Social stratification in Tenza was made up of three layers: priest, townsfolk and peasants.

There being no great landowners, the most powerful and revered figure was that of the priest, whoever was the holder of the office. Next came a few dozen families of townsfolk, traders, artisans and local officials, at whose apex were a rustic impoverished elite of 'notables' *(principales),* descendants of families which at an earlier period were estate owners and *encomenderos.* Some 'retired' peasants and widows also lived in the town, as well as recently arrived officials, teachers, etc.

The remainder of population were peasants living scattered in the 12 landgroups, a few of whom were distinguished by ownership of archaic sugar mills of which one fifth were moved by motor and the rest by oxen.

No attempt can be made here to describe the complex system of church organisation, with its brotherhoods and sisterhoods fitting parishioners of different age, sex and rank, nor the church building tithes, first fruits, missions, bazaars and impositions by which the institution and its incumbent were maintained. It amounted to a complete moral control by the priest over all the parishioners, with some minor protests from the notables only, and a generalised attitude of submission and fatalism in the peasantry. The priest is the executive and head of the local church which as fabric and organisation embraces the largest part of corporate aesthetic expression and diversion through its ceremonies and bazaars, its processions and robes, pageantry, rhetoric, music, fireworks, architecture, statuary and painting.

He has direct access to all adult citizens through confessions and the sermon, and becomes arbiter of personal and public moral issues. This degree of pre-eminence over a long period has led naturally to a situation in which the individual with his hopes and fears tends to conceptualise his situation in terms of symbols which the church is able to manage.

We must also note that, in the nomination of officers for guilds, section organisations, brotherhoods, and so on, the priest confers status-ranking on those who have no other qualification to enjoy it, and confirms the rank of those who owe it to some other attribute. At the same time, by his occupation of the Presidency General of each of these organisations, the institutional statuses to which he nominates parishioners are always inferior to his own. The most commonly expressed aspirations of the peasants were not concerned with making progress or 'getting on', but with fulfilling religious duties, working hard, minding the family and avoiding doing ill to neighbours, and their most common grumble was that rising prices and falling production, and also the threat of external violence and 'communism', were making it difficult for them to fulfil their duties. The apparent passivity and resignation is to be appreciated in the answer to the question: what would you do if you had the worst farm in the region?

Seventeen out of twenty-six said they would 'get used to the fact' (mostly *accordarse* or *conformarse*) five of these adding that it would be God's will . . . *Estaria de Dios y que se iba a hacer.* Five claimed that they already had the worst. Only five said they would fix it *(arreglaria)* of whom one spoke with aggressive conviction: 'I would fight to put it in order' *(Bregaria por arreglarla).*

A further essential element in the picture of change in Tenza is the continuing stream of migration, whereby the population remains constant in spite of a natural increase of about 2% per year. If one considers who migrates and in what circumstances, and the relation of migration to social ascension, it helps to explain why an apparently archaic and obsolete system of social control should continue immaculate and intact in conditions which would seem to lead to increasing tension and conflict.

Of the sons and daughters of our 145 families studied, one hundred and ninety were reported to be living outside the municipality of Tenza. Their present occupations were given as follows:

TABLE 16

OCCUPATIONS OF OUT-MIGRANTS FROM TENZA

	Men	Women	Total
Agriculture	20	2	22
Clergy and nuns	5	6	11
Domestic tasks (mainly housewives)	0	48	48
Students (including secondary)	4	8	12
Teachers	6	5	11
Military and police	9	0	9
'White' collar	33	15	48
Workers	4	3	7
Salary earners	4	0	4
Graduates	2	0	2
Unknown	6	10	16
Total	93	97	190

We can safely assume that not more than 15% continue in 'peasant' status, that is to say work on their own farms or the farms of others, or are married to men who do. Of the women, a certain number which we were not able to determine exactly, but probably between five and ten, are employed as domestic servants, and another seven men and women are labourers *(obreros)* in town establishments. The rest have been able to enter urban life at a level superior to the majority of the existing urban population. Thus, the picture is not essentially one of migration forced on a peasantry by a desperate shortage of land, but rather one of migration to the town as a crowning achievement for children of families who meet with most success in their agricultural labours. This interpretation of migration was clearly born out by examining the average number of migrants per family according to tenure groups. (The result is shown in Table 15).

In the lower categories (tenure-groups 5 and 6) the family is engaged in the harsh struggle to eat, (22 of the 50 families with less than 1 hectare reported that they were unable to buy meat). The labour of the younger members of the family is required for basket making and for countless penny-pinching tasks, and there is nothing to spare to dress a child adequately even to finish his primary schooling at the *pueblo* school. There is no respite in the daily struggle allowing for the minimum of planning and saving required for a reasonable exit.

Tenure groups 2, 3 and 4 are under less insistent economic pressure and the young people who leave are likely to go provided with the prime necessities, not only as regards clothes and completed schooling, but with definite job opportunities in front of them.

Pueblanos and families of tenure group 1 are already placed above dependence on cultivation of the soil and crafts, being either owners of a few head of cattle, or else in entrepreneurial or urban occupations. Since therefore neither the land nor the declining urban activities of the *pueblo* offer much possibility of satisfying livelihood expectation for the young generation, and since no secondary education is available, emigration is taken for granted, and plans are made to use available facilities (influence, city connections, savings, urban manners, scholarships, etc.) to effect the upward outward step.

Thus the most common mode of ascension involved the accumulation of land or investment in a grain or sugar mill, the construction or purchase of a town-house, and the migration of the children. This in itself, however, did not enhance the local status of the parents. Moreover, the migrated children seldom helped the family left in Tenza, but showed relief at the cessation of the tie of paternal obedience which migration broke. Thus one is led to the conclusion that the increasing failure of the peasant calling to provide a livelihood, and the irksomeness of subordination did indeed urge the young to look for an alternative way of life, and to assert their rights to freer and newer forms of behaviour, but also accustomed them to disassociate these aspirations from the Tenza routines, which were allowed to continue undisturbed.

Thus, military service, with few exceptions, separated the young from Tenza, not only by offering new openings (especially a career in the police) on completion of their service, but also by 'breaking the spell' of obedience and submission to the whole system of parental and community control. One old informant, describing an earlier period, told us that the boys always came home after completing their military service, but they were no longer the timid youths who had bidden a tearful farewell to their parents and relations. On the day of their return they would go on a terrible blind, beat up folks, get into all kinds of trouble and have to be locked up; and within a few days they were off again to jobs as policemen or labourers in Tunja or Bogota. *(Cuando llegaban del servicio ya no eran los muchachos llorosos y miedosos qui se despedian de sus papas y familiares. El dia de llegada era una borrachera terrible y le pegaban a la gente, siempre armaban problemas y habia que encerrarlos.)*

Is it possible to summarise these various forms of change in any more general fashion? The lot of Tenza and its neighbours seems to have been that of an area of consistently high population since the conquest, with rich soils and a benign climate differentiated according to altitude. The variety of its organic and inorganic products made a high degree of local autarchy possible. Two negative factors seem to have allowed the area to achieve a certain degree of balance in its peculiar local economy over an extended period:

i. non-occurrence of any important exotic crop in demand in the export market, and

ii. comparative inaccessibility during a long period in relation to large population centres requiring food supplies.

During a long period of comparative isolation the system developed was not that which is still found in many zones of family producers, namely family self-provisioning organised around a single crop such as wheat, corn, plantain, potatoes, and so on, with the export of a few surpluses in order to purchase necessities not produced by the family. It took the form, rather, of a degree of local autarchy, with variations in the type of crop produced according to geographical conditions and custom, and a development of rural crafts. Between these different forms of production there existed a system of exchange based on 10–12 market centres, amongst which there was much mobility and within which money was the means of exchange, though the local price system was not necessarily congruent with that of the remaining parts of the country, nor with that which operated in and around Bogota.

The older internal ordering of the region's economy and social relations based on relative isolation has recently been exposed to the irresistible embrace of the larger society. This implies a number of different kinds of phenomena, whose sum is a chronic syndrome of maladjustment to modern conditions.

In place of local autarchy, each family must now sell the product of its resources and skills in the national market, and with the money derived therefrom buy the necessities for survival, and in addition as much as possible of those goods and services which larger horizons make desirable. This task becomes daily more burdensome, since the resources have been over-used and are declining absolutely, while the great variety of skills manifest in Tenzan productive activity become daily more irrelevant to livelihood as they compete with new raw materials and machines. Thus, one step forward by innovation is overtaken by two steps backwards due to the obsolescence of the whole received technological heritage.

In comparison with the two cases described from Chile, Pupuya and Lo Abarca, Tenza itself is not subject to any process of social differentiation, the reason for this being that there is no advance in production, but rather slow economic decline, and a tight control of institutional penetration by the ecclesiastical institutional monopoly, which also managed the schools. Not only was there no basis for the expansion of nexus functions but much of the trade had been subtracted from the nexus centre by the decline of crafts and by the extension of motor transport which brought lorries from the capital for the purchase of baskets, and buses which enable the peasants to get to other markets more easily. Thus the notables, nexus men by tradition, lived on old glory and a few surviving privileges. While the grown-up children of the townsfolk, studying for professions in the city, returned at holiday time to thumb their noses and perform symbolic acts of protest and playful revolt.

Pupuya, Chile[3]

The emergence of new middle strata out of the peasantry, and its tendency to urban cultural standards and new modes of local domination is one of the forms of disintegration of the landgroup. It was not seen to appear in Tenza because of the growing redundancy of the rural centre, and the fact that institutionalised outward migration provided a form of social ascension without building a local class, and because of the cultural domination of a highly traditionalistic church. The particular form taken by the process under conditions of rapid growth of capitalist productive relations will be seen in the case of Lo Abarca.

The case we shall examine here is one in which the process of social bifurcation stands out clearly, perhaps on account of certain idiosyncratic features. The district of Pupuya in the commune of Navidad had twice enjoyed intense market relations with the production and export of wheat, and later with lentils, and at the moment of the study had just reverted to a subsistence system based on the production of wheat, following the recession of mercantility due to pestilence which attacked lentils. While market production had been an important factor of economic differentiation, the catalyst of class formation in its social aspects was what we have called institutional penetration, and the intensification of communications circuits linking it up with the national capital.

Pupuya appears to have been settled in the first decades of the last century, by freeholding families which for the first two or three generations had ample lands for family production. Lying to the south of the Rapel River, communications with the central valley required a long day's ride on horseback and even after the construction of the railway from San Fernando to Pichilemu, the nearest railway station, Alcones, was 60 kilometres away. However, although remote from cities, the peasants could ship their wheat from a small port (Matanzas) at a few kilometres distance, and thus participate in the thriving export trade which reached Peru, California and even Australia. This export trade declined and disappeared in the 1870's.

However, the lentil which grew well on those dry slopes, was much in demand in the capital, and became a profitable export crop. From 1940 onwards, the river Rapel could be crossed by a motor ferry, and in 1942 the commune of Navidad, of which Pupuya is a district, became a part of the Department of San Antonio, Province of Santiago, thus changing the geography of its nexus. In 1952 the Rapel was spanned by a bridge and Pupuya could now be reached by fast motor traffic from the capital. In the fifties, a number of other powered machines made their appearance, including grain mills and diesel motors, two tractors and a number of motor pumps. The agents of these innovations as well as many minor elements are said to have been the merchants who came to buy lentils and sell articles of consumption.

Pupuya has a Mediterranean coastal climate, and consists of hills of sandy lands grouped along a stream. Only about 50 of its 5,000 hectares are irrigatable (without the use of pumps) and these are used for the cultivation of tiny gardens *(chacras)*, though the stream itself dries for varying periods in summer. Its 250 homes mostly follow the course of the stream for some 5 kilometres, though a certain number of the houses are dispersed on the hillsides. It forms a loose collection of ill-defined landgroups whose houses and lands have accumulated and fragmented around the original holdings of the first settlers. Near the centre there are signs of an unsuccessful attempt at establishing a *plaza,* and an urbanised centre.

Loss of the lentil as an export crop reversed earlier trends towards capitalist agriculture. The subsistence system which was re-instated did not require wage labour or notable investments of capital in the productive process. Each family whose livelihood depended on agriculture sought first to produce the year's supply of wheat for family provision, seed and petty exchange, considered to be 20 quintals of grain, requiring 2–3 hectares. Although there was some local sale of wheat, it was not a profitable market crop. Chick-peas, however, fetched a fair price, and this crop was planted to supply cash needs, although the labour input was higher than for wheat, so 59% of the land was in wheat and 14.6% in chick-peas.

Although the distribution of landed property was highly unequal, and probably represented entrepreneurial success during the 'wheat' period, the disappearance of wage labour tended to restore equality since excess land could not be cultivated and was let out in share-tenure to those who lacked land, but had surplus family labour. The productive potential of each farm, therefore, rested on the amount of family land and labour, and the possession of oxen, the essential draught animal. Of the sample studied, 54% reached the considered subsistence norm for a family of six (20 qq.), 46% falling below it. The sale of wheat was limited to 17%, amongst whom were those who enjoyed other sources of income, and received share-rents in wheat. Other elements of the subsistence system were exchange of labour, 'lending' wheat or meat, collective labour for threshing by the horse-trampling method, and so on.

Having in mind the close correlation between land held and levels of consumption and prestige found in Tenza, we looked for a similar stratification, but did not find it. Nor did the inclusion of draught animals possessed alter the picture significantly. What the data yielded was a threefold division of the households between:

i. Those which had access to land, either their own or that of others, and cultivated wheat along with other products, thus providing for their families with greater or lesser adequacy within the limits set by the subsistence system. They consumed most of the product and sold or exchanged a remainder for the purchase of imported necessities. This group constituted the majority, or almost 80% of the households, and is referred to (sociaeconomically) as of 'common status'.

ii. A second group was distinguished as enjoying non-agricultural sources of income, and hence freed from the necessity of performing agricultural labour. These did not necessarily have more land than those of common status, but usually enjoyed share-rents for their land, which were an adjunct to family incomes derived from commerce, remunerated services, official positions, pensions, etc. These are referred to as of 'superior status'.

iii. A third group consisted of households unable to provide for their own livelihood on account of a defective labour force, i.e. invalid fathers of families, abandoned women, widows, etc. or owners of neither land, nor animals nor tools, and are referred to as of marginal status.

These qualitative differences stood out quite clearly in the data for the sample families studied. Selected 'judges' in the landgroup were asked independently to name the people of most prestige, or importance, and this list tallied with those of 'superior status' characteristics.

All in some form or other could be said to have a 'slot' in the larger society, either by exercising a permanent trading role, or by being agents of one of the four active political parties, or by an administrative role in church or civil service, or by being related to persons with official or property-owning positions outside. It was this connection, coupled with knowledge and experience of urban ways and bureaucracies, which gave them importance, and affirmed locally enjoyed status. All but three had lived some period of their lives outside the area, in an urban situation.

Their nexus function was assured by the fact that they were accepted and trusted (at least by their partisans and relatives) and had qualified for their belonging either by being native born or linked by kinship to the native born. (The exception to this rule was the agricultural extensionist assigned to the zone, who lived in the house of the leading merchant, and had been made godfather of the latter's child). Their nexus function was also facilitated by the high level of interaction they enjoyed with the neighbours by virtue of their occupational or lay roles, i.e. a renter and repairer of machines, a shopkeeper, a restaurant keeper, a charitable dispenser of medicines, seven local politicians, a leader of community activities, an extensionist, a teacher and two members of the agricultural committee, each of whom talked to many neighbours daily. None had less than six years primary schooling and eight had post-primary schooling.

The 'institutional penetration' which played an essential role in the process of class formation fell mainly within the activities of the Plan Navidad, which began operations in the area in 1960, some five years before the study referred to was made. It consisted of a programme of development and welfare launched by the government with the explicit aim of relieving the economic distress caused by the loss of the market crop, and at the same time spreading cultural improvements, and implicitly of counteracting the political exploitation of discontent by local opposition elements. Its contents centred around the provision of credits in the form of agricultural inputs for marketable lines of production, and especially for a new type of wheat, and the necessary artificial manures, but there were experiments with other lines as well.

The plan operated at first through a group of local residents of 'superior status', the chief of whom was the main trader and representative of the governing political party. With the change of government in 1964 the plan was taken over by the

National Smallholders' Institute (INDAP) and its local management was vested in a 'Smallholders' Committee' of all agriculturalists who wished to join, with officers forming a 'Directive'.

The committee's tasks are given in resume form as follows:

To seek the improvement of husbandry, productivity and commercialisation by means of a joint effort based on mutual assistance and cooperation;

To seek better living standards and the enjoyment of the fruits of civilisation (culture, arts and science);

To obtain better public services, i.e. in health, education, communications, etc.

And to see to it that credits came on time.

The committee was to serve as a community council for mobilising activities and at the same time as a pressure group vis-a-vis the government.

Elections set up a directive dominated by the same group of superior status people, who did not depend upon their own labour for livelihood.

It is not difficult to see the mechanism by which the programme crystallised and augmented class differentiation. The early emissaries of the plan found their level most easily with the superior status people, who responded with understanding to the benefits of the programme as explained to them. Even the trader whose business might be diminished by cooperative organisation, preferred to put himself at its head, rather than remain outside it. But perhaps more important was the fit between the aspirations of the majority of the superior status people and the committee. For this majority was not simply a category: its members formed a group, an elite defined especially by control of the flow of communications and facilities between the larger society and the locality. So membership of the committee increased this control and gave it legitimacy. It also put them in continuous interaction with town people, technical officers, officials, politicians, international guests, and so on, and lent force to an impulse to urbanise life style, and look to the town for their models, thus coming closer to their town visitors, and adding to the distinctions between themselves and the peasantry.

However, the upshot was not a new structure of dependence upon bureaucratised *caciquismo* as we have seen elsewhere, but an attitude of rejection of the Plan by a large sector (probably between 30% and 40%) of the working peasants. (This must be seen in the light of a process of politicisation owing its origins to experience in the nitrate fields two decades earlier, and maintained by political activists since.) Thus the inevitable political overtones of the programme, connected with the government and the monopoly of management by the elite, ensured that the programme became an element of dissension rather than cooperation.

Pupuya represented a rather unusual combination of factors: a persistent move towards urbanisation resulting from the new transport and communications link, and the historical and contemporary importance of migration; a reversion to subsistence agriculture *without* isolation; and the coincidence of party-political activities emanating from the national capital, with local factional differences based on rivalry between clusters of families and conflicting socio-economic statuses. The incongruity of the situation owed much to the biological chance which destroyed the cash-crop, lentils.

e. Lo Abarca, Chile

Until the 1920's Lo Abarca was a rural centre set at the junction of three streams in the dry hills behind the Chilean coast, at the latitude of Santiago. Most of its male population, including the shopkeepers, worked as share-tenants on the estates surrounding it, planting wheat on the dry hillsides after the first showers of the year (in Mediterranean style) and harvesting it for the provision of their families and for sale.

By the 1960's a complete alteration had taken place and a group of peasant entrepreneurs had come to dominate the scene, by the introduction of horticulture and mechanical irrigation. I shall attempt to set out the relevant facts and the generative situation in this transformation. The conclusions to be drawn support the position expressed by Warren Dean (1966) in his study of São Paulo entrepreneurship namely that the main burden of explanation concerns the circumstantial conjuncture, rather than the cultural or personality propensities of a particular group of persons who became entrepreneurs. (This, of course, without denying wide differences in effectiveness to be found in any restricted group of people.)

Lo Abarca gathered local importance in the nineteenth century, becoming administrative centre of an extensive commune, a religious centre famous for its annual festival dedicated to the Virgin Mary (La Purissima), and a trade centre with four thriving stores supplying the estate populations with consumer goods brought from Santiago or directly from the port of Valparaiso. It also harboured a number of cattle dealers, and its traders dealt in some degree in other estate products. As a social group in addition to those playing rural centre roles, it provided dwelling for praedial dependents of the estates and a number of small proprietors.

It was in the 1920's that Lo Abarca's fortunes declined. She was overshadowed as centre by the growth of the coastal resorts at a few miles distance, and in1923 the administrative offices of the commune were transferred to Cartagena, the largest of them. The railway joining Santiago to the port of San Antonio and to Cartagena passed her by. In 1924 a severe drought caused the death of many of the cattle and the loss of the wheat harvests (always a risky crop in those conditions) damaging estate owners and share-tenants alike. With the decline of wheat-growing and stock-raising, land values declined and landownership was extended amongst poorer villagers. Land values began to recover from 1940 onwards, but the estates have tended to division by inheritance or sale. Eucalyptus plantations, some specialised fowl and pig rearing, sheep, and cattle raising, aided by the building of dams, have replaced the old estate agriculture. Some of the villages worked in afforestation and continued to plant wheat for family provision. Others, aware of the summer market for vegetables in the coastal resorts, as tenants or as owners, began planting the alluvial valley bottoms hitherto neglected as under constant threat of both drought and flooding. Their use became profitable through the introduction by a Spaniard, Ibanez, of the *pequen* (Rowley, 1969), a primitive pump and well system by which the underground waters of the valley bottoms could be drawn and used for the irrigation of small plots. In the late 1940's the first motor pump was introduced, and intensive horticulture has since then become the main productive activity of the population, alternating seasonally with the cutting of firewood from the eucalyptus plantations for domestic use and for bakeries in Santiago.

Thus, economic growth in the larger society involved:

i. the growth of Santiago as a consumer centre;

ii. the application of power to vehicles and pumps, and

iii. the spending of upper and middle class incomes

in summer vacations. This created a *de facto* redistribution of productive resources in Lo Abarca so that access to one hectare of the unstable valley bottoms came to out-value hundreds of hectares of prestigious but useless hillsides.

Most characteristics of the landed society faded away, and the conformation of a new rural capitalist socio-economic structure took place, with a much higher level of mercantility. Attempts have continued to be made by former owners of unirrigated lands to produce wheat but these have had little success or importance in the picture, which is occupied by vegetable production on small parcels of irrigated valley lands. The new producer-entrepreneurs include a few of those who bought land when it was cheap and have retained it, and a larger number of cash and share-tenants cultivating lots of between 4,000 square metres and 3 hectares. For 7 months there is a great demand for labour by the producer-entrepreneurs, which is quite well paid by local standards. During the off-season, work is scarce and badly paid, and consists mainly in wood-chopping for the firewood contractors. Tenants of irrigated land were able to average production to the value of 1,500 escudos per hectare, and the producers on an average produced double that by planting two hectares which yielded 3,000 escudos.

However, real economic dominance went to those who had been successful in accumulating enough to buy lorries, and take over the role of trader. This did not in itself require additional capital, since payment was made on delivery in the city, and accounts squared the same evening with the producers. But once ensconced, the possibilities of fast capital accumulation presented themselves, and also the elaboration of a system of control by the trader-lorry owners. These were able to acquire woodyards, and during the winter months, they employed the otherwise idle tenants in chopping wood bought from the plantations on the estates. They also forwarded money to their cash-tenants for their expenses before the first harvests gave them an income, receiving repayment by fixing a lower price for the produce.

Lo Abarca presents us with a classic case of the penetration of the landed society by the expanding industrial-urban system. We note that inevitably the stimuli have come from outside – the building of roads and rail, the sale of radios, the broadcasting of news (including the daily market price of tomatoes!), the sale of lorries, tractors, motors for pumps and saws, the demand for fresh vegetables, for firewood, etc. Within Lo Abarca, however, certain conditions other than the geographical ones must be taken into account. The previous land-labour situation, i.e. the cultivation of dry wheat on estate lands by share-tenants, already evinced a commercial-capitalist structure, so that the proprietors' half share of the crop plus any surpluses which the rudimentary techniques allowed the peasants, went to the market. Secondly, both land and labour were already mobile. For a time, the estate monopoly of land broke down, as a result of the decline of the cattle/dry wheat regime due to drought, thus establishing a new fluidity in proprietorship. Labour, too, had at some earlier stage been freed from praedial dependence and paternalism, and was concentrated in the village, many families being residential freeholders. Finally the character of the village society is worth comment. No estamental distinction created rigidities in social relations. And even more important: not only did the villagers share locality interests; they were united by a major class interest in the Marxist sense, since it is reported that nearly every family, including the merchants, had a share-tenancy on the lands of the estates. (This well illustrates the value of the concept of the landed society — a system of economic organisation which has room for capitalist forms of production, but in which the level of technology in production and transport is low enough to make necessary continued subsistence agriculture, regionalised rural market complexes, and the predominance of land and labour amongst the factors of production. The structural corollary of this system is the key importance of proprietorship, and the terms of access to subsistence lands. The skeleton of the social organisation is a complex of land-labour relations.) This kind of village, potentially hierarchial, is the exception rather than the rule in Latin America and conformity of Lo Abarca to the pattern is due to (a) the dry-area imperative of placing residences along water courses, and (b) the great earthquake of 1906, which led to the concentration of houses scattered more widely along the streams into what Smole refers to as a 'Strassendorf', fortuitously acquiring the morphology superficially similar to an English village.

It is difficult to estimate the social importance of this form of settlement, but undeniably it meant participation of peasants and non-peasants in common institutions and face to face interaction, and easier access by the peasants than in the dispersed landgroup settlement, the facilities (such as school, founded there in 1890), information and the many associations which have sprung up during the last decades. The peasant of Lo Abarca belonged to the larger society more amply and enjoyed more distant cultural perspectives than most of those we have met from dispersed landgroups.

What was the appearance of this little village society with its 70 odd families, when this study was made, and did it compare with the 'pre-take-off' situation? This was nicely observed by Rowley and Alvayay in their field work. The earlier social life was dominated by the church and its festivals on the one hand, and the patriarchal family penetrated by the norms of a strict catholic ethic. The tone of the society was set by the few well off village notables and commercial families and one estate owner, who gave body to their prestige in their gifts to the church and the positions they occupied in its several festivals, frequented by the rural population from a large surrounding area. One informant said that formerly the church had attempted to mould the customs of the people, and now it tried to keep up with the people, with 'booze-ups' at the Colo-colo club, folk-masses, and 'with-it' parties for the young. What is left of this earlier society is a sense of failure in the old, especially in relation to the 'worthless' behaviour of the young, the dusty harp brought out for the benefit of the interviewers, and the daily religious observations of an exclusive group of the aged pious ladies. (One of these described how she used to ride on horseback twice a week to the nearest railway station and take the train to Melipilla for pianoforte lessons, accompanied by her watchful father.)

The socially dominant group, mature men and fathers of families, who stand around the Colo-colo restaurant and poke fun at the pious old-folk, are those who have lived through and participated in the agrarian 'revolutionette', which meant for most of them improved standards of living. They are much concerned with the development of agriculture, markets, etc., tend to membership of the various associations, and resent the extortions of the lorry-owners/traders, on whom they are all more or less dependent, whether as smallholders, tenants or labourers.

The youngest generation is organised in the Ex-Pupils Centre, for ages 16–25. No principle of social stratification seemed to operate amongst them, and most were obliged to work for a wage in agriculture. Yet their level of aspirations seemed to reach far beyond the village. Of twelve who were asked what they would like to be, the answers were model, cine star, hairdresser, fashion dressmaker, lorry owner/driver (2), qualified electrician, accountant, economist, mechanic, professional footballer and pilot. In their activities they alternated 'sketches' with pop music and fashion shows. In spite of these high-flying aspirations, three quarters of the men said they did not mind being horticultural workers, and only 2 of the 12 interviewed wished to live away from Lo Abarca. What was clear, however, was their break with social tradition, and their willingness to disobey their parents if necessary, to play out their youth game together. Formerly (said one of them) the young only came together as parts of families, now they are doing so because they are the young. Neither family authority, nor church, nor general village reference group canalises their conduct and shapes their values, but rather the impelling images of possible lives held out for them to see by their magazines, the cinema, their visits to the capital, their radios, and which they can themselves act out in the summer on the beaches, and in their sketches, dances and fashion parades. The ex-pupils illustrate the end of the road for the Lo Abarca peasantry. None of the diacritical features remain – relation to family, self-provision, received culture, predominance of landgroup – as orientor of conduct.

f. The collective path of the Mexican ejido

The institutional basis of the new landgroups established by the Mexican agrarian reform reflects a policy of building a peasantry around collective institutions. Lands formerly belonging to large proprietors became the corporate property of collectives of peasants known as *ejidos.* Some encouragement was given to the *ejiditarios* to farm their lands collectively, using the instrument of the Credit Society. *Ejiditarios* who held their land individually were able to form cooperatives originally designed to compensate for the weakness of the small producer in his market relations and his access to the factors of production. Yet at the same time the development path followed by the national economy favoured the individualistic capitalistic operator. The national story is a complicated one in which the collective institutions have great difficulty in surviving. In the case studies which follow, light is shed on the mechanism of attrition.

Case 1 Two units of collective production

This case material is taken from a study by Silvia Gomez-Tagle (1968). It describes the career of an *ejido* established in 1936, when President Cardenas, the most outstanding executor of the Mexican Agrarian Reform, dramatically ordered the expropriation of half a million hectares in the Lagunas area, and within a period of six weeks had the lands, already in industrial production, delivered to 34,743 peasants. The case is interesting from various points of view. We see the state emerge as co-entrepreneur through its agent, the National Ejidal Credit Bank, with the collective of peasant producers strengthening their position vis-a-vis the capitalist market system, but exacting its own price. This partnership is seen against a changing political situation marked in the first phase by the impelling need of the government to count on peasant support, and of the later waning of this need as succeeding governments won the backing of new sectors and interests both within and outside the country.

From the start, Ejido Ana was destined to be a unit of collective production in which peasant families were to participate. Lands were held in common by the ejido, and entrepreneurship and management were exercised by a credit society consisting of the participant peasants who elected their own officers, operating according to a set of norms intended to facilitate use of the bank's services. The credit society was responsible for the bank's credits and the investments made with them for the organisation of collective work, provision of services to members, the marketing of the product and the distribution of profits. The overall aim assigned to the credit society was 'to create productive surpluses which make capitalisation possible and the raising of the level of recompense of its members'.

For the first ten years ejido and credit society coincided, and the members of the first composed the second. Early successes were favoured by the high market price of cotton, the main crop, and the support given by the Cardenas government, especially interested in the success of the policy of collective production. The peasants themselves were also moved by the cooperativist ethos and even abstained from drawing their individual wages (paid as advances on the sale of the cotton crop) on occasions in order to increase collective profits. However, the tide of government favour receded at the end of Cardenas' presidency, and the collective ejidos were left to make their own political and economic bargains with a society in which the most powerful impulses made for capitalist forms of development. It was difficult to establish a properly functioning *nexus* between the peasants, hitherto isolated, and still illiterate and used to clientism, and the bank, with its intricate standardised requirements. Failing to find a sufficiently experienced representative amongst their own people, they appointed a smart town-worker who had helped to organise the ejido, as their effective leader (*representante* of the credit society). He became a typical racketeer-cacique, meriting the epitaph spoken of him by one of the peasants: 'he exploited the members for a long time because they had great confidence in him, and he had them so nicely sewn up that if he hadn't died, he would be exploiting them to this day'. It was said that he knew more and could speak up better than the peasants, and they listened to him at the bank. He based his control on a supporting group to whom he distributed largesse and free drinks on occasions and credited them with work they had not done.

Apart from allowing inflated uncontrolled credits, he misappropriated funds for political joy-rides and installed a store on his own account. The practice of smuggling 'moonlight' cotton became common, that is to say, cotton was sold to private buyers, instead of to the bank. In this period a 'compacted nexus' grew up, if we may use this phrase to describe covert agreements between venal bank officials and the caciques 'representing' the peasants to exploit the relationship between the two institutions for their own individual benefits.

Abuses such as these undermined the cooperative ethos, but the most serious test was probably inherent in the system itself, that is to say, its failure to reward equal work with equal pay. From 1943 onwards the land was parcelled out annually after sowing so that the individual cultivator could be rewarded proportionately to the work and expenses incurred in minding and harvesting his plot.

In 1946, the families which had until then operated as a single collective broke up into four groups, each of which became a credit society, while, of course, remaining members of the same ejido. One of the new units soon dissolved into its individual family units, each of which made its own arrangements for credit, while a second dwindled into a small group of related families, so that the obligations of kinship should structure productive relations where bureaucratic arrangements had failed. This left two groups, one consisting of the rump of the old credit society and the other of the reformers, led by a group with a political commitment to the collective principle.

The story of the two credit societies, which we shall call Rump and Reform, reads like a moral parable about the idle and the thrifty apprentices, and before turning to it, it is interesting to look at this unusual set-up in terms of the distribution and interrelation of the four component functions of the *farm* or unit of agricultural production. For the *ejido* at this stage turns itself into a more complicated pattern as a communal estate. Rump and Reform run two large commercial farms in which 18 and 19 families participate respectively. There is a third commercial farm run by a cluster of six related families. In addition, all the individual families participating in these three credit societies, 43 in number, have their own provision farms (family subsistence plots growing corn which, once collectively ploughed, belong to the families apart from the collective enterprises). The remaining families, apart from the ejidal land tenure, are smallholders with both market and subsistence production.

Let us look at the four essential functions which farm-in-action requires, and the problems of their integration. Landownership is vested in the ejido, and each collective unit uses an area corresponding to the lands allocated to the individual families belonging to it, less the amount which each puts under subsistence crops (corn). No particular problem is recorded under this head, though the complete separation of the ejido from the farm could secrete future conflicts. It is, of course, interesting to note that at this level of development in regard to both technology and market, land ceases to be the central factor about which relations are arranged, its place being taken by the use of common capital and access to credit.

The main weight of *entrepreneurship* moves between the bank and the credit society. The bank is the main financial backer of the enterprise. It advances credit to buy and deliver the inputs and to pay labour against the sale of the crop. It retains the right to decide what crops shall be sown and what technical processes are used, and may withdraw from the contract if these decisions are not observed, or move in and farm the land directly if the crop is threatened by negligence. But in theory, the bank does not carry the entrepreneurial risk, and it is the members of the credit society who enjoy the profits and meet the losses on the operation. In reality, however, the bank did not operate these sanctions, allowing the credit societies to remain in debt. (Indeed, at the time of the study,

75–80% of all the credit societies in La Laguna were said to be in debt.) They became the dependants of the bank as a result, not only economically but politically. On the other hand, where the farm operates with financial success, it is possible for the credit society to develop its own entrepreneurship, using alternative sources of credit, and accumulating its own capital.

Managership is vested in the members of the credit society and its leaders, who appoint a foreman *(jefe de trabajo)* and specialists to run particular lines of production (the herd, the vineyard, etc.) with access to technical know-how through the bank's services. The performance of management is therefore dependent in part on the success of the members in taking and executing decisions within the formal framework of democratic organisation. The problems arising from this novel situation will be dealt with later on.

Both entrepreneurship and managership are ensconced in situations of great complexity and instability, and subject to influences extraneous to the running of the farm. Both depend on relations between the bank and the credit society,

TABLE 17

MEMBERSHIP AND WORK FORCE
OF
COLLECTIVE FARM

	Members	Non-members	
Aged, widows, etc.	θ θ θ θ		
Administrative people	θ θ		
Working members	0 0 0 0 0 0 0 0 0 0 0 0		WORK FORCE
Labourers hired by non-working members		X X X X	WORK FORCE
Labourers hired by foremen		X X X X X X X	WORK FORCE

Source: Gomez-Tagle (1968)

and their economic character is liable to be overlaid by other relations generated by differences in social class and by the mementum of the political struggle. Moreover, the interaction between bank and credit society takes place in face to face encounters between the bank's employees and the society's people, which are not easily controlled by either institution, and it is at this point that the dangers of 'compacted nexus' abuses are most threatening.

The work force consists of the members of the society *minus* non-working members (the aged, widows, etc.) and members with administrative tasks, *plus* workers contracted either by the non-working members or by the foreman according to the needs of the productive process.

The subsistence lands exploited by the individual familes average 0.5 hectares (Rump) and 1.5 hectares (Reform) and are cultivated without manures. Irrigation is supplied by motor pump, and should cost $1,300 per hectare, but it is the usual practice to charge this to the cost of the collective crop. With average yields of 385 and 1,050 kilos respectively, the two groups come out rather below and well above common family consumption requirements. The growing of corn as a subsistence crop is *sub rosa* and contrary to the bank regulations, being regarded as anti-economic, as well as involving misappropriation of irrigation water. It is, nevertheless,. an important security anchor for the peasants.

Work on the alfa-alfa fields is done collectively, as is the planting of cotton and the harvesting of the vineyard. But the main tasks of husbandry for both are done by plots which are assigned to individuals in such a way that an account of the labour input and the resultant product when harvested may provide a scale for dividing up the profit in generally acceptable proportions.

Reform credit society enjoys a collective leadership of 5–6 active peasant members who rely upon one another in taking decisions. But the way these leaders have run the society's affairs has inspired confidence and made it possible for them to obtain further loans from private sources and they were able to buy two further tractors in addition to the one they had bought for cash. In this way they were able to establish a sector of entrepreneurship free from the bank's control. But attempts to profit by the renting out of their tractors were abandoned when they found that they could not compete with the bank's tractors. They also succeeded in obtaining credit from another government agency *(Fondo de garantia)* with which they constructed a stable and bought a dairy herd. By 1968 the capital holdings per head had reached $19,311. In order to maximise their credit with the bank, which financed only their cotton enterprise, they charged many odd expenses to this account and kept their separate current account with income from the hiring of tractors and undercover sales, and from this they could meet special expenses and give loans to members in addition to paying them a four-monthly dividend. Thus the leadership managed to secure considerable freedom of action, but the 'fixing' of the credit bank account made it impossible to analyse their costs and they were left with insufficient data on which to base their entrepreneurial decisions. Sylvia Gomez-Tagle points out that in general co-entrepreneurship between the bank and the credit society is deficient dueto the difficulties of cost analysis and the lack of interest by the bank in the career of the individual credit societies *qua* enterprises, or 'farms' – seeing their activities as just another line of credit which must be squared with the bank's credit policy or manipulated as a means of political control. Nevertheless, Reform credit society has a leadership which is trusted and which came into being as a purposeful reaction to the abuses and frauds perpetrated by the original nexus people. Their strength is manifest in their perception of the ups and downs of the collective in terms of the strengths and weaknesses of their own membership rather than blaming them on the bank as do the members of Rump credit society.

Rump members hold an average of only $6,290 per head in capital and 2.7 hectares in land, as compared with Reform's 5.5 hectares. Their weakness is manifest in the sheer non-performance of the entrepreneurial function, a steady decapitalisation and a virtual surrender to inert dependence on the bank. It is not easy to unravel the syndrome of decline. The restricted land base, inefficient management and a failure to control credits given for consumer goods at the store *(tienda de raya)* left the credit society without profits for several years running, and hence permanently indebted to the bank, while the less successful individual members became personally indebted to the more successful. Indeed, the old pattern of indebtedness, the principle of enthralment in the pre-revolutionary estate, reasserted itself, and with it the attitudes of passivity.

Livelihood is sought in the routine cultivation of the subsistence plot with irrigation water illicitly charged to the bank and the other material needs are satisfied by the presentation of chits at the store for work done on the commercial crops. In the meantime they are able to blame their misfortunes on the bank rather than on their own inability to act collectively. It is the bank which won't give them money, which forces them to sell moonlight cotton, which takes all their harvests and tries to starve them by preventing them from sowing subsistence corn. Even in the early days of the credit society when it corresponded to the whole *ejido,* these peasants could not control their leaders who had to perform in the urban world which they (the members) knew little about. Now they have lost confidence in them and reject their authority but do not feel capable of altering the situation. The bank is like the old patron, and since their indebtedness seems permanent, their policy is to get what they can out of it from day to day.

Case 2 A co-operative for small producers

A second very interesting study of the economic organisation of the ejidos was done by Louise Pare (1968) in the La Balsas area of Mexico, tropical coast lands about to be developed for heavy industry. The study was carried out in an area which formerly comprised a vast estate of 93,000 hectares and two other smaller ones, out of which 8 *ejidos* were created in 1939 with 723 members which since then has risen to 1,149. A cooperative was founded with the functions of providing services to *ejido* members and other small producers, including the purchase of agricultural inputs, consumer goods, transport services, market facilities and backing for obtaining credit. The *ejidos* do not practice collective production, each consisting of a collection of small family farms.

The most important lines of production are cotton, coconuts, bananas and sesame. The first of these is universally grown for subsistence, with surpluses for the market. Sesame and corn are grown together, producing a fair income ($900 per hectare in the first year and a good one ($1,400) in the second. Coconuts net $1,700 per hectare, but only 7 years after plant ing, and thus they require long-term credits. Access to land is widely distributed, not only through the ejidos but also by cash-renting and share-renting agreements between landless peasants and ejido members. The problems for the small peasant are credit and market, and since these are universal peasant themes, it would be prosey to describe in detail the whole complex system of intermediaries between the peasant, his credit and his market. In this case, the peasant must sell his crop to a buyer.

Pare gives two examples of the normal profit margins of the producer and the buyer, showing that in the case of copra the buyer obtained a profit for his services of two-thirds as much as that of the producer, whilst in corn the buyer expected a considerably greater profit than the producer's. The discrepancy is enlarged by the practice of selling in advance of the harvest for three quarters or two thirds of the normal price. Taking into account the fact that one buyer bought from many producers, it is obvious that the system produced very sharp economic inequalities.

Who is the buyer and what special talents does he have with which to earn such a high profit on what he does not produce? The buyer knows the market and can get credit. This is a function of his bureaucratic skills, his political and business friendships and clientships, and his understandings with his fellow buyers. The fact that his profits are more certain than those of the peasant means that he is regarded as a better customer for the bank (or other source of credit) than the producer, and of course his money is turned over rapidly.

But the class of buyer is frequently little different from that of the shopkeepers who retail consumer goods to the peasant. This makes him also *de facto* moneylender, since the peasant's most important credit needs are his own subsistence goods while he is planting and awaiting the harvest of his commercial crops. Moreover, he is likely to own means of transport. Thus, a single individual may well perform the 4 most important commercial nexus functions for the individual peasant. This gives rise to a classic situation of commercial bondage in which the obligation to repay loans forces the peasant into a situation of contractual inferiority in obtaining the other services from the same purveyor. The squeeze is tightened by giving credits and loans not in freely expendable cash but in consumer goods at exaggerated prices, and treating the loans as if they were anticipated sales of the crop and paid at two-thirds or three-quarters of the normal price. Thus, the patron-in-land, eliminated by the land reform, gives place to the patron-in-capital, and the dyadic relationship between this new patron (the *acaparador*) and his peasant client gathers up again the cultural traits of the old relationship and becomes a basic principle of the new ordering of social relations, with its politico-economic caciques, and the followings complexly related to government, administration, corporations, syndicates, etc. Indeed numerous cases are reported in this study of loss of control of the land itself by ejido members. This happens when entrepreneurs and adventurers, with capital and machinery, have begun to make long-term rental contracts with ejido members, whom they retain as wage labourers, for the exploitation of their land. In a case reported from Guacamayas, verbal six-year rental arrangements were made to plant bananas between the existing coconuts. However, the ejido members were never paid their wages since they were obliged to work the land in any case in order to retain their statutory rights to it. Thus, in many of the ejidos studied, members had regressed to the status of indebted peons, while the entrepreneurial scene was dominated by three types of people – caciques of ejidos, some of whom were peasants and others of whom were townsfolk by origin, the *acaparadores* or polyvalent merchants, and the urban 'parachutists'.

These developments have an incongruous appearance in sight of the institutional construction which followed the land reform and set up *ejidos,* credit societies, peasant unions, co-operatives, extension services and credit banks, all with the overt aim of protecting and assisting the peasant producer, whether as an individual or as member of a collective. The situation merits some explanation, which is attempted in the following notes, arising from points made especially in the studies by Louise Pare and Sylvia Gomez-Tagle.

Observations relate to the organisations mentioned above and the extent to which they enable the individual peasant family to control the land allocated to it, either individually or collectively, to produce efficiently and to sell the product on the market for a reasonable return. They fall under two headings: those to do with the viability of the new associations or organisations; and those to do with the contradictions between the rules of the collectivist organisations and the dynamics of a competitive capitalist society.

Problems of the structure of the new organisations

The architects of the reformed agrarian structure were responsible for designing or adopting two new types of primary group through which the collective interest of reform beneficiaries and peasants eligible for government credits were to be defended and managed. One of these was of course the *ejido* itself, a newly constituted land group in which proprietorship of the land was vested, and the other was the credit society, a collection of families supposed to take joint responsibility for the channelling and repayment of loans from the Ejidal Credit Bank. The studies of Las Balsas and La Laguna both pay attention to these groups, giving analytical data about their structure and operation. These data point to the conclusion that their members built them on models derived from accustomed solidary relations, and that the charter or constitution on which they were supposed to operate failed to engage them, and the prescribed procedures for action were for that reason not adopted. Thus, we learn that in Las Balsas, the guarantor groups for shared credit were built around clusters of kin-families. This situation may be desirable in itself but it indicates the lack of any existing models and precedents for bringing into existence groups of peer families which could establish relations of solidarity, based on formal and mutual agreements rather than already ascribed obligations.

An equally common situation is recourse to a cacique, or at least acquiescence in his self-imposition, as we have seen in the case of Ejido Ana in the early years, and in several of the eight *ejidos* studied in Las Balsas. For instance, it is said (L. Pare, 1968:130–1) that Ejido La Mira was dominated by a large acaparador of ejidal lands, offices and products, and that when the co-operative was being formed he organised a boycott of it. As in Ejido Ana, the struggle to get the ejido formed had required 'operators' with town experience who could manage political and bureaucratic relations for the peasants but who after its formation were able to use their advantages to impose the customary exploitative leadership. So many ejidos came to include within themselves the very elements which they had been formed to outflank.

It is reported that the people of the Ejido Naranjito first elected a cacique as representative to the co-operative and when he began to make use of the co-operative's sacks for his own business they withdrew him. This ejido came to function 'democratically'. Others which participated effectively in the co-operative were the groups of squatters in mountain lands unsuitable for machinery and in an economy which did not require wage labour. They were already accustomed to working co-operatively in *combates* (freely formed work-gangs). Others which participated successfully were those from the new population centres. These were still impelled by the emotional momentum of the agrarian struggle. In this case, therefore, a common aim and a common task supported their unity.

They had the common task of establishing their rights and they also shared an awareness of a common enemy. It is too easily forgotten that 'unity' and 'freedom' are best defined by that which in fact or in threat denies them.

The theme of the foregoing is, then, that business associations composed of peer families and regulated by a written scheme of contracts and obligations cannot be created by fiat in societies whose traditional links do not include these social forms. Most of the new landgroups and credit associations which Louise Pare describes take several forms, and are constructed out of traditional bonds such as the cluster of kin families, and the captive group submitted to a *cacique.* The other more marginal groups (the mountain squatters and those from the new population centres) must be thought of as struggling bands freed from bondage and landlessness by the swell of the revolution and united by a struggle to obtain security and legitimation. For them the timely appearance of the co-operative offers a non-exploitative commercial nexus for their relations with the market which have not yet been firmly moulded.

Two of the specific contradictions between known and proven customs on the one hand and demands of the norms of the new associations are:

i. provision for sanctions for the non-performance of norms in the general setting of the new roles, and

ii. the use of 'meeting democracy' and elective procedures as a means of securing majority interests. Louise Pare (ibid.:140–2) says explicitly, 'In all the 50 meetings which we attended, it was possible to see that the democratic election apparatus could not be managed by the peasants, not on account of their illiteracy or lack of training but on account of social inequality and the prevalent caciquism – this implies the permeability of the new associations in respect of the power patterns in the society around it – and apparently the co-membership of persons with opposed interests. Thus, peasant leaders frequently persuaded credit society members against their becoming owners of means of production, not only for fear of responsibility but also because they themselves were the purveyors and renters thereof. Which brings into the foreground once again the inherent, though often latent, contradiction within the peasant sector as between the interests of labour and of agricultural entrepreneurs, and similarly as between the interests of agricultural producers and those of the entrepreneurs of the nexus functions.

Perhaps, therefore, the problem can be restated by saying that power relations in the larger society made it impossible for the poor peasant, interested in producing with his own hands on his own land, to find collective expression for his economic interests where the larger peasants and entrepreneurs were also present.

The apparent contradiction between the norms of collectivism and co-operation and those of a capitalist society in development draws attention to the banks established to attend the needs of the ejido members and small proprietors. According to both studies, the Banco Ejidal and the Agrarian Bank had shortcomings of which one is of real importance – the bank's real aim was a political one – committed to a policy of controlling the *ejido* peasantry by the use of a client system which their credit-giving function made possible by absorbing the worst economic shocks that might befall the peasantry and using their influence to secure peasant allegiance to the official union which was closely woven into the establishment. The consequences of this orientation of the bank were several:

i. The more healthily independent the credit society became, the less it was under political control.
ii. Merchants and *caciques* often were the local advisers of the bank, and naturally hostile to co-operative activities taking the nexus function out of their hands.
iii. The bank had little interest in the educational function.

a. The peasantry and the road to socialism, Cuba

The social order toward which Cuba is being led does not include a significant family-farming peasant sector, even though that sector is still large and important today. Indeed, unlike other socialist revolutions, the agrarian policy-making scene was not dominated by the dilemma of a land-hungry peasantry. The first Agrarian Reform of 1959 expropriated proprietors of more than 400 hectares and abolished rent payments for land and granted property titles to some 100,000 cash, service and share-tenants and squatters over the land which they were working, so that they became proprietors, along with the existing proprietors of less than 400 hectares. The second Reform of 1963 expropriated a further 10,000 proprietors of extensions of 67–400 hectares, leaving a landowning peasantry of approximately 200,000 families averaging some 12–13 hectares each. These were distributed between the main lines of production, as follows:

Cattle, cereals, fruits and provisions ..	79,000
Cane growers	52,000
Coffee growers	30,000
Tobacco growers	39,000

In addition, most of these continued to produce some subsistence crops (Informe, III Congreso ANAP:12–13). These 200,000 family farms came to constitute the private sector, occupying a labour force of some 326,000 including family members and 40,000 permanent labourers (Aranda, 1968: 148).

The rest of the agricultural labour force out of which the socialist sector was built, included workers in the state-administered sugar *centrals* ('co-operatives') and the 'peoples' farms' mainly devoted to the scientific raising of cattle. Chonchol (1961) gives the numbers for these as 163,000 (including 45,000 seasonal workers) and 105,000 respectively, but this was before the 1963 Reform expropriated a further 10,000 farms of 67–400 hectares. If this added a further 100,000 workers to the labour force (and it involved 20% of the arable land), then, even without taking into account the indeterminate number of occasional cane-cutters who worked in other occupations off season, the state-employed labour force is larger than the peasantry.

So the larger part of the labour force, and that which entered the socialist sector, had already been alienated from the land or else had never enjoyed an attachment to the land, and sought employment, social benefits and a dignified status, rather than the security which possession of the land might be expected to give. The long survival of slavery and the importation of labour from Spain, the Canaries, Jamaica and Haiti after its abolition provide the historical grounds for the existence of this rural proletariat, and a reading of 'The Autobiography of a Cimarron' (Barnet, 1966) reveals the gap between the livelihood-image which slavery followed by rural wage-labour permitted and engendered and the common elements of ideology to be found in peasantries. Thus, not only was the bulk of the labour force in the socialist sector already clear of land-hunger, and mobile: it is suggested that the pre-revolutionary production status of many of the new peasants had not permitted them to acquire the landboundness of peasants (Martinez-Alier, 1969). This applies especially to the share-tenants whose entrepreneurial scope was minimised and whose 'tenure' amounted to little more than a system of extraction of labour, not only of the head but of the rest of his family as well.

From 1961 on, the smallholders were organised through ANAP (the National Agricultural Association) whose function is described as 'representing the revolution vis-a-vis the peasants, and the peasants vis-a-vis the revolution'. ANAP took the place of a number of associations which had grown out of voluntary organisations created mainly during the 1930's to defend the peasantry against evictions and rack-renting, and to fight for better prices, in the establishment of which the Communists had been especially active. These associations had later a semi-official status as the government came to play a more active regularising role in agricultural production, and they operated as mechanisms for the distribution of productive quotas. It is not surprising that they came to be dominated by the larger proprietors, and as the socialist nature of the revolution was discovered, they opposed it. These vertical class-dominated associations, organised around each separate product, were replaced by the 'horizontal' organisation, ANAP (Chonchol, 1961:58–59), from which the larger farmers were excluded.

Thus, the post revolutionary peasants found themselves freed from middlemen, rentiers, price fluctuations and avaricious landlords, and their material conditions improved, but they were not given the opportunity to become free entrepreneurs. ANAP, operating through neighbourhood committees known as peasant associations, became the nexus for their participation in production as well as in the political society. Its function was to 'organise, unite and guide the peasants' and provided a restricting matrix for entrepreneurship, controlling prices, credits, access to inputs and even to the necessary voluntary labour as day labourers became increasingly scarce. Price policy was used to protect the town consumer from price fluctuations and to reward the producer according to the quantity and quality of the labour contributed, and at a certain stage provided bonuses for high levels of productivity.

Two other forms of organisation were offered to the smallholding peasants, in addition to the peasant *associations* or ANAP committees. One of these was a co-operative for credit and services, designed to go beyond the peasant association by offering statutory facilities for the collective purchase of inputs and sale of the product on behalf of the group, while the family productive units remained separate, each receiving his due share according to the accounts kept at the office of the co-operative. This form is practised by the majority of the producers of sugar-cane and tobacco, the latter especially in connection with the joint use of machines. The 'highest form' is the producers' co-operative, known as the *agricultural society,* consisting of a group of individual small-holders who have formally unified their properties and work collectively with participation in profits according to the amount of labour contributed. The frequency of these three forms of association is shown in Table 18.

TABLE 18

MEMBERSHIP OF THREE TYPES OF PEASANT ORGANISATION

	No. of Units	Member Families
Peasant associations *(asociaciones agropecuarias)*	1,467	121,833
Credit and services co-operatives *(Co-operatives de credito y servicios)*	884	55,069
Agricultural societies	270	3,200

Source: Aranda (1968:158–159)

Immediately following the second land reform, it was anticipated and intended that the smallholders could be coaxed and educated unhurriedly towards the voluntary formation of the third type, or agricultural society, in such a way that viable large-scale units of agricultural production could be formed, having the necessary conditions for intensive technification.

The patience manifest in the various declarations on the

subject rests partly on an awareness that neither capital nor skilled personnel could be expected to be available for a hurried remaking of the private sector, and partly on the 'political affection' of the leaders in regard to the peasantry.

However, in mid-decade the picture changes. Writing in 1966, Rodriguez gives the number of agricultural societies as 215 while Aranda reports only 270 in 1968 – a relatively minor increase. Apparently answering some chiding from East European socialist experts about the persistence of the private sector, Rodriguez (PEL No.152, 1966) discusses the situation revealingly:

> The situation in Cuba is quite different. To date 70 per cent of the land has become the property of the whole people – the highest form of property. The existence of this state property and the organisation of socialist-type agriculture is a guarantee that, unlike the situation that prevailed for a time in a number of socialist countries, Cuba's economy will not be dependent on the will and actions of the individual peasants. At present the state farms account for just under half the cattle, primarily beef cattle, and they grow 75 per cent of the sugar cane and 100 per cent of such industrial crops as kenaf and cotton.
>
> True, individual peasant farms play the decisive role in growing tobacco and coffee and account for more milk and root crops than the state farms . . . Within the next five years the share of the state sector in sugar-cane will continue to increase much faster than hitherto, since only a negligible increase is envisaged in cane output by the individual farms, while in the state sector it is scheduled to be nearly doubled. If at present the state sector produces less than one-third of the milk consumed by the population, five years hence it will exceed the private sector-four or five times over. As for root crops, realisation of the plans for the state sector in agriculture will enable it to surpass the private sector by 1966. Moreover, the small tobacco and coffee growers are completely dependent on the revolutionary government, which helps them to bring in the crop by enlising students, housewives and factory workers for voluntary work at the height of the season.
>
> Firm control over production facilitates the pursuance of revolutionary policy toward the peasantry. Of course,

> since there is no organised campaign for agricultural co-operatives, the movement in this direction is slow. But this is not the only reason. A more important reason, perhaps, is that in Cuba, where the small peasant has more land than his Russian, Chinese, Bulgarian or Czechoslovak counterparts owned in their time, and where he enjoys state aid in the form of cheap bank credit, advantageous purchasing prices, supply of machinery, technical aid, fertilisers, etc., the small peasant does not feel any urgent pressure to join a co-operative. He can retain the individual forms of property more to his taste and still see his income grow.
> It may be asked: is not this situation likely to lead to the development of capitalism in the countryside? The Cuban revolutionary leadership has not forgotten Lenin's warning that small property engenders capitalism every day, every hour, every minute. But then the small peasants do not carry the same weight in the Cuban economy as they did in nearly all other socialist countries. As we have seen, in Cuba the small peasants are an island in a socialist ocean.

The slowness of the peasants' progress to socialism, coupled with an alteration of developmental strategy, seems to have decided the government to put less faith in the growth of peasant collectives (agricultural societies) and to look for means of incorporating peasant agriculture in the state sector without any breach of faith in regard to peasant property and freedom of choice.

The change of strategy is announced in clear lines in the 1969 report to CEPAL. The government puts first the elimination of external political and economic dependence, considered as the main cause of underdevelopment, and the transformation of internal structures opposed to the general development. This implies the attainment of socialised property *(la propriedad social)* in the strategic sectors and branches, the power to dispose of natural resources in the most advantageous form possible for the country, and full control of foreign trade. This means the avoidance of over-dependence on foreign powers which might restrict policy options, and full command by the state over resources. The report gives primacy to the task of transforming human beings in respect of their skills, their culture and their social consciousness, that is to say, the precondition of the *hombre nuevo,* for the achievement of communism. It then proceeds to declare that the 'fundamental pivot of the politics of accelerated development' is the agricultural sector, with industry planned to service the development of agriculture and to transform its products. The most rapid growth is to be in coffee, meat, citrus and nickel.

In view of the urgency of the agricultural development programme, and the willingness of the government to invest in it, there is little room in the thinking of the planners for the tentative and uneven advances which might be expected from small proprietors, guided by campaigns of extension, guided credit, etc. While there is no talk of a third land reform, and a frequent reiteration of the policy of honouring peasant proprietorship, the peasants' land and labour are required in the framework of larger plans.

The policy of depletion of the peasant sector is composed of 'push' and 'pull' elements, and does not rule out the formation of agricultural societies:

i. The main push factor is the potential for pressure which the government retains in the control of inputs for the peasant economy. This includes the supply of fertilizers and machinery, and perhaps even more important, of labour, since crops like tomatoes and coffee, even when grown on a small scale, require harvest labour. But clearly any excessive use of these pressures could endanger production.

ii. The state enterprises become focal centres of urbanisation and even if the wage-earner status has little attraction, the access to facilities such as better and more sanitary houses, schools, sport and cultural facilities acquire urban magnetism.

iii. The rupture of peasant tradition and succession by the transformation of the cultural aspiration and motivation of the young may be the most important though more gradual means. This is effected by the vast programme of education, and especially the boarding schools set up for peasant children from the more remote areas. In these schools, the young are educated for specialist roles in agriculture, as specialists in mechanical vehicles, in artificial insemination, in grafting, in accountancy, and lead away from the image of peasant livelihood with its polyvalent rudimentary labour. The scale on which these schools operate, with other forms of technical and further education, is expected to leave many peasants without successors wishing to take up the holding.

iv. In cases where no heir wishes to take up his peasant father's farm, the ageing peasant may permute his property for a retirement pension, retaining his house and garden if he wishes. The government is also ready and disposed to buy the farm of any peasant who wishes to move out, provided it is close enough to one of its existing units.

v. Finally, the various state corporations of specialist production (i.e. citrus, kenaf, rice etc.) have recently taken the initiative in approaching smallholding peasants whose lands are suitable for growing their product, offering to rent the property for a fixed sum annually, with the exception of a subsistence parcel around the house. Thus, a peasant might rent to the state 12–13 hectares of his 14-hectare property, keeping 1–2 hectares to use as he pleases. The deal may also include the offer of permanent wage work on the land, held by the state corporation. Thus, the peasant would become rentier-labourer, with his own provision ground – a not unenviable situation, with the added advantage that it provides some local elasticity to food supplies.

NOTES

1. Data used here come from a study done by the author when working with UNESCO in 1959 and studying the possibilities of including local research projects in the curriculum of the Normal School at San Pablo, Canton of Otavalo. The Normal School itself demonstrated the contradictions of the 'estamental' class system. Set in a profoundly rural situation, it was almost entirely recruited from the 'townsfolk' class, and the students distinguished themselves by organising a strike on behalf of the substitution of French language teaching for Quechua, the language of the children they would be expected to teach, and whose language they did not care to know.

2. Work on Tenza was done in 1963 by the author and Salomon Rivera, when the author worked in the Department of Sociology at the National University, Bogota, on behalf of UNESCO. At the time of writing, a re-study of Tenza is in progress.

3. Studies in Pupuya and Lo Abarca both quoted here were done as part of a wider study of small-holding landgroups and villages in Chile directed by the author when working for FAO in Chile with the Instituto Chileno de Investigacion en Reforma Agraria. The Pupuya study was done by Salomon Rivera and that of Lo Abarca by John Rowley.

VII

The Terms of Incorporation

To conclude, an attempt is made to restate the model of the historic dilemma of the peasantry. Attention is drawn to the expansion of industrial production in the developed countries and, in a more sporadic, irrational and disseminated manner, in the dependent developing countries of Latin America, setting in motion in areas of low technology and mercantility which rely upon self-provisioning systems, an outward-moving market frontier of the already nationally articulated network. But in order to assess this vital encounter, it is necessary to have an image of market organisation prior to the consolidation of the national markets.

Throughout most of their post-Colombian history, the economic organisations of the territories may be envisaged roughly as follows:

i. Zones of intensive production of minerals and agricultural goods directly linked to the European market (and later to the North American), in which a small sector of the population also consumed goods imported from these same European markets.

ii. Intermediate regional and local systems of exchange, some linked to the export zones, based on a surplus producing peasantry, an exchange network involving some specialised urban and rural craft production, making possible the maintenance of non-producing sectors of urban population, but restricted in extent due to the difficulties of transport and absence of sources of power and developed technology.

iii. Patches of quasi-autonomous self-provisioning peasant and pre-peasant settlement with a low level of involvement with the other kinds of market systems.

This fragmentary pattern has in the last decades been submitted to the unifying influence of growing national market systems as centres of industrial production have grown up and, with the expansion of road-building and motor transport and other forms of communication, brought within their networks all important centres of economic activity within each nation. Viewed from the rural periphery, this must be seen as an 'incorporative drive' to include the hitherto self-provisioning economies within the national market system, particularly seeking out the marginal sellers of rural produce and cheap labour, as well as buyers of the new factory-made goods.

The encounter between the expanding national and international system and the self-provisioning rural economies has been one of the leading themes of recent history in the Latin American hinterland. In contrast with the persistence of the present expansive movement, past centuries have seen frequent sporadic (and often violent) encounters and equally frequent relapses, market retractions, followed by recoil into subsistence and local systems (Frank, 1969). But the same growth of a national market has had other effects which run parallel to the geographical expansion of the market area itself, namely the headlong expansion of government activity and the bureaucracy, and the growth of the political power of the middle sectors. So parallel with penetration of the market there is an 'institutional penetration' seeking to incorporate the peasantry in a variety of local segments of national organisations, whether schools or home-improvement classes, new church organisations, political parties, peasant unions, co-operatives, and 'pilot schemes' of all kinds. Persistent pressure to expand the range of activities of national institutions and services is one of the main inputs of the emerging middle strata (created by the urban industrial and commercial expansion) whose members, seeking their urban livelihood in a typically atomized style, attempt to increase government allocation of funds to their particular spot in the network, siphoning off what they can from the flow of goods and services between the agricultural periphery and the large urban centres.

The inherently expansive quality of the political administrative nucleus, providing jobs, political followings and the less tangible satisfactions of unremunerative welfare and salvationist roles must be recognised as generative of institutional penetration, and one cause of the frequent incongruence of rural development and welfare programmes with the real needs of country people (Pearse, 1971).

These processes, emanating from the urban industrial core of the national societies, are conceptualised as an overall (and almost involuntary) impulse to incorporate the discrete peripheral social and economic systems upon which much of rural life has rested. It is analysed as a three-pronged process of penetration (market, communications and institutions) whose elements, operating together in the causation of social change, are operationally separable from one another.

Without overlooking the continuing processes of internally generated or endogenous change (such as the generalised decline in resource-ratio) attention is drawn to the way in which this three-fold penetration of the landgroup brings about change in peasant conduct in the framework of general structural change. The central motor force of landgroup momentum is supplied by the daily pursuit of livelihood through agricultural and craft production, using customary technical means worked out within the limitations of the local ecosystem. Closely woven into the complex of productive activities then is the form of social organisation prescribing ways of regulating work, of distributing the product, of transferring and transmitting land and capital goods, of settling disputes, and handling the internal situations affecting the group. So the landgroup system may be seen as a group of families pursuing 'livelihood goals', endowed with a patrimony of natural resources and a set of 'technical and institutional means or instruments' for achieving them.

So long as livelihood goals are tolerably matched by available resources and technical and institutional means, there is no predisposition to change. However, each of these factors is liable to alteration in such a way as to produce incongruity leading to decisions to adopt other conducts, to modify institutions, to change techniques, to make different economic arrangements.

Changes in resource base may arise from natural phenomena such as pests or drought, or from external interference; or there may be a resource-ratio decline due to increasing population, which, as we have seen, is one of the most constant initiators of change. These changes had more importance in pre-industrial pre-national-market conditions. Changes under the impact of this three-fold penetration produces a contrapuntal movement between the means of securing livelihood under new conditions, and a changing field of perceptions and aspirations about the quality and level of livelihood itself.

Although the subsistence system rests mainly on family production, it requires a network of internal exchange of products both of agriculture and of crafts, as well as of labour. The supply of cheap manufactured goods has, under certain conditions, put an end to local craft production, and as sales increase so does the demand for money for individual use. An increase in market oriented production is one method of adding to a family's money income, while the sale of labour to entrepreneurs in other places does the same for the individual family member, whether or not this benefits his family directly. Reliance on market production opens the peasant household to the ups and downs of market prices and changing tastes and standards, and may require industrial inputs, the purchase of which needs credit. It also implies a relationship of daily importance with a usually urban or village trader who, as we have noted frequently, acquires ascendancy by manipulation of the roles of buyer of produce, purveyor of inputs and consumer goods, and 'banker'. These forms of commercial clientalism upset local systems of exchange for obtaining seed, usufruct of land and occasional labour. The decline of the subsistence system and an increasing adoption of town patterns of consumption produces incongruity between amplifying livelihood goals and failing technical and institutional means. Equally common are changes in the conditions of the market for surpluses, either by the termination of demand for a product or simply a decline in the price offered. The quiet joys of a self-provisioned life of homespuns and potatoes begins to pall, and the son of the household is no longer ready to labour for his father in return for his keep, nor to offer his labour without salary to a neighbour in the expectation that the latter will return the day's work to the family economy. The general drift of this kind of change is towards increasing difficulty in meeting local needs from local production and resources and an ever-increasing need for money.

The effect of the general inclusion of all forms of exchange within the domain of the market economy, the spread of the desire and need for urban originated or industrially made goods to all aspects of daily life, and the increased interaction and communication between city and landgroup as money becomes a universal means of exchange, create a situation in which all goods and services get a price, and their free flow along channels of institutional obligation is substituted by an inhibiting accountancy.

The obsolescence of the subsistence system in the economic sense is accompanied by a loss of effectiveness of the landgroup institutions, and under the new circumstances the primary asset is not the control of local resources but ability to manage the nexus with the town and the larger society, not only for obtaining credit and commercial advantage, but also for getting the benefits which the new agencies offer and the prestige which association with them confers locally. As available facilities grow, so new distributive principles begin to operate. Ownership of land and family labour still count, but to a reduced extent. Ability to manage urban cultural forms, the prestige necessary to do business, an entree to the bureaucracy, are assets of equal or greater importance. Local political influence also becomes a powerful asset in bargaining with the establishment and in securing town and nexus allies. Those who achieve a standing in the town are now able to obtain credit, and so free themselves from agricultural tasks, hiring labour for commercial production on their own land and for the purchase of non-agricultural capital goods for processing, elaborating, transporting and trading. Their new livelihood is made by access to cheap labour, advantage in obtaining facilities of urban origin, and profits in what comes into and goes out of the neighbourhood.

So the decline of the subsistence system, and incorporation in the market and political complex, draws out a 'progressive' element within the landgroup. This sector becomes economically differentiated from the rest of the peasantry by its ability to operate on the market, to use rather than be used as labour, and to benefit from new facilities. They are in the same line of business as the old nexus groups of townsfolk and become their rivals and allies. Urbanity, schooling, government legitimised office in welfare organisation and in politics put the official stamp on their distinction. Social differentiation follows the economic, and the cut between social strata no longer divides landgroup from town, but passes through the landgroup, and lines up the 'progressive' smallholders with the townsfolk stratum. Increasingly, they adopt elements of urban culture, and their town acquaintances provide an alternative reference group for their conduct.

Those whose resource base gives them no relief from hardship, and who are unable to deal directly and adequately with the new sources of benefits, and the markets in the town, are obliged to rely upon the new and old nexus men for whatever they can get. But from all that we have seen and read, their situation deteriorates, since it straddles uncomfortably the failing succour of self-provision and a disadvantageous market position for the disposal of their produce. Attempts have been made, both by state organs for promoting credit and co-operatives, and by merchandising and manufacturing corporations (e.g. sugar, beet, coffee, milk and cheese products, etc.) to facilitate and stabilise their production and marketing, with varying success.

Indeed, the majority of the peasantry has neither the resources nor the social advantages necessary to make the full re-orientation necessary to benefit from incorporation, and they are forced into a bad bargain with the society. Dependence on the institutions of the landgroup, now in the process of decay, does not provide security. And if a certain proportion still manages to make ends meet with market-adjunct economies, especially where credits are provided institutionally, increasing numbers become marginal improvisors of livelihood, relying on the sale of their labour in other sectors of the economy.

Does the process of differentiation lead to a class antagonism within the smallholders' landgroup? Insofar as it is worth attempting any general answer, it is that the landgroup as a social system becomes increasingly conflictive and atomized, and that the new bifurcation in regard to the means of pursuing livelihood (as between land-and-labour, and credit and urban connections) is an important element underlying the hostile factions, but other factors confuse any clear confrontation. For instance, insofar as the 'progressives' adopt community leadership roles, they continue to perform a service to the collectivity of members having common local interests. Old rivalries between clusters of kin continue to define factional sides. And clientism still makes many of the Rump peasants the clients of the 'progressives'. A further, often artificial, dimension of the landgroup conflict is the recruitment of rival factions to rival political parties, not so much differentiated by distinct policies as by rival personalities and vote-seeking machines at the level of the town.

So the terms of incorporation are: on the one hand, successful entry to commercial relations in the national market, insertion in communications circuits and adoption of roles in new urban-based political, cultural and welfare institutions by a reduced section of the peasantry, proprietors, traders, commercial share-tenants, technical personnel; and on the other hand, for the majority, a process of forced marginalisation. By this is meant the loss of a clear, predictable and institutionalised means of livelihood: the declining possibility of building livelihood on the landgroup subsistence system and market-adjunct economies, or on estate service-tenancies, the inability of the more productive sectors of agricultural and industrial economy and tertiary occupations to absorb more than a fraction of those with labour to sell.

Marginalisation also aptly describes the effects of this dilemma on social life. Most of the rural population must improvise livelihood by means of occupational polyvalance. This means the sporadic grasping at the possibilities of work, income or land by the individual members of the family wherever or whenever the opportunity arises – upsetting stable family life and persistent community relations which the landgroup made possible for the peasant. As alienation from the land increases, there is a growth of precarious residence in the interstitial or marginal village squeezed between landed properties to whose land they have no access, whose pathological social qualities were already subject to comment with the growth of the Uruguayan *rancherios* in the nineteenth century (Rovetta, 1962), or on the edges of the towns where scanty occupational openings are more diverse, and where more crumbs fall.

The landgroup itself loses its corporate quality, its resources for mutual assistance, as each nuclear family is forced to face the market alone; and each neighbourhood hides growing numbers of destitutes, making possible a 'structural' hunger, or hunger not from pests and drought, but from maldistribution of land and working capital.

Is it possible to quantify this transformation? Domike (1967:10) calculates that of the agricultural labour force in the seven ICAD countries (comprising about two-thirds of the total and also of the rural population of the region):

i. approximately *one half* worked on smallholdings, mainly family properties,

ii. *more than one quarter* worked and lived on estates in which they enjoyed usufructuary rights to land as part-recompense for their labour, and

iii. *less than one quarter* were 'landless or temporary estate workers'.

This distribution refers approximately to the situation around 1960, when one half of the smallholder sector (described as *'minifundio'*) was confined to 2.2% of the total farmlands (Feder, 1966:82), and in fact supported a labour force of 5 times that which these lands required, even at a low level of technology (ibid.:97). This sector received virtually no relief from the Land Reforms, (except perhaps in Venezuela where that problem was not acute) which confined their attentions to the distribution of farms, estates or state lands, and their dilemma takes various forms (Pearse, 1970). Fractioned *minifundia* may be occupied by aged couples whose children have migrated, or mothers of families receiving remittances and occasional visits from husbands earning in distant parts; small proprietors without credit in areas of commercial production may find themselves share-croppers on their own lands, paying half the crop to suppliers of artificial fertilisers, seeds or machinery, or else labourers on their own land, rented out to town entrepreneurs. Much more general is the necessity of finding off-farm labour, earnings from which are padded out by subsistence farming. Is there such a thing as consolidation of smallholdings? In terms of property, there is little sign of this, though in fact a kind of consolidation takes place as single entrepreneurs gain control of the land and labour of various minifundia. Other variations include domestic cottage industries and crafts such as the making of *ojotas* and refabs, needle work, basket making and other manufacturing skills orientated to the urban market and not yet rendered entirely uneconomic by industrial production.

In contrast with the *minifundista* half of the smallholders, there were an equal number of peasants with a more adequate land-base for their family labour. Amongst this sector is to be found an appreciable number of technically well-managed economies, especially where institutional credit is available through government banks or private vertically-integrated corporations. But if the younger members of these families are unable to find *logement* and livelihood in the cities, then they are destined to enter the *minifundio* sector.

Changes on the service-tenure estates (involving Domike's (ii) category peasants) have been more dramatic than those in the smallholders' sector. The catalysts of change are the intensification of market relations, the increasing commercial value of land, and the support obtained by the service-tenants from governments, politicians and unions. Usufruct of land is no longer a sufficient recompense for labour – money and wages are required. And the baroque tangle of particularistic relations between patron and tenant-workers proved to be too inflexible to be organised for more rational production. The risks and inefficiencies of the system have led to the transforming of many of these traditional estates into farms large and small, with a reduced permanent labour force and recourse to the labour market when additional hands are needed. In some cases, estates have been given a 'multifarm' character by being let out to share- and cash-tenants, in others they have been divided and sold to commercial operators frequently of urban origin, using capital accumulated in other sectors of the economy. Governments have also intervened with land reforms expropriating a certain proportion of the estates and have divided them between the share tenants under terms making commercial farming possible (e.g. in Chile) or simply by transferring to the estate peasants the property of their usufruct land (e.g. Ecuador). In this latter case, the tendency is for the estate to be reorganised, making use of the peasant labour from the new *minifundia* implanted around them.

Feder points out that access to land becomes increasingly difficult for the peasant on account of its rising market value, sought after for speculation and as a hedge against inflation, as well as for agriculture. At the same time, the fragmentation of existing smallholders' lands by inheritance goes on, so an increasing number of peasants seek to live off lands which will not expand, while frontier lands taken by squatters and tenants, though they relieve immediate tensions, recapitulate the *minifundio* problem.

The steadily multiplying rural population finds itself caught between the attenuation of its subsistence land base, and the inability of the other sectors of the economy to provide stable livelihood. This is illustrated broadly in the population figures and census data on occupation. The broad picture is well known – the population increase averages 3% per year (see Table 19). There is already a strong flow of migration from the country to the cities, giving an average urban growth figure between 1950 and 1960 of 6%, and still a rural rate of 1.5% increase is maintained. But neither the rate nor the kind of expansion of the manufacturing sector of the economy is able to absorb more than a fraction of the annual increment in the labour force, with a result that the urban sector in which livelihood is eked out in 'non-basic services' grows at a startling 15%.

In Figure 2 I have shown some date (from CEPAL, 1964) about tendencies in employment and levels of production in the Latin American economies, 1950–1985. The economists have attempted to analyse the process of job-formation and labour absorption in the industrial sector, making projections up to 1985 on the basis of what happened between 1950 and 1962. A division has been made between forms of employment in the modern sector, and those of the 'subsistence' sector, including agriculture. (The word 'subsistence' is used here in a different sense from our own and refers to levels of remuneration averaging less than £280 per worker.) Thus,

TABLE 19

GNP ANNUAL GROWTH RATE AND PER CAPITAL FOOD PRODUCTION INDEX FOR LATIN AMERICA

Country	Population 1968	Degree of urbanization	Population increase in last inter-censal period			Annual growth rate of gross product 1955–64	Per capita food production index (average 1964–66 1957–59: 100)
			Total	Urban	Rural		
Argentina	23,616	57.7	1.8	3.0	0.4	0.6	100
Bolivia	4,439	19.6	—	—	—	0.4	97
Brazil	88,105	28.1	3.1	6.5	2.1	2.1	110
Chile	9,343	54.7	2.8	5.9	−0.2	1.0	92
Colombia	20,686	36.6	3.2	7.0	1.7	1.3	100
Costa Rica	1,667	24.0	4.0	4.5	3.8	1.3	88
Cuba	8,019	35.5	2.1	3.7	1.3	—	—
Dominican Republic	4,059	18.7	3.6	9.1	2.7	1.7	82
Ecuador	5,636	26.9	3.0	6.6	2.0	0.8	94
El Salvador	3,217	17.7	2.8	5.8	2.3	2.6	102
Guatemala	4,895	15.5	3.1	5.6	2.7	3.1	113
Haiti	4,973	5.1	—	—	—	−0.9	76
Honduras	2,413	11.6	3.0	8.1	2.5	0.7	110
Mexico	47,335	29.6	3.1	5.2	2.3	0.6	111
Nicaragua	1,904	23.0	2.6	5.9	1.9	0.0	99
Panama	1,318	33.1	2.9	4.5	2.3	3.4	103
Paraquay	2,258	15.9	2.7	2.8	2.6	−0.9	93
Peru	12,771	28.9	2.2	5.7	1.3	2.7	103
Uruquay	2,820	61.3	1.7	3.0	0.6	−0.9	115
Venezuela	10,061	47.3	3.7	7.3	1.4	2.0	128
Barbados	265	—	—	—	—	—	—
Guyana	713	—	—	—	—	—	—
Jamaica	1,792	24.8	1.5	4.1	0.9	—	—
Trinidad and Tobago	1,062	—	—	—	—	—	—

Source: Demographic, Social and Economic Indicators, Table 15 in CEPAL (1967:32–3)

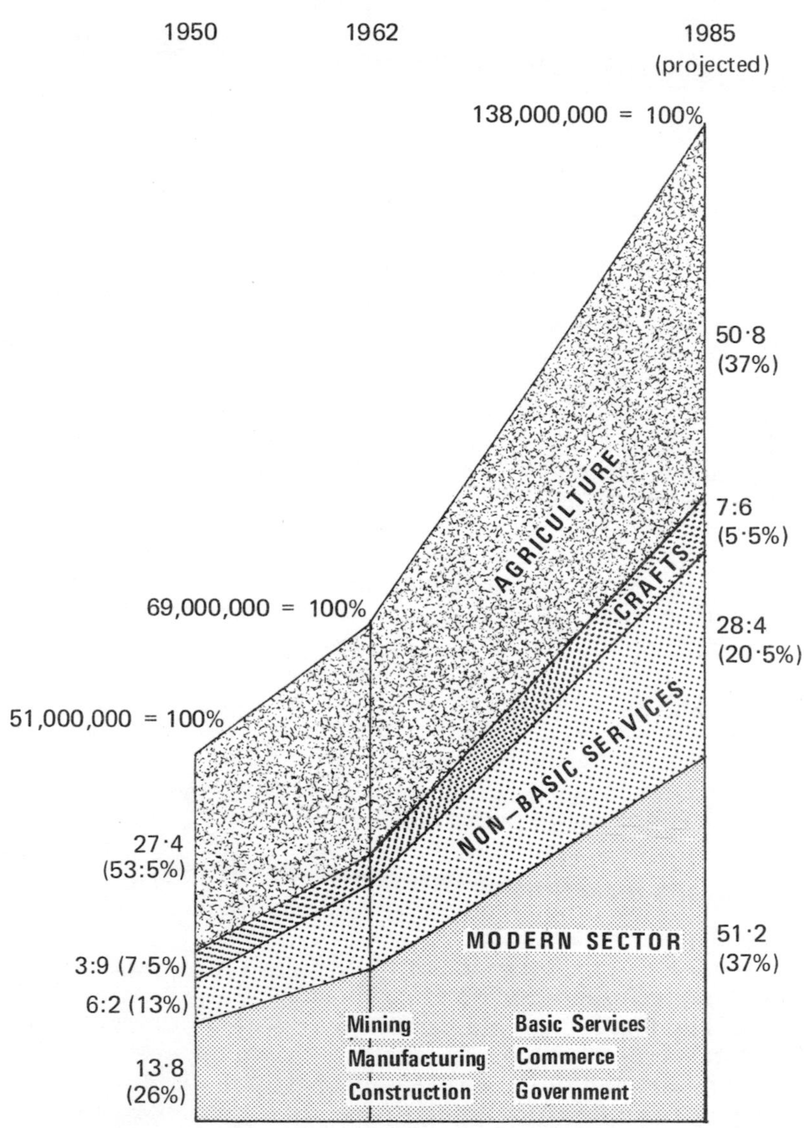
WORK FORCE IN SUBSISTENCE AND MODERN SECTOR
LATIN AMERICA 1950 - 62 - 85
1950
1962
1985
(projected)
138,000,000 = 100%
69,000,000 = 100%
51,000,000 = 100%
50·8
(37%)
7:6
(5·5%)
28:4
(20·5%)
51·2
(37%)
27·4
(53:5%)
3:9 (7·5%)
6:2 (13%)
13·8
(26%)
AGRICULTURE
CRAFTS
NON-BASIC SERVICES
MODERN SECTOR
Mining
Manufacturing
Construction
Basic Services
Commerce
Government

Fig. 2

they expect little improvement in levels of living for most of those who work in agriculture (with the exception of supervisory and technical personnel) and a great increase in 'non-basic services', a term defined as 'the urban catch-all for the effectively workless and underemployed living near subsistence levels' (Domike, 1967:3). This sector is projected as reaching 20.5% of the 'active' labour force by 1985, and is of course that part of the population which is creating the new 'squatments' of improvised housing which have become an essential and growing part of the cities in most developing countries. In addition, it must be pointed out that this sector is largely composed of immigrant peasants and rural labourers, and therefore are the host neighbourhoods to the sons and daughters of peasant families yet to come.

The unsatisfactory nature of these global figures is, of course, their way of hiding real situations in individual countries with more rapidly expanding or already expanded 'modern sectors', or low rates of population growth, which show greater powers of absorption of surplus rural population, while others will continue to struggle with the problems of the landed society by the old methods.

Whatever may be the risks of economic prediction based on observation of 'regular progression of sustained influences' (Cournot, 1923), they are small when compared with risks of positive social or political prediction. However, there are certain very important social consequences of the changes in agrarian structure, and especially in the effects of the loss of tutorial power in smallholders' and estate landgroups and the sudden growth of communications and geographical mobility, which must be taken into account in future calculations. The most important of these have to do with changes in the peasants' capacity for action, a 'deconstriction' resulting from the break down of the system of social control which depended on the quasi-exclusive conduct-guiding role of the landgroup, and multiplication of conduct-alternatives by mass communication and mobility.

In recent years, we have been told a great deal about the limitations of the culture and personality of 'the peasant' and especially the 'Indian'. But it is more realistic to think of sub-cultural systems and the personalities they nourish as responses to real situations. Peasants have a 'limited view of the world' not because this is a universal of peasant psychology but because of the real absence of alternatives. And even where certain constraints and fears become a part of the cultural baggage transmitted in the process of socialising the young, the alteration of the structural matrix of peasant life, the leap forward in the intensification of mobility and communication puts the old norms of upbringing, and the efficacy and appropriateness of traditional socialisation to the new life-situation in doubt. The old saints won't play, the neighbours are obliged to deny co-operation, the old authorities dwindle into figures of obscure custom, the new rich ride athwart the folkways and respect (fear of sanctions for failing to fulfill status-ascribed duties) is dying. Young people of very different character are beginning to appear, and the difference was symbolised in the works of the old informant in Tenza (page 219) who described the return of the peasant conscripts 'no longer the timid youths who bid a tearful farewell to their parents', their night of demonstrative violence, and their departure on the morrow to look for work in the city. A glimpse of the depth of change, implying an outright break with parental authority and norms, showed itself amongst the Ex-Pupils' Centre of Lo Abarco (page 230). These young people became a self-aware group, already emancipated from local control.

Fuenzalida is also very much aware of the categoric nature of the break between the young and their 'traditional' parents in many parts of Peru, most marked perhaps amongst the townsfolk class, but noticeable too amongst the peasants. Speaking of the townsfolk *(misti)* of the rural centre, Pisaj, he says that the young 'think of themselves as a group with a special identity of its own'. They have little interest in exploiting the land, believe in modern things, technical change, left-wing politics, and are more flexible in their attitude to the *indigena.* The peasant young *(majtas)*, though not so radical in their break with their parents, also think of themselves as a group apart; are highly mobile, though they find few job-opportunities and return home pressing for assimilation in *misti* sub-culture, especially in dress and language. They 'move into a more ample network of communications and are more exposed than their parents to urban stimuli . . . they imitate *misti* behaviour and often supplant the latter if the opportunity is offered . . . '.

And, putting together the essential significance of generational status in a period of headlong change, Fuenzalida observes: 'At all levels of rural society, the traditional groups are broken down and reintegrate themselves in the system in new positions by means of their young people' (Fuenzalida 1969:79).

A main feature of these transformations is the breakdown of the landgroup and the loss of its inner logic and conduct-guiding power, and the attachment of the individual rural person (withdrawn from both family and landgroup matrix) to age-sex peer groups and 'vertical' social aggregates and circuits, that is to say, to city-based and probably national corporations, movements, firms, associations, followings, and cults, in connection with political, social and economic aspirations and needs. This means that the conceptual apparatus we have used so far is inadequate to explain the new scene.

Thus at first sight the distinguishing features of the coming situation are two:

> A prolonged and interrupted collision between the generational effluence of the dissolving peasantry, part rural and part urban, encouraged by schooling and by constant public promises to look forward at least to the decent appurtenances of livelihood in return for labour, yet denied and rejected by the economy and condemned to uncertainty about next year's food and welfare.
>
> An available political force likely to be captured by new forms of populism and adventism, subject to ingenious palliatives and repressive policies, and ultimately able to support a leadership offering revolutionary re-ordering of society and redistribution of the means of livelihood.

Bibliography

Abascal y Sousa, José Fernando, 1944, *Memoria de Gobierno Tomo I, Viceroy of Peru 1806–1816,* Sevilla.

Acosta, José de, 1940, [1950], *Historia Natural y Moral de las Indias,* Mexico.

Ahumada, J., 1966, 'Hypotheses for the Diagnosis of a Situation of Social Change: The Case of Venezuela', Ch.1 in *Studying the Venezuelan Polity,* Cambridge, Mass.: Harvard University Press.

Antezana, Luis E., 1955, *Resultados de la Reforma Agraria en Bolivia,* Cochabamba. Privately printed by Imprimeria F. O. Guenca Sucs.

Aranda, Sergio, 1968, *La revolución agraria en Cuba,* Mexico, Siglo XXI.

Arcila-Farias, Eduardo, 1957, *El régimen de la encomienda en Venezuela,* Caracas.

Aron, Adrianne, 1966, *Local Government in Bolivia,* presented to American Anthropologists' Association meeting, Pittsburg, Pennsylvania.

Azevedo, Maria, 1963, *Camaçari, Estrutura Agrária,* Relatório Preliminar, Instituto de Ciências Sociais da Universidade de Bahia.

Bagú, Sergio, 1952, *Estructura Social de la Colonia,* Buenos Aires.

Bandelier, 1880, *On the Distribution and Tenure of Land Among the Ancient Mexicans,* reprinted by Peabody Museum, Harvard.

Barcelli, S. Augustin, 1956, *Mediosiglo de luchas sindicales revolucionarias en Bolivia,* La Paz.

Barnes, Kathleen, 1965, Mimeographed drafts for report on Land Tenure in Bolivia by the Interamerican Committee for Agricultural Development.

Barnet, Miguel, 1966, *Biografia de un Cimarrón,* La Habana: Instituto de Etnologia y Folklore.

Barran, J. P. and Nahum, B., 1967, *Historia Rural del Uruguay Moderno*, Montevideo: Ediciones de La Banda Oriental.

Basadre, J., 1937, *El régimen de las mitas,* Lima.

Belaunde, Guinassi M., 1945, *La encomienda en el Perú,* Lima: Editorial Mercurio Peruano.

Bendix, R. and Lipset, S. M., 1968, *Class, Status and Power,* London: Routledge.

Blasier, C., 1966, 'Power and Social Change in Colombia – Cauca Valley', *Interamerican Studies Journal,* July, 386–410.

Bonifaz, Miguel, 1953, *Legislación agrario-indigenal,* Cochabamba: (probably private).

Borde, Jean and Góngora, Mario, 1956, *Evolución de la propriedad rural en el Valle del Puangue,* Santiago de Chile: Universidad de Chile.

Bourricaud, F., 1962, *Changements à Puno,* Paris: Institut des Hautes Etudes de l'Amérique Latine.

Brandão Lopez, 1968, *Desenvolvimento e Mudança Social,* São Paulo: Companhia Editôra Nacional.

Cândido, Antonio, 1954, 'A familia caipira', *Sociologia,* XVI: 4, São Paulo.

Cândido, Antonio, 1964, *Os parceiros do Rio Bonito,* Rio de Janeiro: Livraria José Olympia.

Canelas, Amado, 1966, *Mito y Realidad de la Reforma Agraria,* La Paz.

Carter, William, E., 1964, *Aymara Communities and the Bolivian Agrarian Reform,* U.S.A.: University of Florida Press.

Castro, J., 1965, *Une zone explosive: le Nordeste du Brésil,* Paris: Editions du Seuil.

CEPAL (United Nations: Economic Commission for Latin America), 1967a, *Estudio Economico de America Latina,* Santiago.

CEPAL, 1967b, *Urbanización y tendencias de cambio en la sociedad rural en Latino-America* (mimeo), Santiago.

Chevalier, François, 1963, *Land and Society in Colonial Mexico,* Los Angeles.

Chevalier, François, 1968, 'La expansión de la gran propriedad en el siglo XIX', *Communidades,* III: 8.

Chonchol, Jacques, 1961, *La Reforma Agraria Cubana – Realizaciones y Perspectivas,* (mimeo), Havana.

CLAPCS, Centro Latino-Americano de Pesquisas em Ciências Sociais, 1960, *Resistências à Mudança,* Rio de Janeiro.

Clark, R. J., 1968, *Land Reform and Peasant Market Participation in the Northern Highlands of Bolivia,* Washington: Pan American Union.

CNRS (Centre National de la Recherche Scientifique), 1967, *Les Problèmes Agraires des Amériques Latines,* Paris.

Collarte, Juan Carlos, 1969, A paper read at the Latin American Centre, Oxford.

Comitas, Lambros, 1968, 'Educación y Estratifacación Social en Bolivia', *América Indigena* 28, 631–651, La Paz.

Condarco Morales, Ramiro, 1965, *Zárate, El Temible Willka,* La Paz.

Cook and Simpson, 1948, 'The Population of Central Mexico in the Sixteenth Century', *Ibero-Americana* 31, Los Angeles.

Correia de Andrade, 1964, *A Terra e o Homem no Nordeste,* São Paulo: Editôra Brasiliense.

Cournot, 1923, *Essais sur les fondements de nos connaissances,* Paris.

Craig, Wesley W., 1969, 'Peru: The Peasant Movement of La Convención' in *Landsberger* (ed), 1969, pp.274–296.

Cuba, 1969, *Informe de la delegación de Cuba a CEPAL,* (mimeo), La Habana.

Cunill, Pedro, 1966, *L'Amérique Andine,* Paris.

Dandler-Hanhart, Jorge, 1967, *Local Group, Community and Nation,* Bolivia (1935–1952), M.A. Thesis, University of Wisconsin.

Dean, Warren, 1966, 'The Planter as Entrepreneur', *Hispanic American Historical Review,* XLVI: 2.

Debien, G., 1956, *Etudes Antillaises,* Paris.

Delgado, Oscar, 1968, Mimeographed drafts for report on land tenure in Bolivia by the Interamerican Committee for Agricultural Development.

Dennis, Pierre, 1911, *Brazil,* tr: Bernard Miall, London.

Diégues, Jr., Manuel, 1960, Regiões Culturais do Brasil, Rio de Janeiro: Ministério da Educação e Cultura.

Dión, H. G., 1950, *La Agricultura en el Altiplano,* La Paz.

Domike, Arthur

Du Moulin, J., 1965, 'Monocultivo y proletarización: dos ejemplos de Las Villas' in *Ciencias Sociales Contemporaneos,* I: 1, La Habana.

Duran, Marc Antonio, 1965, 'El estancamiento en la organisación interna do los ejidos', *Trimestre Económico, Vol. XXXII,* No. 127, Mexico.

Eckstein, Salomon, 1966, *El ejído colectivo en Mexico,* Mexico: Fondo de Cultura Económica.

Erasmus, C. H., October 1967, 'Upper Limits of peasantry and agrarian reform', *Ethnology* 6: 4, Pittsburgh.

Feder, E., 1968, *Review of Land Tenure changes and of Land Reform in the 1960's.* Draft – mimeo (for U.N.).

Feder, Ernest, 1966, *Societal Opposition to Peasant Movements.* Paper given at Cornell Seminar on Latin American Peasant Movements.

Feder, Ernest, 1971, *The Rape of the Peasantry,* New York: Anchor Books.

Finlay, M. I. 1969, *Slavery in Classical Antiquity,* London.

Flores, Edmundo, May 1964, 'Land Reform in Bolivia', *Land Economics,* XXX: 2.

Frank, A. G., 1969, *Capitalism and Underdevelopment in Latin America,* London: Monthly Review Press.

Friede, Juan, 1944, *El indio en lucha por la tierra,* Bogotá: Ediciones Espiral.

Friede, Juan, 1963, *Los Quimbayos Bajo la Dominación Española,* Bogotá.

Fuenzalida, V. Fernando, 1969, 'El mito de la Sociedad Triétnica' (mimeo), IX Congreso Latinoamericano de Sociologia.

Gage, Thomas, (ed. A. P. Newton), 1946, *The English-American: A New New Survey of the West Indies,* London.

Garica, Antonio, 1970, 'Los Sindicatos en el Esquema de Revolución Nacional', *El Trimestre Económico,* XXXIII: 132.

Garcilaso de la Vega, 1943, *Comentarios Reales de Los Incas,* Buenos Aires.

Gibson, Charles, 1964, *The Aztecs under Spanish Rule,* California: Stanford University Press.

Gibson, Charles, 1967, *Spain in America,* New York: Harper and Row.

Gomez-Tagle, Silvia, 1968, *Organización de las Sociedades de Crédito Ejidal en la Laguna,* Master's Thesis, UNAM, Mexico.

Guerra y Sanchez, R., 1964, *Sugar and Society in the Caribbean,* Newhaven: Yale University Press.

Hanke, Lewis (ed), 1969, *History of Latin American Civilization: Sources and Interpretations.* Vol. 1, 'The Colonial Experience', London: Methuen.

Haring, C. H., 1947, *The Spanish Empire in America,* New York.

Hassaurek, 1868, *Four years among Spanish-Americans,* New York.

Head, F. Bond, 1967 [1826], *Journeys across the Pampas and among the Andes.* London.

Heath, Dwight B., 1960, 'Land Tenure and Social Organisation: An ethno-historical study from the Bolivian Oriente', *Inter-American Economic Affairs,* 13: 2.

Heath, Dwight B., 1966, 'The Aymara Indians and Bolivia's Revolution', *Inter-American Economic Affairs,* XIX: 4.

Herbert, Jean-Loup, 1969, *Una comunidad frente al capitalismo de una estructura colonial* (mimeo). Presented at IX Latin American Congress of Sociology, Mexico.

Hewitt, Cynthia, 1969, 'Brazil: The Peasant Movement of Pernambuco, 1961–1964, in *Landsberger.*

Hill, G. W. and Gollas, Manuel, 1968, *Minifundia, economy and society of the Guatemalan Highland Indian* (mimeo) Land Tenure Centre, Wisconsin University.

Hobsbawm, E. J., 1967, 'Problèmes Agraires à la Convención' in *CNRS* pp.395–407, Paris.

Huizer, Gerrit, 1969, Mimeographed report to the International Labour Office on peasant organisations in Latin America.

Humboldt, A. von, 1811, *Political Essay on the Kingdom of New Spain*, New York: John Black.

Hutchinson, H. W., 1957, *Village and Plantation Life in North-eastern Brazil*, Seattle: University of Washington.

ICAD (Interamerican Committee for Agricultural Development), 1966, *BRAZIL, Land Tenure Conditions and Socio-Economic Development of the Agricultural Sector. BRAZIL, Pôsse e uso da terra e desenvolvimento socio-económico do setor agricola*, Washington.

ICAD, 1966, *CHILE, Tenencia de la tierra y desarrollo socio-económico del sector agricola, Santiago.*

ICAD, 1965, *ECUADOR, Tenencia de la tierra y desarrollo socio-económico del sector agricola*, Washington.

ICAD, 1965, *GUATEMALA, Tenencia de la tierra y desarrollo socio-económico del sector agricola*, Washington: Panamerican Union.

ILO (International Labour Office), 1964, *Agrarian Reform, with particular reference to employment and social aspects*, Geneva.

ILO, 1955, *Living and Working Conditions of Indigenous Populations in Independent Countries*, Geneva.

ILO, 1966, *Plantation Workers*, Geneva.

ILO, 1957, *The Landless Farmer in Latin America*, Geneva.

Juan, G. and Ulloa A. de, 1955 [1772], *A Voyage to South America* in Keen, 1955.

Julião, Francisco, 1968, *Cambão: La cara oculta de Brasil, Mexico:* Siglo XXI.

Katz, F., 1966, *Situación Social y Económica de los Aztecas Durante los Siglos XV y XVI,* Mexico: Universidad Nacional Autónoma de México, Instituto de Investigaciones Historicas.

Kay, Cristobal, 1971, *Comparative Development of the European Manorial System and the Latin American Hacienda System,* Doctoral Thesis, University of Sussex.

Keen, Benjamin, 1955, *Readings in Latin American Civilisation,* Cambridge, Mass.: The Riverside Press.

Koster, H., 1816, *Travels in Brazil,* London.

Kubler, George, 1952, *The Indian Caste of Peru, 1795–1950: A Population Study based upon Tax Records and Census Reports,* Washington, D.C.: Smithsonian Institution, Institute of Social Anthropology.

Kubler, G., 'The Quechua in the Colonial World' in *Steward,* 1946–50.

Landsberger, Henry, A. (ed) 1969, *Latin American Peasants Movements,* London, Cornell University Press.

Leons, Madeleine, 1965, 'Changing patterns of social stratification in an emergent Bolivian Community', Ph.D. thesis in Anthropology at the University of Los Angeles.

Lewin, Boleslao, 1957, *La Rebelión de Túpac Amaru y los origenes de la emancipación Americana,* Buenos Aires.

Lévy-Bruhl, Henri, 1934, 'Theorie de l'esclavage', in Finlay, 1959, p.151.

Liévano, 1962–63 approx., *Los Grandes Conflictos Sociales y Economicos de Nuestra Historia,* 4 vols., Bogotá: La Nueva Prensa.

Lins do Rêgo, 1932, *Menino do Engenho,* Rio de Janeiro: José Olympia.

Lins do Rêgo, José, 1966, *Plantation Boy* (tr. of Menino do Engenho), New York: Alfred Knopf.

Lliévano, Indalecio, 1972, *España y las lachas sociales del Nuevo Mundo,* Editora Nacional, Madrid.

Lora, Guillermo, 1967, *Historia de Movimiento Obrero Boliviano,* La Paz.

Lynch, John 1958, *Spanish Colonial Administration 1782–1810,* London: The Athlone Press.

Martinez-Alier, Juan, 1969 (approx.). Manuscript, Notas sobre la primera reforma agraria en Cuba.

Mathiason, J. Roland, 1967, *Political Organisation and Attitudes among Venezuelan Peasants,* Ph.D. Thesis, Massachusetts Institute of Technology.

McBride, George M., 1923, *The Land Systems of Mexico,* New York.

McBride, George M., 1936, *Chile, Land and Society,* New York, American Geographical Society, Research Series.

McBride, Jorge, *Chile, su tierra y su gente,* Santiago: Prensas de la Universidad de Chile.

McEwen, W. J., et al., 1969, *Changing Rural Bolivia* (Research Institute for the Study of Man, Bolivia Project), New York.

Means, Philip Ainsworth, 1932, *Fall of the Inca Empire and the Spanish Rule in Peru, 1530–1780.*

Mellafe, R., 1964, *La Esclavitude en Hispanoamerica,* Buenos Aires: Editorial Universitaria de Buenos Aires.

Metraux, Alfred, 1960, 'Résistance au Changement', in CLAPCS *Resistências à Mudanca,* pp.71–81.

Miranda, Nestor, 1969, *Kolonialklientelism: Eine ethnosoziologische Analyse des Repartimiento-Encomienda-Systems Antillen 1492–1525,* Thesis, Heidelberg University.

Monbeig, P., 1952, *Pionniers et Planteurs de São Paulo,* Paris.

Mora, José Maria Luis, 1837, *Obras Sueltas,* Paris.

Moral, Paul, 1961, *Le Paysan Haïtien* (Etude sur la vie rurale en Haïti), Paris.

Mörner, M., 1965, 'En Torno de la Penetracion Mestiza . . . ', *Revista Historica,* XXVIII, Lima.

Mörner, Magnus, 1969, 'The Theory and Practice of Racial Segregation in Colonial Spanish America' in Hanke (ed), 1969, Vol. I.

Muratorio, Blanca, 1966, *Changing bases of social stratification in a Bolivian Community.* Paper given at American Anthropologists' Association, Pittsburg, Penn.

Muratorio, Blanca, 1969, 'Participación Social y Politica de los Campesinos de Nor Yungas, Bolivia', *Revista Mexicana de Sociologia,* XXXI: 4.

Nash, Manning, 1960, *Primitive and Peasant Economic Systems,* San Francisco: Chandler.

Naciones Unidas, 1958, *El desarrollo economico de Bolivia,* Mexico: Naciones Unidas.

Oberg, Kalervo, 1957, 'O campônio marginal no Brazil rural', *Sociologia,* XIX: 2, Sao Paulo.

Ortiz, Suttie, 1963, *The Economic Organisation of a Paez Indian Community,* Thesis, University of London.

Ots, Capdequi, 1958, *Las instituciones de Nuevo Reino de Granada al tiempo de la independencia,* Madrid.

Oviedo y Valdés, Gonzalo Fernandez de, 1955 [1944–45], 'Historia General y natural de las Indias, Asunción, Paraguay, in *Keen* (ed), 1955, translated from the original by editors.

Paim, G., 1957, *Industrialização e economia natural,* Rio de Janeiro; Instituto Superior de Estudos Brasileiros.

Paré, Louise, 1968, *Los endrogados,* Master's thesis, UNAM, Mexico.

Paredes, M. Rigoberto, 1965, *La Altiplanicie,* La Paz; Ediciones Isla.

Paredes, M. Rigoberto, 1965, *Tiahuanaco y la Provincia de Ingavi,* La Paz: Ediciones Isla.

Parry, J. H., 1966, *The Spanish Seaborne Empire,* London: Hutchinson.

Parsons, E. C., 1945, *Peguche,* University of Chicago Press.

Payne, James, 1965, *Labor and Politics in Peru,* Newhaven: Yale University Press.

PEL (Panorama Económico Latinoamericano) 1966, No.152, La Habana.

Peinado, Marcelo, 1971, *Land Reform in Three Communities of Cochabamba.* Distributed in mimeographed form by the Land Tenure Centre, University of Wisconsin, Madison, Wisconsin.

Pearse, Andrew, 1969, 'Subsistence farming is far from dead', in CERES II: 4.

Pearse, A. C., 1973, 'Structural Problems of Education Systems in Latin America' in *Knowledge, Education and Cultural Change,* London: Tavistock Publications.

Peñaloza, Luis, 1946, *Historia Económica de Bolivia,* Vol. I: 1953–4, Vol. II, La Paz.

Penny, D. M., 1969, *Bulletin of Indonesian Studies,* February, 9, p.73.

Perez, Elizardo, 1963, *Warisata,* La Paz.

Perreira de Queiroz, M. I., 1967, 'Petite Léxique de la Vie Rurale Bresiliènne' in CNRS 1967.

Piel, J., 1967, 'Un soulevement rural péruvien: Tocroyoc (1921)', *Revue d'histoire moderne et contemporaine,* XIV.

Pitts,-Rivers, Julian, 1965, *'Who are the Indians?'* Encounter, XXV: 3, London.

Posada, Francisco, 1967, *El Camino Chibcha a la Sociedad de Clases,* Mexico.

Powell, J. D., 1966, 'Venezuela: the Peasant Union Movement' in Landsberger, 1969.

Prado Jr., Caio, 'Contribuçáo para a análise da questão agraria no Brasil', *Revista Brasiliense,* 28, pp.163–238.

Prado Jr., Caio, 1945, Historia económica do Brasil, São Paulo: Editôra Brasiliense.

Prado Jr., Caio, 1963, 'O Estatuto do Trabalhador Rural', *Revista Brasiliense,* 47.

Prado Jr., Caio, 1965, 8th ed. *Formação do Brasil Contemporâneo (Colônia),* São Paulo.

Preston, David A., 1969, 'The Revolutionary Landscape of Highland Bolivia', *Geographical Journal,* 135.

Pugh, Ramón, 1969, Los Campesinos Venezolanos: Organisacion Politica Liderazgo y Economia, IX Latin American Congress of Sociology.

Ramirez, Pablo, 1967, *Cambios en las formas depago de mano de bran en el Valle Central* (mimeo) ICIRA, Chile.

Rangel, I. M., 1956, 'Desenvolvimento e projeto', *Revista da Faculdade de Ciencias Econômicos,* 5: 9, pp.65–173.

Rene-Moreno, G., 1959, *La mita de Potosí en 1795,* Potosí.

Reyeros, Rafael, 1937, *Caquiaviri,* La Paz.

Reyeros, Rafael, 1949, *'El Pongueaje',* La Paz.

Reyeros, Rafael A., 1963, *Historia Social del Indio Boliviano,* La Paz: Editorial Fenix.

Rios, José Arthur, 1969, 'The Cities of Colonial Brazil', in Hanke (ed.), 1969, pp.329–340.

Rodriguez, C. R., 1966, *La revolución cubaine et le paysannat,* Havana.

Romano, Ruggiero, 1966, *Cuestiones de historia económica latin-americana,* Caracas.

Romano, Ruggiero, 1965, *Una Economia Colonial: Chile en el Siglo XVIII,* Buenos Aires.

Rosenblat, Angel, 1935, *El desarrollo de la población indigena de América,* Buenos Aires.

Rosenblat, Angel, 1954, *La población indigena y el mestizaje en America,* Buenos Aires.

Rovetta, Vicente, 1962, *Peón rural y rancherío,* Montevideo.

Rowe, J. H., 1957, 'The Incas under Spanish Colonial Institutions', *The Hispanic American Historical Review,* XXXVIII: 2.

Rowley, John D., 1968, *El desarrollo sin la solidaridad communitaria,* Manuscript circulated in ICIRA, Santiago.

Salz, Beate, 1955, *The Human Element in Industrialisation,* Chicago: American Anthropological Association.

Sanginés Uriarte, Marcelo, 1968, *Educación Rural y Desarrollo en Bolivia,* La Paz: Editorial Don Bosco.

Santivañez, J.M., 1871, *Reivindicación de Los Terrenos de Comunidad,* Cochabamba.

Santos de Morais, Clodomiro, 1966, *Comportamiento de las Clases y Capas del Campo en el Proceso de Organización,* (mimeo), ICIRA, Santiago.

Santos de Morais, Clodomiro, 1969, *Algunas consideraciones en torno de las Organizaciones Campesinas en Latinoamerica* (mimeo), Mexico.

Schejtman, Alexander, 1968, *El Inquilino del Valle Central* (mimeo), ICIRA, Santiago.

Schickele, R., 1968, *Agricultural Revolution and Economic Progress, A Primer for Development,* New York: Praeger.

Service, Elman R., 1955, 'Indian-European Relations in Colonial Latin America', *American Anthropologist,* 57, June.

Service, Elman R., 1951, 'The Encomienda in Paraguay', *Hispanic American Historical Review,* XXXI.

Simpson, L. B., 1966 [1950], *The encomienda in New Spain,* Los Angeles: University of California Press.

Stavenhagen et al, 1968, *Neolatifundismo y Explotación,* Mexico.

Steward, J., 1946–50, *Handbook of South American Indians,* Washington: Government Printing Office.

Stinchcombe, A., 1968, 'Agricultural Enterprise and Rural Class Relations' in Bendix and Lipset, 1968.

Traven, Ben, *The Ride to Monteria* (novel).

Udy, S. *The organisation of work.*

UNESCO, 1962, *Social Research and Rural Life in Central America, Mexico and the Caribbean Region,* Paris.

Urquidi, Arturo, 1966, *El Fuedalismo en America y la Reform Agraria Boliviana,* Cochabamba, Editorial: Los Amigos del Libro.

U.S. Department of Agriculture, 1958, *Agricultural Geography of Latin America,* Washington.

Valcarcel, Carlos A., 1915, *El Proceso de Putumayo,* Lima: Imprenta 'Comercial' de Horacio la Rosa y Co.

Vasquez de Espinosa, A., (tr. C. V. Clark) 1955, 'Description of the West Indies' in Keen, 1955.

Verlinden, Charles, 1958, 'Esclavitud medieval en Europe y esclavitud colonial en America', in *Revista de la Universidad Nacional de Córdoba,* Córdoba.

Verlinden, Charles, 1964, 'Esclavage Medieval en Europe et Esclavage Colonial en Amérique', *Cahiers de l'Institut des Hautes Etudes de l'Amérique Latine,* VI, Paris.

Vilhena, Luis dos Santos, (ed. by Braz do Amaral) 1923 [1802], *Recopilação de Noticias Sotero-politanas e Brasilicas,* Bahia.

Villava, Victorián de, 1871, 'Discurso sobre el mito de Potosi', *Revista de Buenos Aires,* XXIV, Buenos Aires.

Vollmer, Gunter, 1967, *Bevölkerungspolitik und Bevölkerungsstruktur in Vice Königreich Peru zu Ende der Kolonialzeit (1741–1821),* Berlin.

Weeks, D., 1947, 'The Agrarian System of the Spanish American Colonies', *Journal of Land and Public Utilities,* XXIII.

Whetten, N. L., 1962, *Guatemala: The Land and the People,* Newhaven and London: Yale University Press.

Whitehead, Laurence, 1969, *The United States and Bolivia: A case of neo-colonialism,* London: The Haslemere Group.

Willems, Emilio, 1961, *Uma vila Brasileira,* Sao Paulo.

Wolf, Theodor, 1892, *Geographia y geologia del Ecuador,* Leipzig: Brockhaus.

Wolf, Eric, 1966, *Peasants,* Englewood Cliffs, N.J.: Prentice Hall.

Zavala, Silvio, 1935, *La Encomienda Indiana,* Madrid.

Zavaleta, René, 1969, in 'Marcha', October 8, Montevideo.

Zondag, Cornelius H., 1966, *The Bolivian Economy 1952–65,* Praeger Special Studies in International Economics and Development.

Zorita, Alonso de (tr. Keen), 1963, *Life and Labour in Ancient Mexico,* New Brunswick: Rutgers University Press.

Index

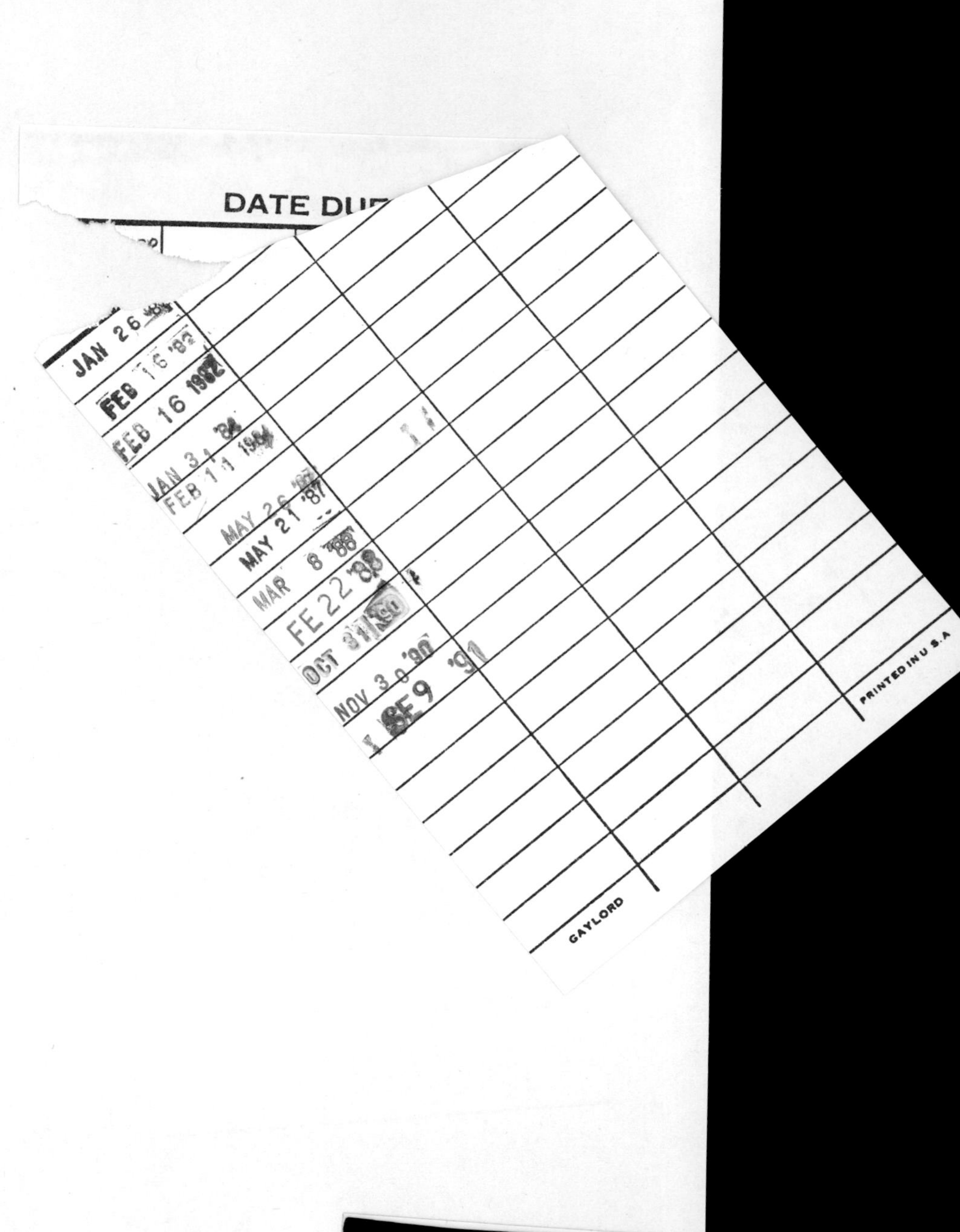

DATE DUE
JAN 26
FEB 16 '82
FEB 16 1982
FEB 11 1984
MAY 21 '87
MAR 8 '88
NOV 30 '90
GAYLORD
PRINTED IN U.S.A.